Politics and Change in Singapore and Hong Kong

In democratization theory, Singapore continues to be a remarkable country for its extremely low level of contentious politics despite rapid economic development. In contrast, many different groups in Hong Kong have taken their demands to the streets since the 1970s. Even though there is an obvious difference in the willingness of the population to actively challenge the regime, the political developments of the two city-states show a similar pattern of political mobilization and government reaction.

This book examines the changing pattern of contentious politics in the democratization process of these Asian city-states. It explores the causal connections between popular contention and democratization, using a multi-disciplinary approach with theoretical insights from the political sciences, sociology and psychology. The political process model is applied to provide further understanding of the patterns of interaction between contenders, opposition groups or social movements and the ruling elite. The book argues that differences in the strategies applied by the ruling elite explain why members of the opposition were empowered or obstructed in challenging the government.

Stephan Ortmann is Assistant Professor of Comparative Politics at the Fern Universität in Hagen, Germany. He is the author of *Managed Crisis: Legitimacy and the National Threat in Singapore* (2009).

Routledge Contemporary Asia Series

Politics and Change in Singapore and Hong Kong

Containing Contention

Stephan Ortmann

Routledge
Taylor & Francis Group

LONDON AND NEW YORK

First published 2010
by Routledge
2 Park Square, Milton Park, Abingdon, Oxfordshire OX14 4RN

Simultaneously published in the USA and Canada
by Routledge
711 Third Avenue, New York, NY 10017

Routledge is an imprint of the Taylor & Francis Group, an Informa business

First issued in paperback 2012

© 2010 Stephan Ortmann

Typeset in Times New Roman by
Taylor & Francis Books

British Library Cataloguing in Publication Data
A catalogue record for this book is available from the British Library

Library of Congress Cataloging in Publication Data
Politics and change in Singapore and Hong Kong : containing contention / Stephan Ortmann.
   p. cm. – (Routledge contemporary Asia series; 21)
Includes bibliographical references and index.
1. Singapore–Politics and government–1965-1990. 2. Singapore–Politics and government–1990- 3. Protest movements–Singapore. 4. Opposition (Political science)–Singapore. 5. Hong Kong (China)–Politics and government. 6. Protest movements–Hong Kong. 7. Opposition (Political science)–Hong Kong, I. Title.
   JQ1063.A91.O77 2009
   320.95125–dc22
                              2009015978

ISBN13: 978-0-415-55291-2 (hbk)
ISBN13: 978-0-415-62752-8 (pbk)
ISBN13: 978-0-203-86769-3 (ebk)

**This book is dedicated to my wife, Hongzhuan Li,
whose loving support always kept me focused.**

Contents

Figures and tables

Figures

Tables

Abbreviations

AMP	Association of Muslim Professionals
ASEAN	Association of South East Asian Nations
AWARE	Association of Women for Action & Research
BBC	British Broadcasting Corporation
CCCs	Citizens Consultative Committees
CCMCs	Community Center Management Committees
CCP	Chinese Communist Party
CCTV	closed-circuit television
CDO	City District Officer
CEC	Central Election Committee
CEO	Chief executive officer
CIC	Christian Industrial Committee
CNA	Channel NewsAsia
CNN	Cable News Network
CPF	Central Provident Fund
CPI	Corruption Perceptions Index
DBs	District Boards
DMCs	District Management Committees
EAG	Education Action Group
EDB	Economic Development Board
ExCo	Executive Council
FEER	Far Eastern Economic Review
FTU	Federation of Trade Unions
GDP	gross domestic product
GIS	Government Information Service
GLCs	Government Linked Corporations
GPCs	Government Parliamentary Committees
GRCs	Group Representation Constituencies
GSNTU	Government School Non-Graduate Teachers Union
GST	Goods and Services Tax
HDB	Housing and Development Board
HK	Hong Kong
HK$	Hong Kong Dollar

HKFS	Hong Kong Federation of Students
HKJA	Hong Kong Journalists' Association
HKPTU	Hong Kong Professional Teachers' Union
ICAC	Independent Commission Against Corruption
IHT	*International Herald Tribune*
IMF	International Monetary Fund
IPS	Institute of Policy Studies
IRs	integrated resorts
ISA	Internal Security Act
ISD	Internal Security Department
KMT	Kuomintang
LegCo	Legislative Council
MACs	Mutual Aid Committees
MDA	Media Development Authority
MICA	Ministry of Information, Communications and the Arts
MM	Minister Mentor
MOE	Ministry of Education
MP	Minister of Parliament
MRT	Mass Rapid Transit
NCMP	Non-Constituency Member of Parliament
NKF	National Kidney Foundation
NMP	Nominated Member of Parliament
NPPA	Newspaper and Printing Presses Act
NSP	National Solidarity Party
NSP	National Solidarity Party
NSS	Nature Society (Singapore)
NTUC	National Trades Union Congress
OB	out-of-bounds
PAP	People's Action Party
PRC	People's Republic of China
RCs	Residents' Committees
ROC	Republic of China
S$	Singapore Dollar
SAF	Singapore Armed Forces
SAR	Special Administrative Region
SARS	Severe Acute Respiratory Syndrome
SCMP	*South China Morning Post*
SCOPG	Standing Committee on Pressure Groups
SDA	Singapore Democratic Alliance
SDP	Singapore Democratic Party
SIA	Singapore Airlines
SJP	Singapore Justice Party
SM	Senior Minister
SMEs	small and medium-sized enterprises
SoCO	Society for Community Organization

SPH	Singapore Press Holdings
SPP	Singapore People's Party
ST	*The Straits Times*
TUC	Trade Unions Congress
UMELCO	Unofficial Members of the Legislative and Executive Councils
UMNO	United Malays National Organization
UrbCo	Urban Council
WP	Workers' Party
WTO	World Trade Organization

Acknowledgments

The idea for this book dates back to my final years as a master's student at the University of Erlangen-Nuremberg, when I learned about Singapore, a country that had stubbornly defied the modernization paradigm that positively links economic growth with democracy. I wanted to understand why this tiny city-state, an economically developed country without natural resources, had somehow resisted the pressures of modernization and not democratized or even shown any development toward democratization. Initially, this was a very difficult undertaking because it is always easier to explain something that has occurred than something that has not. I was, therefore, looking for a case that was similar enough in terms of size, politics, and history to allow for a meaningful comparison. After a long period of gestation, I finally realized that Hong Kong would be an almost perfect match. Especially intriguing for me was the fact that in 1975 two political scientists, Chan Heng Chee from Singapore and Ambrose King from Hong Kong, had independently written very similar articles about their respective city-states. Both claimed that there was an administrative state and a depoliticized population. Since then, Hong Kong has experienced a mushrooming protest movement while Singapore's opposition has largely remained quiescent. This, however, meant that I needed to place a special focus on Hong Kong during the 1970s and early 1980s, because it was during this time that the early seeds of the political transformation of the city-state were sown.

I am indebted to Mark R. Thompson of the University of Erlangen-Nuremberg, who first stirred my interest in studying Asian and, in particular, Singaporean politics. As my mentor for many years, he has guided my research and theory building. I should also mention Mark's graduate colloquium and the faculty's Asia Pacific Colloquium, whose members provided me with important constructive comments that helped me improve my arguments. Furthermore, I had many long conversations with Phillip Kuntz, who patiently listen to my ideas and provided me with invaluable feedback.

Furthermore, I would like to thank the German Academic Exchange Service (DAAD) for financing a research trip to Singapore. I am also indebted to the East Asian Institute (EAI) of the National University of Singapore (NUS) for inviting me as a visiting scholar and allowing me to use the enormous resources of the university. I am especially grateful to Wang Gungwu, who not only invited me to the institute but whose comments were invaluable for the writing of this book. I would also like to offer thanks to Chua Beng Huat, whose critical insight and profound knowledge challenged me to refocus my central argument.

While in Singapore, I have also met a lot of Singaporeans who shared some of their time and knowledge with me. I cannot mention them all. However, I would like here to thank Chee Soon Juan (chairman of the Singapore Democratic Party), Jacob George (former member of Think Centre), Goh Meng Seng (member of the Workers' Party), James Gomez (Singaporean political scientist and member of the Workers' Party), Arthero Lim (member of the Singapore Democratic Alliance), Sylvia Lim (chairman of the Workers' Party), Alexius A. Pereira (sociologist at the National University of Singapore), M. Ravi (Singaporean lawyer), Melvin Tan (member of the Workers' Party), and Yap Keng Ho (social activist).

For my research on Hong Kong, I would like to thank Joseph S.Y. Cheng, who is not only an academic but also a participant in the opposition movement of the late 1970s and early 1980s, for giving me the opportunity to discuss my ideas with him. I also need to thank the University of Hong Kong and especially Norman Miners, whose archive of newspaper articles and other material from the 1970s has allowed me to construct a very detailed picture of the city-state during this time.

My colleagues at the Fern Universität in Hagen, Germany, greatly assisted me in the completion of my book. I am particularly thankful to Tobias Fuhrmann and Stephan Bröchler, whose feedback was essential for this publication. Furthermore, I am grateful to two anonymous reviewers whose comments greatly improved the final manuscript. In this context, I also need to mention the helpful assistance and patience of Madhavi Bhargava and Dorothea Schaefter from Routledge, who were always ready to answer my many questions. I am also indebted to Victor Seow and Nathaniel Eschler for proofreading parts of this book. While so many have helped me in the process of writing this book, the remaining errors are of course my own.

1 Introduction and methodology

Containing contention in Hong Kong and Singapore

"Our movement, our campaign for democracy, will grow and gain momentum and strength," Dr Chee Soon Juan, a prominent Singaporean opposition politician, optimistically proclaimed while leading a small unlicensed protest for three days during the 2006 IMF/World Bank meeting in Singapore (*IHT* 19 Sep. 2006). This protest stands in contrast to Hong Kong, where, already in 1980, organizers could mobilize 2,000 protesters against poor living conditions (*SCMP* 24 Nov. 1980). Only a few years earlier, Hong Kong citizens had equally been described as apathetic and depoliticized. What has led to this change and why are Singaporeans much less inclined to challenge the government than their Hong Kong counterparts?

Modernization theory predicts that during periods of rapid economic growth there is an increasing likelihood that a country will become democratic. The effects created by industrialization, urbanization and social stratification, lead to greater competition between different social forces. Consequently, this results in an increase of contentious politics, such as labor strikes, rebellions, riots, or demonstrations, which target the ruling elites. However, Singapore attracts attention because there were hardly any visible acts of contentious politics from independence in 1965 until 2005, in spite of more than three decades of rapid growth.

The case of Singapore, therefore, suggests that modernization theory is either mistaken or, more likely, as Inglehart and Welzel (2005) contend, in need of modification. The question that arises is how Singapore's rulers were able to contain the threat of contentious politics that leads to disorder and tension between various social forces. To better understand this, it is useful to consider another city-state, Hong Kong during the 1970s and 1980s, in an era when a nearly dormant opposition movement was revived.[1] In contrast, in Singapore, a small but vocal opposition movement returned only in 1981. Since then, challengers have made some progress. Public demonstrations even made a comeback in Singapore in 2005, but their minuscule size still stands in stark contrast to the thousands of activists in Hong Kong. While recent events in Singapore suggest that contentious politics is again on the rise, the focus of this book is on how the Singapore government, unlike its counterpart in Hong Kong, was able to consolidate its rule and nearly eliminate all forms of opposition, despite the pressures of modernization.

Singapore and Hong Kong in the 1970s: most similar cases

The two city-states have often been considered most similar cases, as is witnessed by an abundance of studies which compare Hong Kong and Singapore (e.g. Geiger and Geiger 1973; Castells, et al. 1990; Chiu, et al. 1995; Wong 2002; Sing 2004a; Cheung 2008). This is not surprising, considering the many similarities between the two small city-states (Table 1.1).

While Hong Kong is not an independent state, it has enjoyed great autonomy since World War II which can be described as "de facto independence" (Harris 1982). This has meant that the influence of the British administration has remained virtually nonexistent during this time. Both cities have been strongly influenced by British administrative practices, due to their colonial history. Even though Singapore gained autonomy from Britain in 1959, and independence in 1965 after it split from Malaysia, it is remarkable how much of the British administrative apparatus has survived the transition. At least on

Table 1.1 Some indicators for Singapore and Hong Kong[1]

	Hong Kong	*Singapore*
Size	1,092 sq km	692.7 sq km
Population (1970)	3,959,000	2,075,000
Population (1980)	5,063,100	2,414,000
Popularion (2008)	7,018,636	4,608,167
Ethnic groups	Chinese 95%	Chinese 76.8%
	Filipino 1.6%	Malay 13.9%
	Indonesian 1.3%	Indian 7.9%
	other 2.1% (2006 census)	other 1.4% (2000 census)
GDP per capita (1970)	US$959	US$914
GDP per capita (1980)	US$5,692	US$4,859
GDP per capita (2006)	US$27,071	US$30,082
Freedom House (2008)	Political Rights: 5	Political Right: 5
	Civil Liberties: 2	Civil Liberties: 4
	Status: Partly Free	Status: Partly Free
Economist Index of Democracy (2008)	Rank 84 (hybrid regime)	Rank 82 (hybrid regime)
Corruption Perception Index (2008)	Rank 12	Rank 4
Human Development Index (2008, data for 2006)	Rank 22	Rank 28
Index of Economic Freedom (2009)	Rank 1	Rank 2

Note: Due to lack of historical data for many of these indexes, more recent data has been used in this table.

1 Freedom House data has not been cited because the Hong Kong scores for the 1970s, which are not published on the website, are problematic. Upon request, Freedom House has sent a file with Hong Kong scores, which rates the city-state as "free" for most of the 1970s and gives it high marks for "political freedom" despite of the lack of most Hong Kongers to participate in politics.

Sources: CIA 2009; NationMaster.com 2009; Transparency International 2008; Economist Intelligence Unit 2008; UNDP 2008; Heritage Foundation 2009.

the surface, Singapore has preserved a great deal of the institutions from the British colonial era. There are, for example, the parliament, the judiciary, the school system, the English language, and also some of the more infamous aspects such as the Internal Security Act (ISA), which allows for detention without trial. Hong Kong, on the other hand, never became independent and remained a part of the British empire until it was handed over to Chinese rule in 1997. Formal democracy, as in Singapore, did not become a political feature of colonialism in Hong Kong until the late 1980s, but liberal attitudes toward free speech and freedom of assembly were largely respected in colonial Hong Kong, while control of the media and severe restrictions on political expression were and still are unabashedly justified by Singapore's leadership. While today Singapore is considered noncompetitive and Hong Kong semi-competitive (Sing 2004b), in the 1970s Hong Kong was equally noncompetitive.

Due to the fact that the majority of the population in both city-states originates from the Chinese empire, there is also a strong similarity in cultural practices. Singapore's government regards so-called "Asian values," which contain many Confucian virtues, as its basic cultural foundation. A study has found that while 65 percent of the Hong Kong elite believe in the existence of "Asian values," 93 percent think it would not be good to emulate Singapore's political system (Beatty 2003: 47, 64). While in the 1970s, Chinese culture was sometimes used as an argument to explain the politically apathetic population (Lau 1982), the decades after 1980 proved that this was not the case. Nevertheless, this has led some to conclude that Singapore's cultural heritage is one reason for the population's lack of interest in political affairs. This becomes even more complicated by the fact that Singapore's population, with about 76 percent ethnic Chinese, is much less homogeneous than Hong Kong's, with 95 percent considered Chinese, which suggests that Singapore could be more rather than less prone to social conflict.

In both city-states, entrepôt trade and international corporations play an important role, and both have experienced rapid economic growth, due to export-oriented industrialization. Their developmental experiences gained these two city-states the designation as tiger states, or dragon states, and they have often been seen as direct competitors. Furthermore, since the 1970s both states have been regarded as relatively free of corruption. While both proclaimed economic freedom as essential, the British colonial regime in Hong Kong felt the need to maintain an economic system that was based mostly on laissez-faire, with little government intrusion. Singaporean leaders, obviously influenced by their initial collaboration with the Communists (Bloodworth 1986), decided to control the local economy, which was accomplished to a large part through an emphasis on government-linked corporations. Furthermore, the Singapore government developed economic plans that included targeted subsidies for multi-national corporations (MNCs), which were carefully selected according to certain criteria. This also sets it apart from Hong Kong, where the government supported MNCs only insofar as it maintained extremely low taxes and provided the infrastructure for businesses.

Both states have been characterized as administrative states with small ruling elites, which have successfully depoliticized their populations (King 1975; Chan 1975). Despite the differences in economic development, the two city-states have also experienced similar political developments. Initially, the emphasis was placed on the business elite, while social movements were discouraged, demobilized or entirely destroyed. In particular, the labor movement experienced strong government control. While the Singaporean government decided to replace the numerous labor unions with a government-controlled national trade union, the Hong Kong government, in unison with business leaders, more subtly controlled union activism, which was already mitigated due to a divided labor movement.

Finally, since the 1970s and early 1980s, we can observe in both states the return of an oppositional movement that increasingly challenged the ruling elite. In Hong Kong, this occurred during the 1970s, an era of government expansion and heightened expectations. It was during this time that there was also an explosion of pressure groups and other political groups, some of which staged protests. The loss of legitimacy of the colonial regime in 1984, coupled with the introduction of greater representation, led to a strengthening of the community movement and a greater tendency to form alliances. In the case of Singapore, the 1981 election of an opposition member to parliament marked a change in the fortunes of the opposition. Beginning in 1991, the government has also allowed the development of a limited civil society. The Singaporean opposition has, however, still made very limited progress.

The similarity between the two cases makes them ideal for an analysis of the origins of contentious politics. As Rustow (1970: 350) points out: "The many possible variables that can affect the origins of democracy and the even more complex relations among them can best be sorted out by looking at their total configuration in a limited number of cases—perhaps no more than two or three at the start." When we assume that contentious politics is directly related to the process of democratization, an analysis of these two states should provide evidence for the tactics of ruling elites and their challengers in their quest to influence the political development in these authoritarian states with democratic features.

The comparison of these two "Chinese societies" may, finally, also shed some light on future developments in the People's Republic of China, which openly favors the Singaporean model in containing the rise of contention. Of particular interest is Singapore's ruling party, the People's Action Party (PAP), whose dominance of the political system provides a role model for the Chinese Communist Party (CCP), which also tries to encourage pragmatic and technocratic policies while at the same time wanting to monopolize power.

Defining democracy

Before we can analyze the impact of contentious politics on the political development and democratization of the two city-states, we need to understand what is meant by that elusive concept "democracy", and how it can be distinguished from other regime forms. It has to be acknowledged that the line between what have commonly been considered authoritarian and democratic regimes is not as clear as the terms might suggest. In reality it is a matter of degrees. However, in order to determine these degrees, it is necessary to set parameters that distinguish a predominantly democratic from a predominantly authoritarian regime, or even other regime types. This book uses a procedural definition of participatory democracy similar to that of Lipset, who writes:

> democracy (in a complex society) is defined as a political system which supplies regular constitutional opportunities for changing the governing officials. It is a social mechanism for the resolution of the problem of societal decision-making among conflicting interest groups which permits the largest possible part of the population to influence these decisions through their ability to choose among alternative contenders for political office.
>
> (Lipset 1959: 71)

Robert Dahl (1971), furthermore, provides three main requirements for a democracy. All citizens need to be able to formulate their preferences, be able to express or signify these preferences to the government, and have their preferences receive equal weight in the conduct of government. Dahl makes it clear that his definition is an ideal type of democracy, which has not yet been achieved in any country in the world. For this reason, he argues that existing democracies should be called "polyarchies."

Having set the parameters for an ideal typical democracy, it becomes necessary also to identify the characteristics of other regime forms. While many studies in the past merely used a dichotomy between an ideal typical democracy and an ideal typical authoritarian regime, more recent research has focused on a broader classification of authoritarian regimes, because it became evident that the type of regime has an influence on the democratization process. Dahl (1971), for example, distinguishes between four different ideal typical regimes: closed hegemonies, competitive oligarchies, inclusive hegemonies, and polyarchies. The closed hegemonic regime is defined as a regime in which there is neither public contestation nor any participation in elections or office. When a closed hegemonic regime liberalizes, i.e. increases the possibilities for public contestation, it becomes a competitive oligarchy. When it increases its inclusiveness, which means that more people are able to participate in the political process, an inclusive hegemony is the result. Both Singapore and Hong Kong have, according to this definition, developed in the direction of inclusive hegemonies, as they have tried to allow more participation without also increasing contestation. Of the two cases in this study, Singapore may be considered closest to this ideal type, because the state has created a number of political offices and functions to incorporate participatory elements while the ability to contest the political regime has remained virtually nonexistent.

While Dahl makes use of only two different criteria, contestation and participation, Linz and Stepan's regime typology includes four different characteristics, namely pluralism, ideology, mobilization, and leadership. These four characteristics yield five different ideal regime types, which are called democracy, authoritarianism, totalitarianism, post-totalitarianism, and sultanism. For example, pluralism is legally protected in a democratic regime; limited but not responsible political pluralism characterizes an authoritarian regime; lack of pluralism marks totalitarian regimes; limited, but not responsible, economic and institutional pluralism is a feature of post-totalitarian regimes; and economic and social pluralism which is subject to unpredictable and despotic intervention exists in sultanistic regimes (Linz and Stepan 1996). In the context of this book, however, it is not necessary to go into detail of this classification, because this regime typology describes the spectrum of regimes from authoritarian to closed totalitarian but neglects the range from authoritarian to fully democratic regimes. Furthermore, this classification is also unsatisfactory because it leaves little room for hybrid forms, which may play a crucial role in how or even whether a country democratizes. Consequently, political scientists have come up with hybrid regime forms such as "electoral authoritarianism" (Diamond 2002), "competitive authoritarianism" (Levitsky and Way 2002), "illiberal democracy" (Zakaria 1997) or "semidemocracy" (Case 1996).

The concept of semidemocracy, first used by William F. Case to illustrate the cases of formal democracy in Southeast Asia, describes a regime that allows electoral participation but prevents "opposition parties from winning elections and replacing the government as in full procedural democracy" (Case 1996: 439). He considers Singapore to be a prime example of this regime form. Zakaria, who labels this type of political system an illiberal democracy, has noted that an increasing number of "democratizing" countries follow this pattern. In order to avoid the impression that this hybrid regime form could be regarded as a transitional stage in a one-directional democratization process, Levitsky and Way (2002) have reconceptualized it as a competitive authoritarian regime: a regime in which "formal democratic institutions are widely viewed as the principal means of obtaining and exercising political authority" (ibid.: 52). In general, these hybrid regimes try to follow a thin red line between democracy and authoritarianism in order to maintain the hegemony of the ruling elite.

Making elections the touchstone of these hybrid regime forms, however, neglects the many similarities that exist between authoritarian regimes that maintain democratic institutions and/or practices but not necessarily elections. It is only when we emphasize the procedural factor that colonial Hong Kong is not part of this hybrid form and is instead regarded as "semiauthoritarian." This is because the city-state is characterized by "liberal participation without electoral contestation" (Case 1996: 438). However, an elected legislature is not a necessity for an authoritarian regime to claim popular legitimacy, which, for example, in the case of Hong Kong, has been achieved through popular support for the regime. While the only partially elected institution in Hong Kong, the Urban Council, did not significantly contribute to the legitimacy of the government even though the low voter participation in Urban Council elections was often used as an argument against further democratization (see Chapter 3), a largely impartial judiciary, a free press, and the existence of pressure groups conferred legitimacy on the government because these democratic "features" enabled it to claim that it was acting in the "interest of the people." It is therefore possible to consider colonial Hong Kong as a democracy in principle, even though it lacked electoral procedures for the legislature or executive.

Because of the similarities between the political systems of Singapore and Hong Kong in the 1970s this book uses the classification "authoritarian regime with democratic features" to describe political regimes in which authoritarian elements dominate but institutions commonly associated with liberal democracy exist. The important aspect of such a regime type is the domination of the political system by a small ruling elite with minimal influence on the political system from other groups. In such a regime, outsiders can hardly influence policy making, even though certain democratic procedures and institutions are maintained. At the same time, these democratic features, regardless of their content, provide serious obstacles for further democratization of the political system because they allow the ruling elite to claim that the masses are already represented. Both Singapore and Hong Kong (at least in the 1970s) can be considered authoritarian regimes with democratic features. The emphasis on democratic features is important because, in part, these allow the regime to claim legitimacy. The "democratic features" have to be understood as the claim to some sort of democratic mechanisms, which aggregate the will of the people and grant significant legitimacy to the political regime. In the case of Hong Kong it was the perception that there were a free media, a fair judicial system, the right to assembly and free speech, among other aspects. This contrasts with Singapore, which maintains free and relatively regular elections, while the ability to influence politics through the media is extremely limited and protests are virtually prohibited.

Explaining contentious politics

Recently, research into democratization has moved away from exploring the reasons for democratization, to the study of the consolidation of democracies and the reasons for the development of hybrid democratic regimes with various flaws or defects. However, despite the global trend toward democratization there are still many countries that can be labeled authoritarian. This is reflected in the 2008 Freedom House report, which rated about half of the world's countries as "not free" or "partly free". Most of these countries can be classified as open or closed authoritarian, while only a few have shown a tendency to move toward liberal democracy. While most of the consolidated democracies can be found in Europe, Asian and African states have remained much less fertile ground for liberal democracy.

At the same time, a number of studies have suggested the resilience of authoritarianism in Asia, which could become a viable alternative to Western democracy (Fukuyama 1995; Huntington 1996; Nathan 2003). These regimes, the argument goes, have learned from the example of other authoritarian countries and have perfected their rule in order to avoid the pressures for democratization. External factors also play a role in a recent study by Barmer, Ratner and Spector (2008), which suggests that integration into the international economy and the lack of a normative commitment to institutional and electoral notions of democracy are the reason for this authoritarian stability. They argue that the literature on democratic transitions has over-emphasized domestic factors in its explanations of this kind of authoritarian stability. A close analysis of particular cases, however, clearly suggests that external factors are only relevant if they directly influence internal power struggles. Furthermore, studies that emphasize the stability of authoritarian regimes tend to neglect the changing political environment of these countries, which may eventually threaten this stability. In contrast to democratic regimes, autocracies face a number of problems, such as the lack of balance of powers, reliance on economic growth for legitimacy, the need for an orderly leadership transition, and the lack of responsiveness of the government to the people, among others.

A discussion of the reasons for the stability of authoritarian regimes as well as their political development should include a review of important research into successful democratizations, which has received much attention during the "third wave" of democratization (Shin 1994). This research tradition has even produced a number of studies that probe the lack of democratization, or "non-transitions," in some states, even though they overestimate the determinacy of democratization (Hawkins 2001; Thompson 2002). These studies provide an essential foundation for evaluating political change, which can be integrated into a broader framework of political change in stable authoritarian regimes. Therefore, to return to the arguments of modernization theory, it is necessary to combine an analysis of these changes which increase the chances for democratization, but also of those that contribute to authoritarian stability.

Democratization and the lack thereof can be attributed to the pattern of political contention, which is reflected in the interaction between the ruling elite and the opposition as well as their potential supporters. Democratization, if not imposed from outside, has to be regarded as the result of a negotiated compromise between the goals of the ruling elite groups and those of oppositional groups. Therefore contentious politics has been closely tied to democratization. This, however, still remains a "much misunderstood but crucial relationship" (McAdam et al. 2001: 265). While contention plays an important role in democratization, this question can best be analyzed by a comparison of a non-transition with one that has significantly liberalized. Contentious politics is not absent in authoritarian regimes with democratic features, which means that the forms of contention are decisive in democratization processes. If we understand how the tactics and goals of opposing societal groups influence the interaction between these groups, we will be better able to understand how and why authoritarianism persists and how the inevitable decay of an authoritarian regime could lead to liberalization.

An important contribution of this book is the focus on political change, which allows us to separate political developments from the idea that authoritarian regimes necessarily lead toward liberal democracy. Instead, I want to contribute to our knowledge of the changing societal forces that accompany rapid economic development and industrialization, often called modernization, of late-developing countries. While researchers have found a close link between economic development and democratization, as well as between economic crisis and democratization, they have failed to reveal the causal link between the two. The major problem is, therefore, to understand why the structural factors that improve the chances for democracy do not necessarily lead to democratization. As we all know, historical developments often occur because of the decisions of individual political actors which, however, cannot be viewed in isolation from their environment. This interrelatedness requires a new approach, which combines aspects of previous theories from modernization theory, social movements theory, and so-called "transitology".

This new approach can be achieved through a modified version of the political process model that was developed by Doug McAdam (1982) in the context of the study of social movements and insurgency. While McAdam sought to explain the rise and evolution of social movements, the dependent variable in this context is the development of contentious politics. This broadens McAdam's model, on the one hand, to include the whole breadth of oppositional activity (from informal to formalized), and on the other hand, to include the role of the opponents of the movements, the rulers, and their supporters. For the latter group, it is essential to minimize the development of contentious politics, because this contributes to the relative stability of the authoritarian regime. This political process model of democratization then leads to the actor-centric independent variables, namely the tactics and goals of the ruling elite and oppositional groups as well as the institutional and historical factors in which the interaction between the two sets of groups is grounded. With this model it is possible to integrate the explanatory factors of structure and agency in a more balanced understanding of political changes.

The application of this model requires us to make a basic underlying assumption, namely that it is possible to roughly categorize every society into two sets of contending groups: ruling elite groups and oppositional groups. While the former are interested in maintaining or enlarging their power, oppositional groups try to increase their power. While it is difficult to determine these groups in liberal democracies because of constantly changing constellations, this dichotomy is of particular importance in authoritarian regimes, because the ruling elite groups hold all levers of power and oppositional groups are unable to participate in the decision-making process. Modernization processes redistribute the resources between contending groups and thus lead to an increase in so-called "contentious politics." For an authoritarian regime, this means that the ruling elite groups need constantly to adapt their tactics to maintain their hegemony in the political system.

The interaction between challengers and the ruling elite, therefore, has to be seen in the context of historical developments and the institutional frame in which this interaction takes place. This affects the organizational strength of a group, the group's perceptions of the environment, and its tactics and goals, which in turn have an influence on the relationship. Legitimacy, furthermore, constitutes a background variable that has an impact on the actions of a single group and on the interaction between the groups. While the group interaction is largely seen within a local context, external groups do influence the relationship of the ruling elite and the opposition, which means that they will have to align themselves with either group. For example, U.S. President George W. Bush's support for the Singaporean regime placed him on the side of the ruling elite groups,[2] while Amnesty International's condemnation of Singapore's poor human rights record establishes the group as part of the opposition (Amnesty International 2008).

The first hypothesis states that, even though modernization potentially changes the opportunity structure in favor of oppositional groups, the opposition still needs to take the initiative and challenge the ruling elite. At the same time this hypothesis also implies that the ruling elite may be able to adapt to these changes and thus mitigate their impact, which would stabilize the authoritarian regime (Huntington, 1968). For this reason, efficient management of the economy and society reduces the pressure for greater political competition. However, external shocks could still remain a potential threat to those in power, with the most serious challenge coming from within the regime itself, namely the perception of inefficient policies, which could potentially lead to serious economic difficulties. The inability to provide "good government," therefore, leads to greater political contention between political actors because it generates opportunities for political actors willing to challenge the ruling elite.

While "good government" provides an authoritarian regime with performance legitimacy, the changes in the opportunity structure also require a strategy of co-option and coercion. The government must be aware that it has to follow the following axiom: co-opt when you can, coerce when you must. A government that is overanxious in applying coercion risks the development of a powerful underground opposition. For this reason, ruling elites must attempt to include potential members of the opposition in political institutions that do not threaten the power base of the elite. In rare cases of dissent, however, the rulers must also be willing to undermine potentially powerful opposition figures. This varied strategy uses a divide-and-conquer approach that successfully demobilizes dissenters. If the government is not decisive enough and fails to co-opt opposition members into the government apparatus, and the government faces significant social pressure, it will likely lead to greater social mobilization.

While the ruling elite groups significantly shape the constraints on the behavior of the opposition, it would be wrong to assume that the decisions of opposition members do not matter. The opposition's choice of tactics and goals also has an impact on the choice of strategies of the ruling elite. If the majority of the opposition accept the oppressive conditions of an authoritarian regime and propagate only reforms to the ruling elite's program, they have very little chance of challenging the regime. On the other hand, a vocal opposition which is willing to resort to non-institutionalized tactics, such as demonstrations, sit-ins or hunger strikes, and demands fundamental changes (i.e. revolutionary goals), can strengthen its organizational base and improve its capability to challenge the regime. However, this approach also increases the potential for repression, or in McAdam's terms, strong social control response, which, however, depends on the strength of the ruling elite groups.

This can best be exemplified by a comparative analysis of ruling elite and oppositional groups in Singapore and Hong Kong. These two cases demonstrate the impact of these processes, because the two city-states share periods of rapid economic growth but differ significantly in the degree of political mobilization. While in Singapore political activity is heavily circumscribed, in Hong Kong activism has become a normal part of the political system. In terms of democratization theory, Hong Kong has already experienced an initial transition to representative government, even though full democracy has been denied (Thomas 1999). In contrast, Singapore's regime has been extremely successful in stabilizing authoritarian rule (Chua 1994; Trocki 2006).

Methodology

Analyzing the complex interaction between oppositional and ruling elite groups requires multiple levels of analysis, with a combination of primary and secondary sources. In the case of Singapore, a significant body of research has been published on opposition parties,[3] civil society,[4] the state,[5] the institutions,[6] and the elite.[7] To a lesser extent, there are also a number of very important studies on Hong Kong in the 1970s,[8] although newspaper archival work has been used to augment deficiencies in the literature whenever possible.

The changes in the political opportunity structure will be analyzed using historical analysis. In this part, the most significant events that contributed to an increase of political opportunities will be discussed. Because those political opportunities arose within an institutional framework, the historical analysis will be augmented by an institutional analysis. The focus will be on institutions that either provide the basis for oppositional activity or that limit the development of opposition.

In order to understand the motivation, the beliefs, and the perceptions on which the actions of the various groups are based, a combination of historical analysis and discourse analysis will be used. Speeches, books, party news-papers and websites, newspaper articles, and independent web logs (blogs) complement interviews and conversations with important actors in the oppo-sition to capture the perceptions, goals, and strategies of the political groups. In the summer of 2005, I was able to observe the Singapore Democratic Party during one of its meetings and I spoke with the head of the Workers' Party, Sylvia Lim. Other people in the opposition whom I have met include James Gomez (political scientist and 2006 Workers' Party candidate), Yap Keng Ho (social activist), the human rights attorney M. Ravi, and others. Using e-mail, I have also been able to interview a number of other members of the opposition (such as Glenda Han, the youngest opposition candidate in the 2006 election), which has been very helpful in the course of my research.

The historical nature of my comparative case, Hong Kong, required a different research strategy that focuses mostly on archival research. Very helpful in this regard was an internet newspaper article database which contains mostly English-language articles collected by Dr Norman Miners of the Department of Political Science at the University of Hong Kong. This database comprises of more than 150,000 articles covering from the early 1970s to 1994. While most of the material from this database comes from the two largest newspapers, the *South China Morning Post* and the *Hong Kong Standard*, there is also a large amount of source material from oppositional groups, such as the Hong Kong Professional Teachers' Union and the Reform Club. This proved to be a very good and efficient resource for conducting thorough research of political groups during the 1970s and early 1980s. Furthermore, a number of book publications from oppositional groups augmented this analysis. Finally, my research into Hong Kong's past greatly profited from e-mail correspondence as well as an interview with the one-time president of the now defunct Hong Kong Observers, Joseph S.Y. Cheng.

Chapter outline

The book is organized into three sections. The first part (Chapter 2) develops the theoretical framework for the comparison of the two cases in which I will adapt the political process model by Doug McAdam to explain the develop-ment or lack of contentious politics in the two city-states. While the original model only concentrated on the role of the challenger group and considered the ruling elite merely in terms of its response to oppositional activity, my expansion will focus on the role of the tactics and goals of both the ruling elite and challenger groups.

The second part (Chapters 3–8) makes a systematic comparison between the two cases, based on the different aspects of the political process model. In this section there are three chapters on Hong Kong and three on Singapore, in an alternating pattern in order to draw attention to the comparative aspects of the two cases. In each case, Hong Kong precedes Singapore. This order has been chosen because Hong Kong's development of oppositional activity has not only preceded Singapore's but has also superseded it in many ways. In the first two chapters of this section, the different political groups will be placed in a historical and institutional context, to reveal the changing political opportunity structure as well as the restrictions on oppositional groups. In the next two chapters the ruling elite groups, their perceptions, and their strategies and tactics will be discussed. This will be repeated in an analogous manner with two chapters on oppositional groups.

The last chapter, (Chapter 9) draws attention to crucial aspects of the comparison. The ruling elites of the two cases have both faced the challenges of modernization, but levels of contention differ significantly. This chapter will show that, in comparison, the "threat" of losing power is significantly reduced when the ruling elite can maintain the impression of "good government," when it can adapt its output to changing conditions, and last but not least, when it is successful in weakening oppositional groups through a combined strategy of coercion and co-option. Political opportunities that develop due to an erosion of regime legitimacy provide the basis for oppositional activity, and a legitimacy crisis potentially provides the trigger for contentious politics because oppositional groups, which perceive a real chance to gain influence, are emboldened to challenge the ruling elite. Finally, this chapter will also suggest future scenarios for the political development of the two city-states.

2 Modernization and the political process model

Modernization and industrialization result in an increasingly complex political system. New political actors emerge and are vying for influence. Ruling elite groups become aware of the challenges and defend their power. The challengers in authoritarian regimes with democratic features, such as Singapore and Hong Kong, continue to face a strong regime. Both city-states reveal that attempts to contain the increased potential mobilization resulting from modernization are achieved with different success. This raises the question of how we can explain that modernization on the one hand leads to increased political mobilization, while on the other hand it also potentially reinforces existing political structures. To answer this question, we need to determine what factors influence the degree of politicization of a society. While modernization processes provide political opportunities for members of the opposition to challenge the political regime, modernization theory fails to explain how and when this translates into political contention that could eventually pose a serious challenge to the regime.

Containing contention in Singapore and Hong Kong

Many social scientists have provided explanations for the lack of political activity in the two city-states. When we go back to the first half of the 1970s, both city-states were described as depoliticized and consequently devoid of significant political activity (King 1975; Chan 1975). To explain this, scholars have suggested a plethora of different explanations, which include political culture, the interests of the middle class, government effectiveness, and the use of coercion.

One of the most widely discussed reasons for the apparent lack of political activity in Hong Kong during the 1970s and in Singapore after independence in 1965 has been the political culture of the two city-states. It is argued that most people are apathetic toward politics and instead merely pursue material benefits. In Hong Kong, this seemed to be reflected in the low participation in Urban Council elections, and in Singapore, the lack of interest in political events is taken as evidence of a population that is totally uninterested in politics.

In regard to Hong Kong, Lau Siu-kai has argued that the society was largely governed by utilitarianistic familism, which he defined as "the normative and behavioral tendency of an individual to place his familial interests above the interests of the society and of other individuals and groups, and to structure his relationships with other individuals and groups in such a manner that the furtherance of his familial interests is the overriding concern" (Lau 1982: 72). The interests of these familial groups were supposed to be largely materialistic, to have a short-term horizon and to place a high emphasis on social stability. The potential usefulness of family members was the central concern in this conception, and recruitment of new members was based largely on this notion. The family orientation in turn created what Lau has termed "aloofness" toward the society (ibid.: 87), which was mainly to blame for the lack of political participation in Hong Kong. He concludes that Hong Kong, in an ideal-typical sense, corresponds to a "minimally-integrated social-political system," which presupposes the existence of two separate major groups: the Chinese society and the expatriate-controlled bureaucracy, with very few linkages between the two. He claims that both bureaucratic polity and Chinese society are "boundary conscious," with a minimum consensus on the division of labor and a fairly high degree of insulation of the two groups. Lam Wai-man (2004) has seriously challenged this argument, criticizing Lau's narrow conception of political participation. In Lau's opinion, the low level of participation was reflected in the very limited direct contact between the people and the political decision makers, as well as the low voter turnout in Urban Council elections (Lau 1982). In contrast, Lam argues that Lau neglected unlawful political activities, which played an important part during the 1970s (Lam 2004). Instead of being a structural feature, Lam Wai-man argues that the government actively pursued the depoliticization of society. This was accomplished by promoting three related discourses: the discourse of prosperity and stability, the discourse which marked political activists as "troublemakers," and the discourse of the social activist groups' denial of their role in politics (Lam 2004). With regard to Singapore, Vennewald (1994a) notes that the widespread apathy is the result of the extreme centralization of power in the state, which causes individual citizens to resign from politics. This argument could easily also apply to Hong Kong.

Another aspect of the two city-states' political cultures refers to the assumption that Asians are more oriented toward consensus than are other people. On the one hand, there is the suggestion of cultural relativism, which suggests that Singapore, as part of an ancient Asian cultural region, is not suited to democracy. This is mostly advanced by the ruling elite, which claims that so-called "Asian values" are essentially the root cause of stability. Singaporeans, it is argued, are genetically inclined to strive for a society based on consensus and cooperation. Conflict, in this context, is an aberration born out of unstable times. One of the first proponents of the Asian values discourse was Lee Kuan Yew, who considered Confucian ethics as part of Singapore's economic success and the reason why Singaporeans reject notions of so-called "Western" democracy. Michael D. Barr has argued that "Asian values," like his earlier idea of socialism, were for Lee Kuan Yew only a means to an end, namely creating prosperity and a social consensus (Barr 1998). Others have argued that Asian values accompany the state's attempt to co-opt the rising middle class while trying to avoid democratization (Thompson 2001). Elsewhere Thompson (2004) also argues that in Singapore, "Asian values" were only used to justify authoritarianism after the city-state had become a developed country, which shows that these ideological claims do not provide legitimacy to the regime. In Hong Kong, surveys suggested that many preferred a strong paternalist state, which indicated that the colonial regime matched with the political values of the people (Lau and Kuan 1988). However, in a later study of three Chinese societies (China, Taiwan, and Hong Kong), Kuan and Lau (2002) have come to the conclusion that traditional values have very little impact on political participation.

Furthermore, especially in the case of Singapore, the virtual lack of political activity is attributed to middle-class support for the present political regime. This has to be seen in contrast to modernization theory, which claims that economic development produces a middle class whose interests are the establishment of a democracy. Rodan (1996) argues that while the middle class in Singapore has sought autonomy from the state, it has found it in the shopping malls and not in parliament. Furthermore, the rising middle class's moderate demands of the state are due to "Singapore state's ability to heavily condition the avenues of effective capital accumulation" (ibid.: 39). Elsewhere, Rodan (1992) also argues that the middle class has been a major beneficiary of PAP policies. The government's intervention in the economy, the size of government-linked corporations (GLCs), and the official ideology of paternalism have enabled the ruling elite groups to maintain control over the demands of professional activists. The class-based approach is therefore able to trace the structural conditions that maintain the regime's status quo.

Scholars have also suggested that the *strength* of the government is responsible for the lack of political contention. This augments the class-based approach, because it highlights the importance of leadership and organizational structures. The effective strategies of the regime for dealing with social and economic problems, as well as the ability to deliver the economic goals, have eliminated the need for political opposition (Lau 1981; Hussin 1997). According to this opinion, the outcome has been that people are content with the success of the ruler—in Hong Kong with the colonial regime under Governor Murray MacLehose and in Singapore with the People's Action Party. The economic performance and the efficiency of the government guarantee continuing support (Neher 1999). There is no doubt that economic success and performance contribute to the legitimacy of the regime. This book will also show that the opposite, namely relative lack of performance in the form of economic problems, has created opportunities for the return of the opposition.

In both city-states, authoritarian rule is justified by the extraordinary need for political stability.[1] In Hong Kong, it was argued that China would object to democratization because it could create an independent entity. As this would be against Chinese nationalist aspirations, it would be obliged to annex the colony by force (Lau 1981). In Singapore, the PAP has claimed that its domination of politics is essential for the survival of the nation in the face of threats from neighboring countries, race riots, and cultural changes, among many others. In its opinion, the party's ability to confront the "national threat" was proven in the struggle against Communism as well as communalism at the time of independence in 1965 (Quah and Quah 1989). Some have argued that the survivalist claims no longer serve as a possible legitimation for the political system, with its focus on developmentalist goals (Koh 1997). However, the PAP still portrays various problems, such as the Severe Acute Respiratory Syndrome (SARS) crisis of 2003 or the water dispute with Malaysia, as national crises which threaten the survival of Singapore. This suggests that, to a certain degree, the ideology of survivalism still legitimizes the ruling elite's hold of power, at least in its own perception (Ortmann 2009).

In both Singapore and Hong Kong, the government has also tried to co-opt a number of potential challengers into political institutions to preempt the development of contention. This was meant to "steer change in Singapore down a preferred path of political co-option rather than political contestation" (Rodan 2006b). Similarly, Lau has argued for Hong Kong in the 1970s that "co-option of potentially disaffected leaders into the government machinery deprives protest movements of leadership and makes mobilization of the mass for political movements extremely difficult" (Lau 1981: 197). While this strategy is indeed very effective in containing contention, we need to know how it affects the opposition's goals and tactics. Co-option, this book argues, tends to split the opposition into moderates and more aggressive members, which weakens their organization. At the same time, co-opted moderates tend to accept their role in the political system as one of constructive opposition that denies them the right to increase their strength.

Finally, researchers studying the Singaporean opposition have noted the importance of coercion and fear. In Singapore, coercion is not used indiscriminately against any kind of opposition. Rather, as William Case (2005) notes, the government employs "artful manipulations" of the system and selective repression of oppositional behavior, which serve as a warning against anyone wanting to get involved in politics. Cherian George, in his analysis of the press controls in Singapore, has called this balanced tactic "calibrated coercion" (George 2007). While in Hong Kong coercion was not as important for the rulers, the government did arrest members of the opposition and closely monitored the activities of pressure groups.

While many of these explanations account for the relative lack of contention in Singapore and Hong Kong, there are obvious differences between the two city-states in the level of contention. It is evident that since the late 1960s Singapore's leaders have been far more effective in containing contention than have been their Hong Kong counterparts since the 1970s. Only a comparison of the two cases, therefore, will allow us to understand what determines this disparity. This will shed light on the mechanisms behind contentious politics. Despite some structural differences between the two cases, the similarity of two city-states undergoing tremendous economic changes while the governments try to contain the contention that results from new demands to the political system allows us to evaluate the containment strategies and distill the factors that are important for their success.

In order to assess the processes that underlie political contention, this book employs the political process model. This model was originally conceived by Doug McAdam (1982) to understand the generation of insurgency during the civil rights movement. In the tradition of James Rule and Charles Tilly (1975), from whom he borrowed the term *political process model*, McAdam tried to understand the development of social movements and their decline. In Rule and Tilly's model there are three types of groups that play an important role: government, contenders, and challengers. While the government holds the principal ability to coerce others, those that use resources to influence the government are called contenders. "To the extent that a contender can routinely lay claim to the generation of action or yielding of resources by agents of the government, the contender is a member of the polity, which consists of all contenders successfully exercising routine claims to government response" (Rule and Tilly 1975). Finally, the groups, which are not part of the polity, are the challengers. They lack sufficient resources to exert influence on the government. While the government and the contenders form the ruling elite groups, challengers are marginalized and potentially form oppositional groups.

Ruling elite groups and oppositional groups

The interaction between different groups within a society (and even across borders) is decisive to understanding the development of contention and, eventually, pressure for democratization. Alfred Stepan points to the importance of the democratic opposition during democratic transitions when he asserts: "In order to understand how a democratic opposition can attenuate the bonds of authoritarianism, we must first consider where the opposition stands in relation to the other components of the regime" (Stepan 1990: 159). To accomplish this, it is necessary to distinguish between different groups with unequal power and resources. Stepan (1990) distinguishes between five different groups:

1. the core group of regime supporters
2. the coercive apparatus that supports the regime
3. the regime's passive supporters
4. the active opponents of the regime
5. the passive opponents of the regime (Stepan 1990: 160)

This book argues that in Singapore and Hong Kong, these five groups can be reduced to a basic underlying dichotomy. On the one hand, there is the regime and its supporters, and on the other hand, opposed to it, are the opponents and its supporters. The terms "ruling elite groups" and "oppositional groups" will be used to describe the distinction between regime and opposition. The second group in Stepan's list describes the institutional frame in which the groups interact. This also gives the ruling elite groups the ability to exert power over other groups. In this sense it is an obstacle and a tool at the same time. The passive supporters are "quasi-members" of each group and, in theory, can potentially be mobilized to join the respective group. In reality, however, they will play only a limited role, namely providing moral support to a group. Moral support, however, is an important asset to a political group.

The term group in this context needs to be defined. In social psychology, a group is described as an "aggregate of individuals who interact with and influence one another" (Bordens and Horowitz 2002: 289). Other characteristics of a group are the need for the group to have a purpose, the existence of group norms, a prevailing role distribution, and effective ties and interdependence between group members. In the context of social groups within a state, however, it is necessary to define groups as so-called *affiliative* groups, because they exist for more general social reasons (ibid.). People often join these groups voluntarily because they feel close to the groups' values and norms. Examples for these groups are religious sects, fraternities, or political parties.

Second, it is important to understand the distinction between ruling elite and opposition and why the term "oppositional group" is used. The ruling elite is understood as an aggregate of social groups that is in a position of political power and is able to manipulate the resources of a country to obtain a favorable position for members within the groups. The different groups are not mutually exclusive and multiple memberships are quite common. Elite groups also tend to be closely connected through a common ideology. Oppositional groups, on the other hand, are a mixture of social groups that are excluded from political power or have very limited influence over political decisions and need to compete for resources with powerful contenders from within the ruling elite. They are often seen as members of opposition parties and civil society, of which the latter refers to groups that are independent of the state and often act in conflict with the state (Kim 2000). However, the concept of oppositional groups must also include less formally organized social movements and unofficial networks that act in opposition to the government (Geddes and Zaller 1989). They are usually more fragmented, because they do not share a single ideology and they usually disagree among each other on the choice of tactics and goals.

This distinction is necessary in order to understand how, when, and why oppositional groups will challenge the ruling elite groups and how, when, and why the ruling elite groups respond. This naturally presupposes that there is a continuous struggle between opposing groups. This conceptionalization adapts parts of Schubert et al.'s 1994 model of strategic and conflictual groups. The groups in their model are defined by their position in the production and appropriation process, by socio-structural characteristics, by ethno-cultural characteristics, and the power resources that each of these groups has. The latter refers to their potential to engage an antagonistic group, which is of great importance to challengers, who are interested in wrestling for power. Members of the ruling elite in this concept are not only those that are part of the regime but also those that support the regime (Schubert et al. 1994).

Elite groups and oppositional groups are, however, not seen as unchanging opposites, but as continuously developing or declining social groups that can trade places at any time. Elite groups and oppositional groups are not homogeneous groups, but are malleable constructs that help us to better understand the relationships between different groups. A ruling elite may consist of many different, in themselves competing social groups, and at any point in time this group alliance may break apart, initializing a new power struggle. However, elite groups, under normal circumstances, tend to have a common interest which creates a union and even fusion between the different groups. Oppositional groups, on the other hand, are often marked by internal fissures and lack significant power in the political system. In democratic societies, oppositional groups and pressure groups can indeed exert tremendous influence on the government, even if they are unable to directly influence the outcome. In authoritarian regimes, opposition, if it exists, can sometimes not even exert indirect influence on the political process.

The degree of power a group can exert depends on its location within the political system. An environmental group may have a relatively high impact on the decision to eliminate environmental hazards, but it may not have any power over how it can create awareness for its cause. The military, usually part of the ruling elite coalition, may have great influence on strategic decisions but very little on military funding. The degree of power, however, may change over time, as one group is able to increase its power even within one of the two sets of groups. Especially within the elite, certain groups can act as oppositional groups in order to increase their power. To complicate matters even more, groups within the elite and oppositional groups cannot always be clearly separated. There are many links between different groups within each set, and even links between the two opposing groups.

In spite of these differences, the political process model of political change in this book analytically simplifies the interactions in order to analyze the development or decline of contentious politics. This is possible because the two cases in this study are authoritarian regimes with democratic features that clearly separate the ruling elite from the opposition. Figure 2.1 shows the interaction between the two sets of groups, which will be explained in the following sections.

Expanding political opportunities and the institutional structure

While social movement theorists have focused solely on the reasons for the development, rise, and decline of social movements, this book is interested more in the conditions that could change the power relationship between

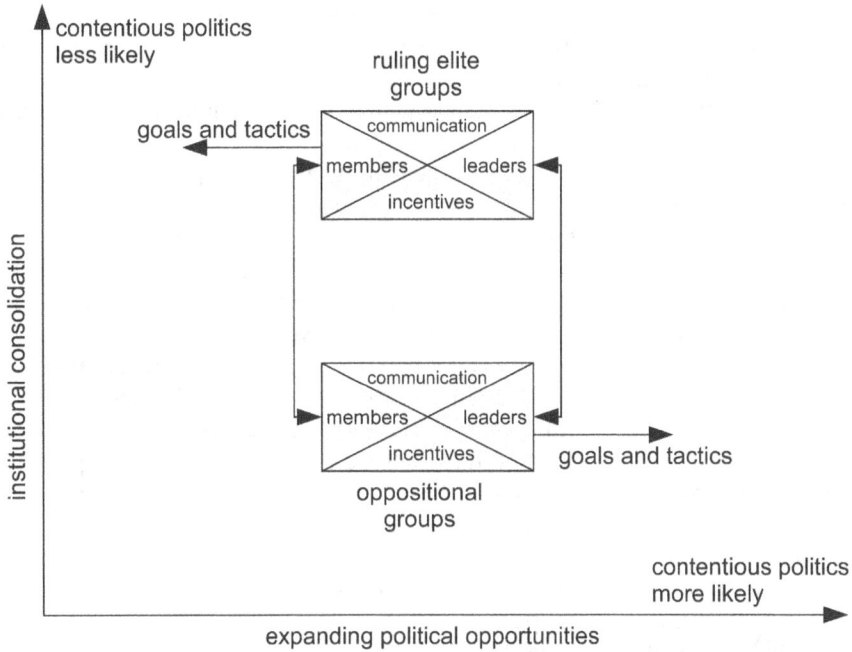

Figure 2.1 The Political Process model of contentious polities

excluded contenders and powerful ruling elite groups. McAdam's initial assumptions are not necessarily only about social movements per se: "Under ordinary circumstances, excluded groups, or challengers, face enormous obstacles in their effort to advance group interests. Challengers are excluded from routine decision making processes precisely because their bargaining position, relative to established polity members, is so weak" (McAdam 1982: 40). This description closely resembles the relationship of various groups in authoritarian regimes, where a small elite monopolizes power and oppositional groups have very few resources to challenge it.

The development of social movements, McAdam asserts, is dependent on changing political opportunities that arise over time. Any event that changes the power relationship, the assumptions, and calculations of the opponent is seen as a disruptive occurrence in the political process. Examples of events that threaten the status quo are wars, industrialization, changes in the international arena, economic crises, and large migrations. Modernization can therefore be regarded as one reason for changing political opportunities.

It is important to recognize the significance of political opportunities in the democratization process, because without them excluded groups cannot challenge the predominance of a strong, cohesive ruling elite group. Moreover, the changing conditions can weaken the elite group coalition, which can lead to greater fragmentation of the political system and thus to power struggles between opposing forces. While it is not easy to generalize the content of changing political opportunities, it is important to recognize that political processes are not static and are subject to constant changes. For example, modernization processes such as industrialization create greater complexity in the political system. This complexity in turn changes the conditions for competing political groups.

Opportunities have to be understood as motivators for oppositional groups. The opportunity structure is always related to the ruling elite groups, which through their ability to deal with challenges either provide an opportunity for challengers or weaken the chances of potential contestants. They have the potential to essentially reduce the power discrepancy between the two opposing groups. The following four dimensions have been identified: the first dimension regards the relative openness of an institutionalized political system, the second deals with the degree of ruling elite cohesion, the third considers the existence of allies within the ruling elite groups, and last but not least, the fourth deals with the state's ability and willingness to use repression against its opponents (McAdam 1996). All of these dimensions have one thing in common: they are based on the legitimacy of the political regime. An erosion of legitimacy, therefore, provides challengers with an opportunity to challenge the regime. The concept of legitimacy will be discussed in detail in the context of the cognitive perceptions of the different groups.

In this context it is important to note that the improved bargaining position of the oppositional groups increases the costs of repression for the ruling elite groups. Often, groups are only attacked when they are challenging the system and when they are vulnerable (Gamson 1975). This is similar to Robert A. Dahl's (1971: 15) second axiom: "The likelihood that government will tolerate an opposition increases as the expected costs of suppression increase." For Dahl, the opposite is also true: when the costs of toleration of the opposition decrease, repression will be less likely. This might suggest that repression may not be necessary for ruling elite groups to maintain their dominance. For Dahl, a competitive regime is most likely when "the costs of suppression exceed the costs of toleration" (ibid.: 15). This is, however, only the case when the two groups are able to find a compromise, through which a competitive system can be institutionalized.

Recently a number of theorists have challenged the political process model's structural bias. Goodwin and Jasper's criticism is directed at the assumption of widening political opportunities as an explanatory variable for the development of social movements. They claim:

> Whether this thesis makes sense depends, of course, on what is meant by "political opportunities." The broadest definition makes the definition tautological: Movements cannot emerge where people are unable, for whatever reason, to associate with one another for political purposes. (Imagine the fictive society described by George Orwell in *1984*).
>
> (Goodwin and Jasper 1999: 30)

By taking an extreme example of a totalitarian country, the authors neglect the possibility of countries that have independent groups but also a number of strict restrictions on political group behavior. In authoritarian regimes with democratic characteristics, for example, the right to free speech or the right to assemble are restricted and controlled by the government.

The ability of groups to organize under these circumstances, however, is not static but depends on changing conditions in the society, which, when they are conducive to oppositional forces, are considered political opportunities. As Tarrow (1996: 61) argues, "Movements arise as a result of new or expanded opportunities; they signal the vulnerability of the state to collective action, thereby opening up opportunities for others; the process leads to state responses which, in one way or another, produce a new opportunity structure."

While modernization results in the development of opportunities, formal institutions such as the bureaucracy, parliament, procedures, and rules and regulations restrict the extent to which they can have an impact on oppositional groups. In the political process model, institutions are part of the changing opportunity structure and of the use of social control response by the regime (McAdam 1982). Institutions have a long history and therefore also provide a structural constraint on oppositional groups. An analysis of institutions enables us to understand the frame in which the two groups interact. Institutions give the ruling elite the tool with which they can suppress the opposition. Institutions alone, however, do not explain why political groups act in a certain manner. This can only be understood through an analysis of their organizational structure, their cognitive perceptions, and their choice of tactics and goals.

Therefore, opportunities have to be considered within the institutional context of a political regime. Institutions regulate the behavior of ruling elite and oppositional groups. While ruling elite groups have great influence over the development of these institutions, oppositional groups are almost entirely excluded from them. They, furthermore, give the ruling elite the tools with which it can control oppositional activity. However, they are also closely linked to political culture and societal values, which are more difficult to change. Institutions often inherit these structures from previous governments, which explains why revolutionaries often attempt to completely replace these institutions.

Organizational strength

Political opportunities and formal institutions are not enough to understand the development of contentious politics. In order for the disadvantaged and powerless to take action, there need to be existing organizational structures in the society that enable the development of challenger groups. In McAdam's opinion the presence of networks and organizations is of great importance to the development of social movements. In terms of oppositional or excluded groups, the importance of organizational strength, therefore, cannot be neglected

(McAdam 1982). For the ruling elite, group cohesion and strength determine the groups' ability to act decisively against the challengers. A cohesive ruling elite is better capable of managing the state and suppressing the opposition. The relative strength of a group determines the success of a group, and for challenger groups it also determines the level of social control, because the costs for repressing a strong group are much higher.

While changing political opportunities provide the historical frame of continuously changing interactions, the analysis of the organizational structure appears static. The analysis of the organization can admittedly only capture a moment in time. It needs to be recognized that the two groups are subject to membership fluctuations whenever conditions change. Nevertheless, an analysis of the organizational structure provides an important insight into a group's present position and allows the researcher to determine the problems and challenges that the group may face in the future. McAdam (1982) identifies four aspects that determine organizational strength: members, leaders, established structure of solidary incentives, and the communication network. These factors play an important role for the ruling elite groups, as well as for the challenger groups. The former have to maintain their advantages in these areas, while oppositional groups will have to attempt to increase their strength. In the following sections, each of these aspects will be introduced.

Members

The role of members is important for ruling elite groups as well as for challenger groups. The study of elites usually focuses on the leaders, who undoubtedly play the most important role in any group. However, those who follow the leaders and who strengthen their power are at least as important. Even within groups, there are power struggles, and so it is only reasonable to assume that this is also the case within the elite. Strong supporters and bureaucrats, who can be considered members of this group, are of great importance to the stability of the group. It is important to take into account factors such as the number of members, their education, and their ideology, among others, in order to understand who the members are that support the political regime or involve themselves in oppositional politics.

While recruitment of members of the elite usually follows predefined paths, oppositional groups usually find their members "along established lines of interaction" (McAdam 1982: 44). This means that before joining a challenger group, members tend to be in formal or informal organizations out of which the group develops. For example, students in Hong Kong who had been part of the student movement were more likely later to become members of pressure groups (Leung 2000). McAdam's model does not cover, however, an essential aspect of movement development, namely the increase in members over a period of time. These new recruits often join an organization or group because of its rising strength or because of other apparent benefits.

Leaders

Second, the leaders are of great significance to any group because their decisions determine the direction of the group. This is especially important when we consider the actor-oriented approach of democratization, whose proponents claim that the primary reason for the development of democracy is the agents who decide to pursue democratization. For instance, leaders of the ruling elite have tremendous influence on the development of a country. Their decisions, among other things, shape the institutions and determine the reaction to oppositional activity.

It is the prestige and the organizational capabilities of leaders that lend credibility to a group, and also may lead to its downfall if they are lacking or become problematic. Disagreements between various leaders can also be an impediment to the development of group alliances or may lead to the breakup of existing alliances. The split of a ruling elite coalition into "soft liners" and "hard liners," which is a precondition for top-down democratization, is a good example of this development (O'Donnell and Schmitter 1986).

The structure of incentives

The benefits that members get from a group are the focus of an analysis of the structure of incentives. In McAdam's model, only solidary incentives play a role, but it has to be recognized that, especially for members of the elite, there are also material and purposive incentives.[2] All organizations must have formal or informal incentives in order to motivate the participation of their members. Moreover, incentive systems can provide "the rudiments of a predictive theory of organizational behavior" (Clark and Wilson 1961: 130).

Oppositional groups, however, often face the problem that potential members may not see the benefit of joining a group if their objectives can also be achieved without their being part of a group. This is termed the "free-rider problem" in group theory (Olson 1965). To solve this problem, a challenger may offer to members the prospect of material improvements. A labor group, for instance, could fight for better salaries and/or provide pastime activities. In some cases, the most important facet might even be idealistic, such as the improvement of society or the individual. This is an aspect of some religious groups, and also of oppositional groups, as this analysis will show. Most groups, moreover, provide their members with multiple incentives in order to attract as many members as possible. This is important because the number of members allows a group to demonstrate strength to its opponents.

Communication network

A final aspect of the organization of a group is its communication network. It determines the strength of an emerging challenger or the degree of control of the ruling elite. There are essentially two forms: internal and external communication.

From the viewpoint of internal communication, group leaders must be able to communicate their ideas to the members of the group. The significance of this element becomes clear when it is linked to the need for coherence within a group. The closer the members are to the leadership and to other members and the greater the ideological homogeneity, the greater is the ability for the group to act as one. Such an informal communication network also provides the individual members with incentives, because it enables individuals to become more important members of a group.

For external communication, it is essential that both oppositional and ruling elite groups exchange information with other groups and with the population. This recognizes the need of these groups to garner support for the group and to build a network of interaction that provides the basis for increasing and maintaining strength. It also raises the question of the means by which groups communicate. These range from personal contacts to the use of modern media to transmit ideas. Access to the press, for example, to communicate the group's goals and strategies increases a group's ability to reach a wider spectrum of people. In authoritarian regimes, this space is often skewed in favor of the ruling elite. Oppositional groups under these regimes tend to have very little or no access to these media. The comparison of Hong Kong and Singapore will show that the ability to communicate has a great influence on the overall relationship between ruling elite and oppositional groups.

Changing cognitive perceptions and legitimacy

Political science, for the last three decades, has often ignored the role of emotions and perceptions (Goodwin, Jasper and Polletta 2001). Rational choice and, in particular, game theory, have been applied to the development of contention and democratization, but since humans are the primary actors in these processes, an analysis of the prevailing perceptions is in order. It is important how people view the political system, socio-economic changes, or their own involvement in politics. For the ruling elite, a sense of purpose and belief in the rightfulness of their actions is as crucial as it is essential for the opposition to be convinced that collective action is needed to achieve its goals. In this context, it is also important to evaluate the role of legitimacy, which has a great impact both on the unity of the ruling elite and on the ability of challengers to confront the government.

The role of emotions in politics is increasingly playing an important role in political science. The focus of this analysis is on the psychological processes of emotions not at the individual level, but rather at the group level. This cultural approach follows Goodwin, Jasper and Polletta (2001), who propose the use of cultural analysis aided by psychological awareness. They describe the role of emotions as follows:

> The emotions most relevant to politics, we believe, fall toward the more constructed, cognitive end of this dimension. Moral outrage over feared

practices, the shame of spoiled collective identities or the pride of refurbished ones, the indignation of perceived encroachment on traditional rights, the joy of imagining a new and better society and participating in a movement toward that end—none of these are autonomous responses. They are related to moral institutions, felt obligations and rights, and information about expected effects, all of which are culturally and historically variable.

(Goodwin, Jasper and Polletta 2001: 13)

This complements McAdam's third component of the political process model. He distinguishes between two cognitive processes that underlie the development of social movements: cognitive liberation and collective attribution. The latter describes the collective processes during insurgency, which maintain the level of urgency and cognitions to sustain the insurgency. It is closely linked to the term cognitive liberation, which describes the psychological conditions that are necessary for the onset of an insurgency. While changing opportunities provide oppositional groups with the ability to challenge the political system, the ability to perceive an opportunity is just as crucial. Since opportunities are not necessarily dramatic, changes of perceptions, however minute, may increase the strength of an oppositional group. This may, for example, be a change in behavior of the elite groups, as McAdam asserts: "the altered responses of members to a particular challenger serve to transform evolving political conditions into a set of 'cognitive cues' signifying to insurgents that the political system is becoming increasingly vulnerable to challenge" (McAdam 1982: 49).

Emotions also play a role in the way that groups conceive of the world in which they interact with other groups. Subjective perceptions about the capabilities and intentions of one's opponent influence the behavior of a group. Cottam and Cottam (2001) have developed an elaborate approach to capture the interaction between groups of different social positions. While their approach mainly focuses on the behavior pattern of nationalists and the interplay between different nation states, it can also improve our understanding of the relationship between challenger groups and ruling elite groups.

Image theory is based on the assumption that humans need to categorize their environment in order to understand a complicated and often confusing world. An image in this context is a cognitive category. Social identity theory is interested in the role of cognitive conceptions of the world in social developments. "Social categories and images of others are shared cognitive constructs. Their existence is commonly recognized and accepted, and they are transmitted in society and across generations through learning and the socialization process" (Cottam and Cottam 2001: 88). Changing an image, therefore, is a process that can take a very long time. In the context of this book it is important only to recognize that these behavior patterns persist, that they pose serious obstacles to changes in the relationship between ruling elite groups and oppositional groups, and that any movement away from these emotions and behavior patterns can signify a change in the overall relationship.

The relevant images in Hong Kong and Singapore deal with the acceptance of the prevailing hierarchical order. Image theory suggests that there are certain behavioral patterns associated with each image. The images, the emotions associated with each image, and the behavior patterns are shown in Table 2.1.[3]

These two images describe prevalent notions and provide a generalization of the groups' perception of the power structure and the opposite group.

The "imperial image" is the dominant image of the oppositional groups in the two cases in this study, which is based on the assumption that inferiority can only be accepted when a group feels that its status is just or when the comparison group is seen as dissimilar.[4] The "imperial image" differs between times of stability and times of conflict. This distinction is made in order to differentiate the perceptional patterns within the classification of the "imperial image". In the two cases in this study, oppositional groups, who hold on to an "imperial image," first and foremost believe that the greatest priority should be the continuation of social stability. This can be regarded as a subjection of the groups' goals to the prevailing social order. Groups who have this sentiment tend also to have a sense of powerlessness, due to an overbearing state that proclaims it is in a superior position to maintain stability.

During times of stability this has the consequence that groups reject the use of conflict to achieve their goals. In the extreme, this may even include doubts about the legitimacy of the group to challenge the regime. The result is submission of the groups' interests to those of the nation as defined by the regime. This strong "imperial image" usually persists in situations in which government repression is strong and opposition members fear this repression. Boudreau (2004: 6) writes accordingly: "State attacks leave legacies of fear and caution that realign authoritarian rule and social resistance for years." As a result, many oppositional groups tend to avoid conflict and submit to the demands of the regime. For instance, most of Singapore's opposition parties usually refrain from directly challenging the ruling party (see Chapter 8).

In times of contention, the sense of stability and weakness may, however, also result in an opposite behavioral pattern. The imperfections of the regime can quickly turn toward discontent and even anger. This in turn leads to a willingness to challenge the ruling elite groups in the interests of stability. This perception is more likely if the government is unable or unwilling to control

Table 2.1   Images, emotions and behavior patterns

	Emotions	*Behavior patterns*
Imperial image	desire for stability, feeling of powerlessness, fear (during stable times), anger (in times of conflict)	Avoid conflict, submit (stable) Willing to use conflict (in times of conflict)
Colonial image	Sense of superiority and legitimacy	Paternalistic dispositions, nonviolent repression

Source: adapted from Cottam and Cottam 2001: 121

the public discourse. In Hong Kong, the press often highlighted the short-comings of the government, which perpetuated discontent. Furthermore, the government's lack of financial resources created serious problems for governmental programs. The result was that the government did not achieve its own targets, which resulted in discontent.

Ruling elite groups are marked by a so-called "colonial image," which is a reflection of their prevailing ideology. They largely consider themselves superior to the opposition, and consequently see it necessary to act as a paternal guardian over these groups. The Singapore and the Hong Kong governments both claim to act in the interest of the people. For example, they have devised ways to help the inhabitants of their cities to improve their behavior. The top-down approach to policy making, furthermore, has resulted in an elitist conception of politics. In Singapore more than in Hong Kong, the ruling elite has seen itself as a special group that has the right to control the lives of the inhabitants because its members are better educated and thus better able to act in the interests of the people. In Hong Kong, the sense of superiority was based less on academic excellence than on racial and cultural stereotypes.[5]

While Cottam and Cottam's concept does not directly discuss the role of legitimacy, it is necessary to include it, from the vantage point both of the ruling elite and of the opposition. As Alagappa points out, legitimacy "frames the discourse among strategic groups—and even between these groups and the public—in their endeavor to control the use of state power" (Alagappa 1995: 3). Mainwaring (1992) also considers legitimacy to be important for understanding the significance of the perception that various actors have of the political regime. This concept recently has also been studied by social and political psychologists. They contend that legitimacy is inherent within the perceptions of individual actors:

> the legitimacy of a government, the authority of its leader, the acceptability of discrimination based on race or gender, has its roots in the perception of moral worth that is an essential part of the perceptional field. People and governments have a moral value that people can perceive, they see in a person, in a nation, or in an action a degree of good and bad that is equivalent to legitimacy.
>
> (Crandall and Beasley 2001: 77–78)

Seen in terms of differing groups vying for power, this perception also influences the decision-making process of these groups. Since the government is seen as one group that is opposed by another, the perception of the oppositional groups by the ruling elite groups is of particular importance.

So, on the one hand, the ruling elite groups are able to strengthen their control over the political system if they are perceived to be the legitimate ruler. This means that oppositional groups are only able to promote democratization successfully if they are able to argue cogently for the development of an alternative to the present situation (Stepan 1997: 662). An authoritarian regime with democratic characteristics that functions relatively efficiently, however, creates significant obstacles for political opposition, because it forces oppositional groups to demand a system that differs from the present only in the degree of democracy. The fact that these regimes can successfully claim that they have functioning legal systems poses problems for a struggle promoting the rule of law. This aspect of the regime, furthermore, reduces the possibility that regime supporters will switch to the opposition (Stepan 1997). Mainwaring also points out that "When authoritarian regimes enjoy considerable support, it is more difficult to mobilize against them" (Mainwaring 1992: 306).

However, on the other hand, the regime's self-perception as the legitimate ruler also affects the relationship between the opposition and the government. This is because effective governance and coercion require cohesion within the ruling elite, and therefore legitimacy. Aside of strengthening elite cohesion, legitimacy also affects the ability to make decisions. In other words, the ruling elite groups are able to perform more effectively if they consider themselves to be the legitimate rulers (Alagappa 1995; White 2005).

The goals and tactics of ruling elite groups

It is possible to distinguish between two ideal-typical goals of ruling elites which, in reality, are complementary: effective and efficient rule (progressive goal) and maintaining power (conservative goal). The latter is perhaps most important to authoritarian rulers such as the PAP in Singapore or the colonial rulers in Hong Kong, who are unwilling to share power with others. In an increasingly complex society, achieving effectiveness and efficiency depends on an increasing number of people, which makes the hegemony of the ruling elite increasingly vulnerable to challengers. This demonstrates that the two goals are not just complementary but also contradictory, and achieving both becomes increasingly difficult. The overarching goal for rulers of both city-states, therefore, becomes the necessity of containing contention in order to ensure stability.

In order to achieve these goals, the ruling elite groups also have the choice between two different tactics: co-option (moderate tactic) and coercion (extreme tactic). Mainwaring suggests that "Often [authoritarian elites'] actions take into account calculations of how the opposition will react, and some government leaders may attempt to co-opt moderate opposition groups" (Mainwaring 1992: 299). An extended form of co-option is also the attempt to preempt the need for political opposition, which can occur through fulfilling the demands of a majority of the population. In both cases, this was the self-proclaimed emphasis on effective and efficient governance. However, since not all members of the opposition can be successfully co-opted, willingness to compromise can effectively weaken the opposition's unity. While the ruling elites in both city-states prefer to make use of moderate tactics, the leaders have also occasionally felt the need to resort to repression. A violent crackdown on the opposition is more likely to have a greater short-term impact on the opposition than a calculated suppression of selected opposition members. The former may have the immediate impact of elim-inating the group, but may pose a more serious threat in the future because the memory of the crackdown can be used to organize or reorganize oppositional groups.

The use of only extreme tactics has the immediate effect of removing com-petition, but poses serious problems once an oppositional movement returns. Only moderate tactics, however, may overly embolden a challenger. In terms of tactics, the right balance is therefore important in order to maintain power. This balance could be achieved by destroying selected opposition members while co-opting others. This effectively drives a wedge into the opposition, which, in consequence, is considerably weakened.

The goals and tactics of challenger groups

The goals of oppositional groups have to be seen as a continuum along which oppositional behavior is aligned. On the one hand, the opposition may choose to demand reform of the existing order. However, if the opposition is able to convince the elite about these reforms, they will strengthen the position of the ruling elite groups. Consequently, they are not likely to generate a strong social control response. The opposite is true, however, for revolutionary goals. Oppositional groups that demand fundamental change are likely to meet with a very strong response from the ruling elite. Usually the goals' of oppositional groups are not either purely reform-oriented or purely revolutionary. Groups such as Communists or even Nazis may be the closest to being almost com-pletely revolutionary. These groups are, however, the exception rather than the rule.

The tactics of oppositional groups can also be divided into two ideal-types: institutionalized, non-threatening and non-institutionalized, threatening tactics. The former include tactics such as contesting elections or becoming nominated members of political institutions, which means that oppositional groups are essentially trying to change the system from within. They do not pose a threat to the existing order and, consequently, the social control response from the elites tends to be small. In contrast, tactics that defy the present order, such as public protests, nonviolent or violent resistance, are perceived to be threatening because they purvey a rejection of the institutional order. For that reason, elite groups are very likely to confront these tactics with a harsh social control response.

While the social control response depends on the type of tactics and goals the groups choose, group impact also depends on it. Ironically, the same tactics and goals that generate the largest control response also have the greatest potential for strengthening an oppositional group or social movement. A group that chooses only reform goals and institutionalized tactics will be very weak, because neither will it be able to effect change nor will it generate much interest in the group. Accordingly, "labor leaders, activists and poets will seek to anticipate, and somehow outflank state repression" (Boudreau 2004: 2).

A balance between reform and revolutionary goals, and between institutionalized and non-institutionalized tactics, therefore, strengthens a group and enables it to have the greatest impact. This is not easy, because the line is never visible and can only be found by trial and error. Finally, a right balance must be found, because an oppositional group needs to achieve significant strength in order to make repression of the group too costly for the ruling elite groups.

Conclusion and outlook

This chapter has adapted the political process model to explain the development and decline of contentious politics, which is regarded as a precondition for democratization (see Figure 2.1). If we assume that regime change is reflected in an increase of contention, then the factors that contribute to and constrain the rise of contention need to be analyzed.

The processes of modernization and industrialization lead to a *rise in opportunities* for oppositional groups to challenge the political regime. The ruling elite groups recognize this and try to adjust institutions in order to mitigate the effects of this pressure. For this reason, it is important to discuss the *institutional structure* of the interaction of political groups. The changes in the opportunity structure and the institutional frame can be seen as the background conditions in which group interaction operates.

The analysis of political groups, first and foremost, requires an evaluation of the *organizational strength* of a group, which determines its ability to interact. The cohesion of a group is reflected in the members, leaders, the structure of incentives, and the communication network. A group that has a large membership, a determined leadership, strong incentives, and an effective communication network is considered to reflect strong cohesiveness. On the other hand, a weak group is small in terms of members, has a divided leadership, provides intangible incentives and is unable to communicate effectively.

Second, the *cognitive perceptions* of a group strongly influence its goals and tactics. The perceptions are cultural constructs, which provide the group with cognitive categories by which it views the world. In this study, groups are largely influenced by either the "imperial image" or the "colonial image." The former describes the opposition's perception of the ruling elite groups, and the latter the ruling elite groups' perception of the opposition. These images reinforce the hierarchical nature of the authoritarian regime and therefore serve to stabilize the political system. An important part of the perceptions is also the factor of legitimacy. For an oppositional group, it is more difficult to challenge a legitimate regime, and a ruling elite group is more successful in implementing its goals and strategies if it is perceived to be legitimate.

Finally, the *choice of goals and tactics* determines the direction of the development of group interaction. The ruling elite groups' goals can be described as either progressive or conservative and their tactics as moderate or extreme. Oppositional groups prefer either reform or revolutionary goals and institutionalized or non-institutionalized tactics. These choices continuously influence the interaction. In the political process model the ruling elite groups' goals and tactics aim for greater institutional consolidation of their power, and reduction of political opportunities. If successful, this decreases the likelihood of contention. Oppositional groups, on the other hand, try to weaken the institutional barriers that confine them and use political opportunities in order to increase their power. Since this increases the level of contention, democratization is also more likely. However, democratization is not inevitable, because much depends on individual choice of certain leaders and fortuitous events.

The next two chapters will analyze the increase in opportunities and the institutional structures of Hong Kong and Singapore. It will be shown that both city-states have had similar development paths and have comparable institutions. The difference lies mainly with the ruling elite groups that have made use of the institutions to achieve their goals. The strength, the perceptions, and the choice of goals and tactics of the ruling elite have had a strong impact on the opposition. While some groups have yielded their interests, others have started to openly challenge the regime. This has increased the level of contention in the political system.

3   Depoliticization and the rise of social protest in Hong Kong during the 1970s

The history of Hong Kong has much in common with that of Singapore. Both city-states originate in the colonial history of the British Empire, which gave them similar institutions. Both were captured by the Japanese in World War II and afterwards slowly decolonized. However, while Singapore became independent, because of Hong Kong's peculiar relationship with the Chinese motherland, due to an "unequal" treaty forced on the Chinese by the British in 1842 and the land lease of 1898, as well as rising nationalist sentiments, the city-state could not become independent. Instead, the British government opted for significant autonomy of its colony, which led to self-sufficiency. Another similarity was the economic modernization of the two city-states, which often pitted them against each other as economic rivals (Jao 1997). At the same time, it provided opportunities for a rising opposition movement that was an outgrowth of the increasing complexity of the state. However, there are significant differences in the economic transformation. While Hong Kong's laissez-faire policy and fortuitous historical events helped to propel the economy, the Singaporean leaders' emphasis on the developmental state closely guided the economy. Finally, a correlation can be made between the 1966/67 riots in Hong Kong and communal and Communist riots in Singapore during the 1950s and early 1960s. These events made it necessary to deal with contentious politics, which often meant co-opting critics into government institutions and also legitimized the use of coercion against more threatening opponents.

In the second part of this chapter, the focus will be on the institutions of Hong Kong's bureaucratic regime. While the city-state had a Legislative Council and an Executive Council, neither of these institutions was very powerful. Instead, power rested with the governor and the bureaucracy, while the latter was perhaps the most powerful. Even though Hong Kong was considered more liberal than Singapore, the city-state had similar regulations, which potentially could be used to contain oppositional groups. Furthermore, while the government promoted the independence of the judiciary to the international business community, there were also those who challenged its true independence, because it was controlled by the administrative state (Downey 1975). Finally, Hong Kong did have some democracy, in the form of the Urban Council. While it provided oppositional groups with an institutional platform for voicing discontent, it also contributed to the co-option of dissent and the depoliticization of society.

Expanding political opportunities

The city-state's modernization, the increasing complexity of the government, and the inability of the government always to fulfill its promise to provide social services resulted in opportunities for newly arising oppositional groups to challenge the ruling elite. These developments were circumscribed by Hong Kong's colonial status, which placed the colony between its imperial master, Great Britain, on the one hand, and the People's Republic of China, on the other. This limited the choices of the government and predetermined Hong Kong's future. After World War II, the British colonial government decided to improve its administration of Hong Kong in order to avoid criticism from the United States or China (Tsang 1988). It therefore decided to support the modernization of the city-state, which became most evident in the growing investments in the local infrastructure and included ambitious programs such as public housing and the construction of a sophisticated public transportation system. Limited efforts in social services, which had been the exclusive obligation of private community groups, the "Kaifong associations" during the early times of the colony, were introduced in order to improve the income discrepancies between the rich and the poor. These developments can be seen as the beginning of a decolonization process, yet without the possibility of independence in the future. Steve Tsang notes that "As the colonial government accepted that its continued existence was at the sufferance of the PRC, it became more responsive to the needs and the wishes of its people and in delivering good governance, though this fell short of introducing democracy" (Tsang 2004: 181).

Decolonization without independence and democratization

The city of Hong Kong originates in the history of the British Empire. With the Treaty of Nanjing, of 29 August 1842, Hong Kong Island, the center of today's Hong Kong, was seceded from the Qing Empire. In 1860, Kowloon was added to the colony and in 1898 the New Territories, the largest part of modern Hong Kong, was leased for 99 years from the Chinese. While British colonialists did not settle on a barren rock, as was often claimed, neither did they find a flourishing Chinese city (Ngo 1999). Originally a trading outpost in the opium trade, the colony soon became Great Britain's major harbor for trade with China. The colony flourished until World War II, when it fell victim to the Japanese army. On Christmas Day 1941, the city was officially surrendered to the invaders. After the war, the colony returned to British control, but the attitude toward colonialism both in Britain and in Hong Kong had begun to change.

Hong Kong's unique historical situation after World War II placed the city-state in a contradictory situation. On the one hand, it was still a colony with a governor at the head of the government and a colonial bureaucracy whose higher echelons were filled with expatriate officials. On the other hand, Hong Kong became increasingly autonomous, with a greater emphasis on home rule. This was, of course, closely linked to the intentions of the British government to disassociate itself from the colonies and the imperialism that was connected with them. Many British law makers thought that the money that was spent on colonies could be better spent at home (Lloyd 2001). The British government, furthermore, tried to leave its former colonies as independent states with a democratic system after a period of "trusteeship," in which the colonial government trained the colonial people for self-government and democracy (Owen 1999). This process of decolonization was not an option in Hong Kong, because the British government had decided that independence for the colony was not feasible. Such a move would have provoked mainland China and might have impelled the Chinese to take the city by force. Furthermore, in 1972 the Chinese government convinced the United Nations to remove Hong Kong and Macao's status as colonies, which reinforced China's territorial claim over the two foreign dependencies (Harris 1978).

The decision to at least partially decolonize Hong Kong resulted in a reorientation of the role of the colonizer from emphasizing only law and order, to increasing concern with the social life of the colony. According to Lee (1967), the change in British colonial policy allowed colonial governments to extend their paternalist rule over a supposedly less advanced population. It was accompanied by the realization that the colonial society was also capable of economic and social development, which motivated the colonial rulers to increase their efforts for the education of their subjects. A related aspect of this decolonization process was the intention to promote the economic and social development of the colonies. At the same time, the British government was not inclined to support this development financially and the colonial governments, therefore, often faced tremendous shortfalls in cash, and in terms of social services they mostly concentrated on education and, after 1945, on social services (ibid.). These general developments also affected Hong Kong, where rapid economic changes increased popular demands on the government to provide more and better social services, better education, and better economic conditions (Lui and Chiu 1999).

Decolonization without independence bore significant challenges for the colonial administrators, who were well aware of the close link between decolonization and the development of a national identity, which was against the interests of the Chinese, and therefore actively discouraged. As a consequence, British colonial rule operated according to a circular logic: "Britain controlled Hong Kong therefore it was the legitimate government; it was the legitimate government because it controlled Hong Kong" (Thomas 1999: 52–53). Even though periods of strong Chinese nationalism obstructed the development of a Hong Kong identity, with the development of a common language,

Hongkongese, a mixture of Cantonese, English and other languages, and relatively high levels of religious activity, "a Hong Kong identity did eventually emerge" (Tsang 2004: 180). This was due to the fact that most of those that had been born after 1950 had no first-hand knowledge of China until the PRC opened up in the 1970s. Furthermore, Communist rule on the Mainland deterred many from returning to China, while at the same time Hong Kong prospered in a socially stable regime. This development of a distinct identity in Hong Kong, ironically, resembled the growth of nationalist movements in other states (ibid.).

The rejection of the possibility of independence for Hong Kong and the prospect of returning the colony (or parts of it) to China in 1997 were seen as a major obstacle in the process toward greater democratization. In the writings of British officials we can see that many saw China opposed to greater democratization on a territory-wide basis because it would entail the development of an independence movement (Faure 2003). While Hong Kong did become very similar to an independent state, at least in administrative terms, when the British government slowly disengaged itself from the city-state it did not become democratic. For Britain, the empire had become very expensive, and it was due to this and its ability to raise enough money that the city-state became financially independent (Scott 1989). Furthermore, the localization policy (although frequently delayed) and the shift toward "home rule" changed the self-perceptions of many Hong Kongers.

The lack of possible future independence was, however, not the only reason why the government was unwilling to broaden the arenas of electoral participation. Another reason was the fear that these democratic institutions could be infiltrated by political groups from the Chinese mainland. In the discussions of Governor Sir Mark Young's plan to introduce greater democratization after World War II, one of the dangers that was discussed was that of political infiltration of the proposed elected institution. Originally, Governor Young saw this threat as coming from the Kuomintang (KMT) but, as the Communists gained control over China in 1949, the fear of infiltration shifted to the Communists. While the Nationalists had been seen as corrupt and easy to influence, the Communists were perceived as incorruptible (Tsang 1988). The Communist threat thus became a serious impediment toward greater democratization, as a British official noted in 1959: "Overt aggression by the Chinese is less likely than an attempt to get the Colony by subversion" (quoted in Faure 2003: 180). This argument may be termed the Communist threat, and largely resembled the reasoning for the Singaporean government's destruction of the political opposition in the 1960s. The threat from Communist China, furthermore, played a significant role in oppositional politics in Hong Kong and created the limits within which interaction was possible.

Democracy was also rejected because of the general discourse that claimed that elected representatives would not necessarily perform better than nominated officials. Most British administrators considered good government to be of greater importance than any development toward greater democratization

(Lo 1997). These attitudes concerning the administration of the colonies reflected the political thought of many prominent Chinese intellectuals at the time, who also tended to place the highest priority on good government. Chinese conceptions of democracy converged with the opinion of colonial administrators in Hong Kong, who thought that Hong Kong was in fact democratic because the government was able to follow the doctrine of *minben* (the people as the basis), and that the only difference was the lack of democratic procedures (Chan 2004). In the Chinese tradition, democracy does not originate from the need to represent diverging interests in society. It is, rather, an attempt to achieve the best government possible for the future of a strong China. Wang and Titunik (2000) argue that China's political tradition stresses the ideal of a selfless and moral leader who makes his decisions in the interests of the people. In this context, the role of the people is only to provide sanction for the legitimacy of the leader (ibid.). Elections, in a definition of democracy that follows traditional Confucian thought, would merely serve as an option for the leader to show that a person still enjoys the trust of the people. The principle of competition between differing groups is therefore entirely absent from this conception. It is not surprising, then, that John Walden, Director of Home Affairs, noted in 1980 that a group of successful Chinese executives in the late 1920s and early 1930s were unanimous in their view "That Hong Kong people think that what is important about the Government is the character and the performance of the individuals who run it rather than whether it is an elected or appointed government" (*SCMP* 18 Feb. 1980).

Economic modernization and the rise of political groups

Perhaps the greatest sign of the proceeding decolonization was the transformation of the Hong Kong economy. In the late 1950s, Hong Kong's economy transformed from an entrepôt economy mainly based on trade with China to an export-oriented economy (Youngson 1982). This was aided by an influx of capital and technology from the mainland and a large number of refugees, which provided the new industrial economy with a source of cheap but relatively skilled labor. The focus of the newly rising industries was on export, mainly in textiles, electronics, and plastic merchandise. Hong Kong's economy was marked by a dominance of small to medium-sized industrial firms, which accounted for its ability to adapt quickly to economic changes (Leung 1996). However, in contrast to developmental states such as Singapore, the government did not guide this transformation (Meyer 2000). Rather, it was the outcome of a fortuitous historical development that was related to the emerging Cold War. It was the UN embargo against China at the time of the Korean War which cut off most of the trade between the colony and mainland China, forcing Hong Kong to reorient its economy. In the 1970s, after the McKinsey Report (see Chapter 5), the Hong Kong government changed its focus from short-term planning to long-term planning, initiating a new phase in Hong

Kong's development toward greater involvement in the economy (Scott 1989). This, in part, reflects a significant shift from laissez-faire economics toward the recognition of the role of the state in the economy. For example, the government began to use its control over land to attract certain industries which it considered preferable to the development of the economy (Miners 1981). Nevertheless, the laissez-faire attitude of many law makers and the dominance of the merchant and business classes in the government still restricted the state's ability to influence the economy.

Hong Kong's economy, furthermore, developed rapidly in the 1970s (despite the oil crisis 1974–75), while the focus shifted from the industrial sector to the service sector, with an emphasis on tourism, finance, and trade (Jones 1990). This not only created new resources for oppositional groups but also provided opportunities for the development of new groups. Lo Shiu-hing attributes the level of group participation in the 1970s to three factors: a split of the societal elite into business elite and the service professionals, which formed the opposition groups. Second, there was increasing political aspiration on the part of working-class representatives, and last but not least there was a considerable degree of liberalization (Lo 1997). The latter reason seems unconvincing, because the government tended to become less tolerant of oppositional politics toward the end of the 1970s. The second argument seems to have played some part in the increase in group activity, because in the 1970s a new, independent labor movement developed (Butenhoff 1999). Before the 1970s, the labor movement in Hong Kong was largely demobilized even though, unlike in Singapore, the government had not directly interfered with labor organizations (see Chapter 4). It did not have to. The labor movement was split into two opposing groups: the right-wing Trade Unions Congress (TUC), close to the Republic of China on Taiwan (ROC); and the leftist Federation of Trade Unions (FTU), close to the People's Republic of China (PRC). The new labor movement, however, remained relatively weak, which becomes evident in the number and duration of strikes, as well as in the number of participants in strikes (Leung 1996).

The most important argument for the development of contention can be found in what Lo (1997) has called the split between the business and the educated elite, the service professionals. This was, however, less a split within the "ruling elite" than a split within the Chinese community. The educated so-called service professionals were the product of the educational politics of the colonial regime and the modernization of the city-state, and therefore more interested in government policies. In this process, society-minded students played the role of the vanguard, as they also did in other Asian countries during the developmental process (Leung 2000; Thompson 2005). After the student protests had declined, service professionals increasingly took their place in the development of a civil society in the late 1970s.

The other group that Lo (1997) identifies is the business elite, which not only shared a different background but also had different priorities than the service professionals. The members of the business elite were either the traditional merchants, who were closely linked to the colonial regime, or the relatively new industrialists. Most of the latter were recent immigrants from China, who had decided to open up their own business because other professions required proficiency in English. Lo (1997), agreeing with Hoadley (1973), argues that this group tended to avoid politics because of its so-called "refugee mentality," because it had experienced the rough political struggle in China and longed for political stability. Furthermore, the reluctance of business owners to participate in politics was probably influenced by the fact that the British colonial government provided them with a legal system that provided them with a secure environment for their activities (Zhang 2006). Business, after all, flourishes best under established rules and is averse to instability.

Significance of the 1966 and 1967 riots

At the crossroads of decolonization and modernization, the late 1960s saw the transformation of Hong Kong's political system from that of a colony to a city-state with increasing autonomy, despite its lack of true independence. This process, however, was not only a logical consequence of British colonial policy but required a number of events that would lead to this transformation. The most important events were the riots in the mid-1960s, which were the trigger that would alter the government's approach, to become more responsive to the demands of the people (Scott 1989; Lui and Chiu 2000). Steve Tsang argues that when John McDouall, then Secretary for Chinese Affairs, retired and the riots swept through Hong Kong in 1966/67, the resistance of the bureaucracy to reforms was broken. "[Governor] Trench thus started a process of transforming the government from an old-fashioned Crown Colony system into a modern administration responsive to public opinion" (Tsang 2004: 190). When the Secretariat for Chinese Affairs was renamed the Home Affairs Department in 1971, this was not simply a sign of the government's willingness to reform but also signified the government's commitment to greater localization, which manifested the end of the colonial phase and the beginning of, albeit still technically colonial, "home" rule.

The two riots, furthermore, set the frame in which political groups interacted during the 1970s. For the government this meant that it had to focus more on "good government" and efficient rule. For the oppositional groups the change of government focus created opportunities for greater influence on the government (Lui and Chiu 2000). With concerted efforts, oppositional groups were increasingly successful in pressuring the government to reform itself. However, it also helped to legitimize the government's authoritarian rule and obstructed the opportunities for alternatives to the political system. The government's reaction to the development of increasingly assertive pressure groups in the 1970s included both co-optation and coercion. While the 1966 riot suggested a disconnect between the ruling elites and the masses, the 1967 riot brought the dangers of anti-colonialism and Communism to the agenda of the ruling groups. The latter made it clear that co-optation alone could not create stable rule, because it directly challenged the legitimacy of the regime. The government's reaction to the two riots serves as a basis for its behavior in the 1970s.

The 1966 riot started when the Star Ferry Company decided to increase its fare and a single protester started a hunger strike. The "Kowloon disturbances" were uncoordinated and occurred on the nights of 6 and 7 April. The real reason for the 1966 riot, however, was probably latent dissatisfaction with the social conditions, which were exacerbated by a minor economic recession. The fact that housing for about 700,000 Hong Kongers was inadequate only shows the desperate situation of many inhabitants (Scott 1989). Despite the lack of organization, it indirectly involved Urban Councilor and social activist Elsie Elliot, who had protested against the price increase. She and another Urban Councilor, Brook Bernacchi of the Reform Club, were also questioned after the riot, which suggested the potential for a future organization of political protest and for a more concerted effort in challenging the government. It is thus not surprising that Elliot's telephone was wiretapped at least from the early 1970s (Tu 2003). The government, furthermore, went to great lengths to investigate the reasons for the riot: "The scope of the investigation was important because it was one of the first attempts by those in authority to find out the sources of discontent and of what the protesters thought of their government" (Scott 1989: 87). This manifested a profound change in the attitudes of a colonial government that had favored a hands-off approach in the past.

The government's investigation into the riots, however, concluded that there was not a problem with the present political system, but rather merely a gap in the communication between the leaders and the public. The report stated "that those who complain are seeking not so much a change in Government, as readier access to Government" (quoted in Miners 1981: 381). The questioning of popularly elected Urban Councilors, furthermore, initiated the government's approach of co-opting its critics by trying to involve them in the policy-making process (Tsang 2004). On the one hand, this allowed pressure groups to influence the government, but on the other, constituted an attempt to preempt those critics who might have called for regime change. The 1966 *Report of the Working Party on Local Administration* made it clear that democratization should be reserved for a later time:

> the members feel that until such time as the public has gained confidence in a system of election by popular vote it is essential to draw upon this valuable reserve of respected, able and public-spirited community leaders by tapping it for participation in the administration of the Colony at the local level as well as at the central level.
>
> (Quoted in Miners 1981: 382)

This resulted in the establishment of local administration in the City District Officer (CDO) scheme in 1968, which had both the stated goal of better understanding the people and the added benefit of depoliticizing the population.

Placed directly under the supervision of the Secretariat of Home Affairs, it was meant to strengthen the ties between the government and the population. The most important reason behind the scheme, according to Ambrose King, was to create a favorable impression of the government: "The CDO, as a political agent at the district level, is not aiming at political mobilization of the populace; in fact, it is trying to depoliticize the political process" (King 1975: 437).

On the other hand, the 1967 riots were much more organized and were directed against what the protesters perceived to be an illegitimate colonial government (Scott 1989). The government, furthermore, linked the riots to the Communists and to the Cultural Revolution taking place in China at the time. The government, after some period of hesitation, however, came to the conclusion that the Chinese government in Beijing was not behind the aggression and there was no secret Chinese plot to overthrow the Hong Kong government (Wong 2001: 77). The disturbances started with labor disputes in May 1967 and turned more aggressive and violent, with human casualties, in June. After the arrest of the three employees of the Xinhua News Agency, the unofficial diplomatic representation of the PRC in Hong Kong, random terrorism plagued the city (Cooper 1970; Scott 1989). From August to December, bomb attacks killed fifteen people and the police uncovered 1,167 genuine bombs. These events allowed the government to capitalize on the Communist threat, which enhanced its legitimacy in the eyes of many Hong Kongers (Scott 1989). It is no surprise that almost 600 different groups announced their support for the government (Cooper 1970).

In response to the riots, the government set up the "Special Group" in the Information Services Department, which was chaired by prominent politicians such as Denis Bray, Robert Locking, and David Ford. The group was set up to assist the government on a day-to-day basis, but its results were never published (Wong 2001). The government's main conclusion from the 1966/67 riots was that they were reflective of a lack of communication between the government and the people. This lack of communication, however, was seen more as a failure of the government to convince the population of its "good" intentions. In this regard, the government recognized the significance of the Information Services Department as its main propaganda organ, as the Secretary for Chinese Affairs, Paul Tsui, made clear in the Legislative Council in 1968:

> This regular flow of factual material may be relied upon in the long run to inform and influence responsible public opinion even in the face of a determined campaign of anti-government propaganda, employing lies and distortion, as the events of 1967 made clear.
>
> (*Hong Kong Hansard* 1968: 15)

Denis Bray, furthermore, said in 1999: "We try [*sic*] to emphasize that we are not suppressing any political movements. But we are simply concerned about law, order and public security" (quoted in Wong 2001: 77). The threat of potential subversion from leftist groups provided the basis for the government to deal with the rise of new pressure groups in the 1970s, even though these groups appeared more moderate. The government's suspicion toward these pressure groups would last well into the 1980s. While the government constantly reiterated its support for freedom of speech and assembly, the claim of public security and the threat of opposition to political stability were used to justify the use of coercion.

The institutional structure

While Hong Kong's institutions have been based on laissez-faire and small government, after World War II they had to adapt to the tremendous changes arising from the economic transformation of the city-state. During that time, an authoritarian regime with democratic features emerged in favor of a more liberal democratic system. The political regime during the 1970s and early 1980s can be classified as non-competitive, partially pluralist.[1] Power in Hong Kong's political system was the sole monopoly of a small group of colonial administrators. This resulted in the development of a bureaucratic regime to which external actors had very little direct access. The only viable options for oppositional groups were to run for elective office in the Urban Council, to petition the government, to stage protests, or to publish critical articles in the newspapers. This, of course, distinguished Hong Kong from present-day Singapore, where the government controls the media and public protests are practically forbidden. Nevertheless, it should not be forgotten that the Hong Kong government had similarly rigorous laws at its disposal. Protests were normally allowed, but Hong Kong had its share of unlawful assemblies that led to arrests. Pressure groups could voice their opinions, but the government closely monitored their behavior and even tried to infiltrate those groups. The newspapers were free to print what they, wanted but their conservative articles showed either their like-mindedness or their tendency to self-censor their reporting. It should not be forgotten that there was legislation that could have been used against the press. Nevertheless, there is no doubt that Hong Kong was more liberal, a place, as Lee Kuan Yew claimed, "where everything goes but nobody cares" (quoted in Walden 1983: 29).

Hong Kong's bureaucratic regime

At the head of Hong Kong's political system was the governor, who was at the same time the representative of the British government. In theory the governor could become a dictator, in practice he needed at least to share power with the bureaucracy, because he needed its cooperation (Miners 1981). This need actually created a bureaucracy much more powerful than the governor, as the civil service, under the leadership of the colonial secretary, conducted the day-to-day operation of the colony (King 1975). As a consequence, Hong Kong experienced what Ambrose King (1975) has called "administrative absorption of politics," which means that the basic functions of the political process had become part of a centralized bureaucratic structure.

The original bureaucracy was very small and nearly totally dominated by British expatriates, and was only intended to maintain the minimum necessary to guarantee peace and political stability. After World War II, however, the bureaucracy experienced tremendous growth rates. While in 1949 it counted 17,500 officials, this number had grown to 45,000 by 1959 and by the middle of the 1970s had doubled yet again. Along with the growth of the bureaucracy there was also a slow process of localization, even though the native population initially received only lower-level jobs while the expatriate British officials continued to dominate the high-level positions. Nevertheless, this process was intended to create the impression of increasing representativeness, even if only in ethnic terms (Miners 1981).

The government, just by its sheer size was able, furthermore, to co-opt potential dissidents. Ambrose King notes that the government constituted the largest employer in Hong Kong in 1972, with around 2 percent of the population working for the government. He therefore argues that "the bureaucracy has contributed a great deal to the stability of Hong Kong by serving as a mechanism for assimilating the potential 'discontented' into the governing machinery" (King 1975: 428).

This monopolization of power within the bureaucracy, however, also contributed to the feeling of powerlessness within the population. For example, one commentator asserted in 1979 that there were only about thirty decision makers who controlled Hong Kong (Lee 1979). As Chapter 7 demonstrates, this opinion represented a widespread perception within oppositional groups, which considered petitions and protest to be the only way to appeal to the government. The government tried to contain this rising contention by improving the "communication channels" and thus co-opting the opposition. In 1979, John Walden, Director of Home Affairs, suggested eleven "channels of interaction," which included advisory boards, informal contacts through City District Officers, petitions to the governor, public statements, commissions of inquiry, the UMELCO office, contacts between the bureaucracy and its clients, letters to the editor, phone-in radio talk shows, public affairs programs, and green papers on policies (Walden 1983). This heterogeneous list, ranging from top-down messages from the government (public statements, green papers) to bottom-up appeals from individuals (letters to the editor, petitions), raises serious doubts about the success of the government's efforts.

The only true link between the population and the government can be found in the co-option of individuals. This was achieved not only through the bureaucracy but also through appointments to advisory boards, such as the Legislative and Executive Councils, which will be discussed in the next section. These measures, however, failed to contain the growth of contentious politics and only reinforced the perception of powerlessness within the population (King 1975).

Legislative and Executive Councils

As a counterweight to the purely bureaucratic, the governor had two consultative councils, the Executive Council (ExCo) and the Legislative Council

(LegCo), at his disposal. The two councils seemed to resemble the two branches of a government with separation of powers, but since both neither were elected nor had any real power, they resembled the Executive and Legislature in name only. Prior to 1976, service in these two councils was even unpaid. Both councils were composed of "official members" and "unofficial members" and, for example in 1975, there were six official (five ex-officio) and eight unofficial members in the ExCo and fourteen official and fifteen unofficial members in the LegCo (King 1975). Ex-officio members were those who held other posts at the same time, such as Attorney General, Secretary of Home Affairs or Financial Secretary (Miners 1981). The development of the Legislative Council shows that there was also a constant process toward greater localization, akin to the bureaucracy. In 1945 there were still fewer than 50 percent Chinese, while by 1970 there were already 84 percent Chinese in the chamber (King 1975).

The unofficial members of these two councils, who were nominated members of society, represented another attempt to co-opt potential challengers. The appointed unofficial members largely belonged to the established and emerging economic elites (King 1975). They were chosen for their likelihood of supporting the governor and, therefore, representative of only the most loyal inhabitants of the colony (Harris 1978). These members had largely conservative attitudes and were defenders of the laissez-faire approach (Wong 2001: 34). Despite the fact that only a small segment of the population could become unofficial members, the government often considered them representative of the interests of the Hong Kong people.

Because the unofficials could not come from all parts of society, the government tried to minimize this problem by means of a more consultative style of governance. This was to be achieved through an office called Unofficial Members of the Legislative and Executive Councils (UMELCO), established in 1963, and expanded in 1970 when it started to work mainly on complaints from the public and conducted research (Miners 1981). As the the Director of Home Affairs, John Walden, pointed out, the government regarded UMELCO as one of the channels of interaction between the government and the people of Hong Kong (Walden 1983). However, because UMELCO's main task was to help people with their daily problems, it often led to charges that it was concerned mostly with petty problems (*Sunday Post–Herald* 1974).

Because the unofficial members showed little opposition to government initiatives and largely played a supportive role, the government's claims of a more consultative style failed to convince the rising pressure groups during the 1970s. The lack of any real opposition from unofficials, for example, led some to believe that they were powerless stooges in the service of the Imperial Power. While their opinion was important to the government and their opposition was avoided (Endacott 1973), in the public perception they were largely seen as "yes-men" (Miners 1994). The unofficial member Woo Pak-chuen, furthermore, asserted that the Legislative Council was part of the governing groups:

We do not regard ourselves, Sir, as being an opposition to the Government.
Indeed we consider it our duty to help the Government in every possible
way to devise the most suitable laws, policies and methods of administration
for this unique twentieth century Crown Colony.

(Hong Kong Hansard 1 Nov. 1972: 51)

This supportive role made it difficult for the government to argue that the
unofficials were acting in the interest of the public, and limited its potential to
co-opt increasingly assertive oppositional groups.

Civil liberties and restrictions

The situation of civil liberties in the 1970s is ambiguous. The Hong Kong
government often prided itself on the high level of personal liberties (see for
instance, Freedom House 2006).[2] However, if we take the laws that were on
the books in Hong Kong during the 1970s, we can find many regulations that
potentially severely restricted oppositional group behavior. As these laws were
mainly intended to create public order, they placed limits on political expression. Lau (1982), furthermore, asserts that the close relationship between law
making and the bureaucracy created a system in which the laws reflect the
prerogatives of the bureaucracy. Perhaps the most significant was the 1967
Public Order Ordinance, which was enacted in the aftermath of the riots during
that year and was primarily designed to crack down on street violence. The law
made it necessary to apply for a permit for public gatherings and placed severe
penalties on unlawful assembly. The illiberal nature of the bill was known to the
colonial government when it was enacted, as the Attorney General, Denys
Tudor Emil Roberts, stated that "If the criticism is made that the Bill errs on the
side of safety, this can be attributed to our experiences in the past few months,
which have reinforced the Government's view that in our circumstances the type
of control proposed in this Bill is unavoidable" (*Hong Kong Hansard* 1 Nov.
1967: 442). During the 1970s, some pressure groups perceived this law an
obstacle to their activities. For instance, H. Tsang, the chairman of the Demar-
cators Association, worried about this law because it was not clear to him whether it superseded their right to picket (*Hong Kong Standard* 10 May 1975).

The law was applied in 1979 when the government arrested sixty-seven
boat people and social workers while they were riding in coaches on their way
to the governor's residence to petition the governor to allow them to be
resettled in public housing. The planned peaceful protest, which had not been
registered with the police, had not yet started. On 12 February 1979, all fifty-six
of those who were prosecuted were discharged and eleven were sentenced, all
of whom were service professionals.[3] Furthermore, the government arrested
other people who showed their support for those arrested (*Hong Kong Standard*
14 Feb. 1979). This event clearly demonstrates that the government was willing
to use the laws in an exemplary fashion and the existence of the ordinance
had some effect on the behavior of oppositional groups.

The Public Order Ordinance was by no means the only item of such legislation that existed during this period. The Control of Publications Ordinance, for example, contained some of the strictest restraints on the press. It stipulated that newspapers were not to publish "false news likely to alarm public opinion or disturb public order" (see: Chang 1982: 82–83). Furthermore, in order to register for new publications, publishers had to pay HK$100 yearly as a registration fee, plus HK$10,000 cash deposit to ensure that a publisher was capable of paying any fines due to legal proceedings. This was comparable to the Licensing Act in England, which was allowed to lapse in 1695. The Hong Kong government was of the opinion that strong regulations were needed to prevent the internal struggles in China from spilling over into Hong Kong. Chang (1982) asserts, furthermore, that despite the legal regulations, the newspapers were free to print whatever they chose because law and reality were two different matters. However, this has to be seen in light to the fact that in 1952 publishers were convicted of sedition under the Control of Publications Ordinance.[4] This likely contributed to an attitude of self-censorship.

During the 1970s, the editors and owners of the English-language newspapers tended to be very conservative, oftentimes openly supporting and even justifying the government, while at the same time the average journalist became part of the rising social movements (Barrett 1979). The conservative English-language newspaper, the *South China Morning Post*, for example, provided a possible justification for Hong Kong's authoritarian bureaucratic regime in 1979: "There are admittedly bureaucratic impediments that block progress and individual initiative here and there. And the Hong Kong resident has to accept that there are a whole range of laws instituted for the general good order of the community which have to be acknowledged and accepted" (*SCMP* 28 Feb. 1979). Even if there are problems with the centralization of power, the paper argues, the government's intent to act in the interests of the people provides it with the necessary legitimacy. The style of this editorial, furthermore, closely resembles Singapore's government-linked *Straits Times*, which often prints justifications for the authoritarian aspects of the government. John Lent, therefore, argues that "reporters find that even though Hong Kong has a relatively free press, there are many doors of government closed to them. Perhaps because of that, they find it easier to act as 'lackeys' of vested interests in government and business, rather than investigators" (Lent 1982: 94).

Other laws allowed the government to arrest anyone for any "offense," while in Britain people could only be arrested for serious crimes. Also there was no requirement for search warrants, and searches could be made with reasonable suspicion. Emergency Regulations, which were withdrawn but continued to hover like the sword of Damocles over society, potentially allowed the Colonial Secretary to arrest anyone without a trial. Many of these laws, even if they were applied only rarely, created a sense of uncertainty within the oppositional groups, which, however, did not hinder some from actively pushing for political change.

An independent judiciary?

In the study of Hong Kong's political system, the judiciary has rarely been closely studied. Norman Miners' classic *The Government and Politics of Hong Kong* (1975–97) mentions the judiciary only in reference to the constitution of Hong Kong, to which he dedicates one chapter in his book. The executive, meanwhile, receives two chapters and the pseudo-legislative three. Peter Harris' book *Hong Kong: A Study in Bureaucratic Politics* only contributes two and a half pages to the discussion of the courts. He mainly considers the judiciary as part of the administrative state and the "courts in Hong Kong ... have no constitutional role and must merely interpret law" (Harris 1978: 85). Lau Siu-kai agrees with Harris when he asserts that "While the bureaucracy monopolizes the law-making and law-enforcement functions, law adjudication is the reserved duty of a relatively independent judiciary" (Lau 1982: 35). The Letters Patent, the de facto constitution of Hong Kong until the introduction of the Basic Law in 1997, placed the power of nominating judges in the hands of the governor. Furthermore, the governor was granted the right to pardon and even to exile political criminals.[5]

While the academic literature generally accepts the notion of an independent judiciary, opinions during the 1970s have pointed out a number of weaknesses in this assumption. For example, in 1974 a lawyer called M.H. Jackson-Lipkin asserted that Hong Kong's judiciary was anything but independent, for three reasons. First of all, the judges were paid out of the government's budget; second, judges were treated as public servants; and third, they were subject to establishment regulations. "They [the judges] have to fill out an annual report at the end of the year. Those in the Judiciary below the rank of Supreme Court judge can be removed for misconduct. They can be fined and they can suffer stoppages of work" (*Hong Kong Standard* 4 May 1974). The issue of lack of judicial independence was so important that even the *London Times* reported that "Many practising lawyers believe that the administration of justice in the colony is in an appalling state" (Berlins 1974). In response, the government introduced a bill that created a commission that was supposed to advise the governor on the nominations instead of just the Chief Justice. The creation of the commission, however, did not end the debate over judicial independence, as the editor of the *Hong Kong Law Journal*, Bernard Downey, wrote in his letter to the *South China Morning Post*: "Unfortunately, the proposals to include the Attorney General and the Chairman of the Public Services Commission as ex-officio members are likely to defeat this purpose, and to strengthen popular impressions or beliefs (held by highly educated members of the community!) that the judiciary is a branch of the Civil Service" (Downey 1975). Another problem for the judiciary was the fact that, while the majority of the population spoke Chinese,[6] the official language of the courts was English. Even after the introduction of Chinese as an official language in 1974, the judge could decide the language in the lower courts, while the higher courts continued to use English.

By the 1980s many again extolled the merits of an independent judicial system. The *South China Morning Post*, for example, wrote: "One point which perhaps not too many in the community understand is that the courts remain completely independent from the executive and regardless of how earnestly the Government or the police may desire a conviction or consider it in the best interests of the community, the decision is ultimately taken by the judge, with or without a jury, or magistrate after carefully weighing the evidence" (*SCMP* 9 Jan. 1980). This commentary seems to suggest that there was still a widespread perception of lack of independence of the judiciary. Chief Justice Denys Roberts, furthermore, emphasized the importance of the judiciary to the stability of the social system because the people considered judicial practices as part of the government. He also noted that the judiciary shared the same goals as the government. "So the courts become important in preserving respect for other institutions of authority as well as for themselves. The maintenance of this respect for the authorities is a potent factor in the stability of society" (quoted in *SCMP* 8 Jan. 1980).

Despite the fact that the judiciary in colonial Hong Kong was a government department, Cheng (1982) argues that its role in political and economic development was largely that of a fair arbiter of rules. This perception of stable laws created an environment that was friendly to investors who valued the security of their financial assets. In part, the judiciary probably also assisted Hong Kong's development as a financial center in East Asia. Furthermore, it should be noted that there were no trials against political opponents that ended in verdicts with exorbitant fines. The rights of assembly and free speech were generally granted, even though there were some notable exceptions, as will be shown later. It is fair to say that the judiciary was merely a passive organ that did not get involved in the political process and generally restricted itself to uncontroversial issues. The perception of lack of independence of the judiciary, however, contributed to the opposition's impression that the government was invincible.

The Urban Council—democratic islet in a non-competitive political system

Colonial government and a non-competitive system officially precluded the existence of pluralist, democratic politics. Despite the non-competitiveness of the political system, a small bastion of democratic activity existed. This democratic islet was the Urban Council, which had developed out of the Sanitary Board in 1936 and whose membership were half elected and half nominated. It provided individuals with a platform to try to influence the process of making policy, as well as its implementation. The literature on Hong Kong's democratization and the development of elected representation only fleetingly discusses the role of the Urban Council before the introduction of District Administration in 1983 (Ma and Choy 2003). This is, of course, due to the role of the Urban Council during the 1970s, which was very limited in both its functions and the representativeness of its constituents. The council's jurisdiction was very limited because it was only responsible for parks, playgrounds, food hygiene, and cultural facilities (management of City Hall, public libraries, museum and art galleries). The franchise for Urban Council elections was very narrow and included both economic and educational restrictions. This had the consequence that, in 1970 for example, only about 6 percent of the population were eligible to register to vote. By 1981, this number had only increased to approximately 9 percent of the population.[7]

At the same time, this quasi-democratic institution provided the government with an argument against further democratization. It functioned to a certain degree as a means for channeling the dissatisfaction of an increasingly assertive intelligentsia and, perhaps more importantly, as a justification for maintaining authoritarian rule. It was often argued during the 1970s that the low participation in Urban Council elections—only 1 percent of the population registered to vote and fewer than 0.5 percent actually voted—showed that there was no demand for further democratization. Many have therefore concluded that the Hong Kong Chinese were apathetic (King 1975; Miners 1981). The low voter registration rate, however, was also due to the complexities in the eligibility requirements and the fact that personal data were collected for the registration. Finally, the Urban Council's makeup[8] provided the government with a justification for nominated members. Elected members, it was claimed, were not necessarily better qualified for their position (Table 3.1).

The development of the Urban Council reflects the conservative attitudes of the ruling groups. Repeatedly, there were proposals for an enlarged franchise and greater responsibilities for the Urban Council. While the franchise was not enlarged before the 1980s, the responsibilities of the Urban Council changed over time. A government White Paper in 1971 considered proposals for the further development of local government, which included significant changes to the Urban Council as well as other possible forms of representative government. The White Paper, however, dismissed the notion of greater representation:

> It is however doubtful whether proposals along these lines would bring greater efficiency to the administration of the urban areas or provide the government with better services, and there has not been evidence of much, if any public interest in the introduction of such systems.
>
> (Hong Kong Government 1971: 1)

Another change in the 1970s limited the ability of the Urban Council. Before 1972 the council had debated issues that were often only slightly related to its duties. Consequently it was frequently used as a platform to argue about issues of current interest. For example, in 1967 Hilton Cheong-leen, an elected Urban Councilor, used the Council's jurisdiction over housing to press for compulsory universal public education. To accomplish his goal, he tabled a motion on the lack of education in the estates and then discussed the lack of public education during the official proceedings of the Urban Council. The

Table 3.1 Urban Council – Voter participation (1965–1981)

Year	Number of registered voters	Number of votes cast	Percentage
1965	29,439	6,498	22.1%
1967	26,202	10,189	38.9%
1969	34,392	8,178	23.8%
1971	38,730	10,047	25.9%
1973	31,384	8,675	27.6%
1975	34,078	10,903	32.0%
1977	37,174	7,308	19.7%
1979	31,481	12,426	39.5%
1981	34,381	6,195	18.0%

Sources: SCMP 1973–1979; *HK Standard* 1975, 1981

government forced the Urban Council to change its rules in 1972 because it seemingly embarrassed the government. Norman Miners expressed his opinion of the government's attempt to reduce the powers of the Urban Council in a footnote: "It is almost incredible that government should have been bothered about this occasional exhibition of free speech, or what harm could come of it" (Miners 1981: 235). Afterwards, discussions on the most important topics (such as the budget) were conducted behind closed doors (ibid.). The consequence was that even fewer people took any interest in the activities of the council.

Even if the Urban Council was the only part of the government that had elected members, its structure was tilted toward the nominated members. The nominated members tended to form a united block, while elected members were unable to agree on most issues. While in plural and competitive democratic systems partisanship is a normal and welcome feature, in Hong Kong's half-elected Urban Council it became a liability. Partisanship inadvertently weakened the elected councilors and prominent social activist and leader Brook Bernacchi, of the quasi-political party the Reform Club, was often blamed for this lack of unity. The function of the Urban Council was therefore twofold: to create the impression of democracy within an authoritarian regime and to provide an argument against further democratization. The most popular Urban Councilor, the nonpartisan Elsie Elliot, frequently complained about this problem and demanded unity among the elected members: "The present leadership has put the council back half a century in history. It is up to the elected side to bring it back and infuse new life into it. If not, it will remain what the Government intended it to be, just a veneer of democracy on a fascist core" (Elliot 1977).

Summary and outlook

The first part of this chapter focused on the historical developments that created the basis for the behavior and the interaction of the ruling groups as well as the challenger groups. Three important historical developments formed the basis of group behavior in the 1970s: the decolonization process, economic modernization, and the riots of 1966/67. The former placed Hong Kong in an odd position because the British government could not allow Hong Kong to become independent. Full democratization was rejected and the government even felt it unnecessary to increase democratic representation on a small level, such as the Urban Council. It considered good government was more important, which was supposedly in agreement with Chinese culture. Economic modernization contributed to the development of new groups of people such as the service professionals, who formed the core of the social movements in the 1970s. The 1966/67 riots should be seen as a turning point in the government's approach. They created a sense that the government needed to involve itself more deeply in society, which was to be accomplished through greater co-optation of members of the opposition. The fear of Communist subversion, which became evident in the second riot, resulted in the government's willingness to use coercion against its political foes.

Next to the historical developments, which changed the opportunities of various political groups, the institutional structure has to be seen as an antagonistic force because the stability of the institutions contributed to the status quo. Hong Kong's bureaucratic regime left emerging political groups very little room to influence the policy-making process. This restricted the options of these actors, as they were forced to resort to petitions, writings, and demonstrations, which created a general sense of powerlessness and inhibited the behavior of oppositional groups. The government tried to co-opt potential challengers into government institutions, but its success was limited because the members of the newly arising pressure groups could only rarely be incorporated into the institutional framework.

In the next chapter, we will turn to Singapore, which has experienced a similar development in terms of changes in the opportunity structure and the return of an active opposition. Unlike Hong Kong, these oppositional groups have, however, been unable to significantly challenge the political system. Singapore's ruling elite groups have been able to better co-opt and coerce the opposition, which has to be mainly attributed to the regime's legitimacy.

4 Expanding political opportunities and limiting institutional structures in Singapore

In contrast to Hong Kong, Singapore's modern history has been dominated by a small, cohesive ruling elite, which has been able to control nearly all aspects of Singaporean life. In order to understand how this came about, this chapter will delve deeper into Singapore's history. In the first part of the chapter the most important events that have influenced changing opportunities for oppositional groups will be summarized. The need for political and social stability has its origin in the unpredictable years between the 1950s and 1965, when Singapore gained its independence. As part of a developmentalist agenda, the need to achieve economic growth necessitated, in the eyes of the ruling elite, a strong state that frequently resorted to authoritarian measures. However, the increasing complexity of the system and the inability to completely fulfill the developmentalist goals led to the resurgence of opposition parties in the 1980s. The election victory of J.B. Jeyaretnam in 1981 is a watershed event in this regard. It heralded the onset of a new opposition movement. However, the return of the opposition did not signify the beginning of a democratization process. Instead, the authoritarian regime was able to adapt to the challenges and consolidate its power. The theme of Singapore's modernization can thus best be described as *guided liberalization*.

The second part of the chapter introduces the institutions that maintain Singapore's stable political system. The bureaucratic state, marked by a strict hierarchy and a close relationship between the ruling party and the administrative state, dominates the Singaporean polity. There is no independent labor movement and the press has become closely linked to the government. Rules and regulations severely restrict oppositional activity. While the judiciary is considered by most to be impartial in business cases, it has been regarded as partisan in political cases by many political activists and scholars. It is beyond doubt that a series of defamation suits against opposition politicians, initiated by members of the ruling elite, have resulted in verdicts with exorbitant fines that have greatly weakened any potential challenge. Still, Singapore claims to be a democracy and maintains periodic elections, which are perceived to be free and thus bolster the legitimacy of the ruling party and the government. Elections have, however, provided members of the opposition with the opportunity to challenge the regime within an institutional context. Nevertheless, there have been fewer instances of contentious politics in Singapore in recent years than in Hong Kong during the 1970s.

Expanding political opportunities

The political developments in Singapore show that the ruling party has been able to successfully monopolize power. This was the result of the particular situation during the years when Singapore became an independent state. During the 1950s, anti-Communism dominated the agenda of the British colonialists and the Communist movement was able to mobilize a large portion of Singapore's ethnic Chinese population, which resulted in a number of strikes, school sit-ins, and riots (Mauzy and Milne 2002). The People's Action Party (PAP) was able to skillfully garner the support of the Communist sympathizers while at the same time establishing itself as a strong anti-Communist party. This was accomplished to a large extent through the successful maneuverings of the party's leader, Lee Kuan Yew. From his point of view, the Communists posed a serious threat to the future survival of the city-state because they aimed to abolish the capitalist system that was seen as the basis of the city-state's economy. To mitigate this threat, Lee forced Singapore into a merger with the Malaysian Union, but his fear of Malay dominance resulted in a break-up only three years later. At the same time, he also destroyed any political opposition and incorporated the labor movement into a larger national movement that was based on developmentalism. The government's policy proved to be successful as Singapore became an economic miracle. At first, these circumstances eliminated virtually all opportunities for oppositional groups. Eventually, in the 1970s and 1980s short-comings in the government's strategy developed into potential opportunities for the opposition. Finally in 1981, the first opposition member since Singapore's independence was elected to parliament. This marked the beginning of a resurgence of oppositional activity.

The birth of a nation and the fight for survival

In order to understand Singapore's political system it is necessary to consider Singapore's colonial heritage and the circumstances under which this island city became a nation-state. When Stamford Raffles discovered an almost deserted island off the coast of Malaya in 1819, he considered it a good location for a trading outpost of the British Empire. He thus founded the lion city, or in Sanskrit, Singapura, which thus became an important part of the British Empire and a harbor for the army of merchants who were interested in trading with the peoples of Southeast Asia. In 1867 the Straits Settlement, named for the small straits that separate Singapore from the Malaysian peninsula, became a separate Crown Colony. While life in Singapore was chaotic and transient, the city was a fast-moving town. The colony was unaffected by World War I, but in World War II, it moved to the front of the war. It was in February of 1942 that the Japanese conquered the supposedly "impregnable fortress" of Singapore with little difficulty (Hack and Blackburn 2004). For many Singaporeans, including the man who would later become the founder of independent Singapore, Lee Kuan Yew, this was a turning point because it proved that the British were not omnipotent, as many had come to believe.

After World War II, support for colonialism had eroded and the British government was intent on a process of gradual independence, which was to occur after the colonies had acquired the necessary political expertise to become democratic republics. The first step in this direction was the election of six members of the Singaporean Legislative Council in 1947.[1] With the rise of Communism, another concern of the British was to avoid leaving a country that was closely aligned with the Communist bloc. In Singapore, the Communists enjoyed a strong presence, which worried the rulers. Consequently, the Communists were often implicated in the political conflicts during the 1950s. When Lim Yew Hock was elected chief minister in 1956, he banned organizations that were considered pro-Communist, which resulted in sit-ins and meetings at Chung Cheng High School to protest against the government. The government, however, was unrelenting and issued an ultimatum for the protesters to disperse. As the deadline approached, riots started and quickly spread across the city, leaving 13 dead and 123 injured. This was the worst violence that Singapore experienced after World War II.

Before independence, the government considered the possibility of a Communist revolution as the greatest threat to Singapore. The British colonial masters and elected local elite considered the threat so grave that they chose to undermine some of the democratic institutions. For example, the elected Lim Yew Hock took the first serious steps to restrict the power of labor unions, which were considered left leaning and therefore close to the Communists. He used the Preservation of Public Security Ordinance to arrest thirty-five people who were considered subversives. At the same time, a new party, the People's Action Party (PAP), was founded that succeeded in rallying the support of the Communists, while at the same time distancing itself from the more radical elements of the Communist movement. This was not an easy endeavor, as the party constantly faced the possibility of being subverted by the Communists. The arrest of the thirty-five leftists in 1957 helped the moderate leadership around Lee Kuan Yew to restore control over the party. Subsequently, the party constitution was revised to only allow cadre members to vote for the leadership (Bradley 1965). This helped Lee Kuan Yew and his close associates to monopolize their power over the party and subsequently to gain control over the whole city-state. In 1957, Lee received overwhelming support from his party for his proposal of adding "non-Communist" to the party platform (ibid.). In the 1959 elections, the PAP ran on a platform of workers' rights, democratic socialism, and an end to Emergency Regulations, as well as anticolonialism (Trocki 2006). In the first elections for a fully elected Legislative Assembly it won a considerable victory, with 53.4 percent of the votes and forty-three out of the fifty-one seats. Lim Yew Hock and his newly formed party were soundly defeated.

After the election, the PAP still considered the Communists to be the greatest threat to the survival of the city-state. As Shee Poon-Kim pointed out in 1978: "The PAP perceives the Communist threat as a life and death issue" (Shee 1978: 195). The PAP's plan to merge the city-state with Malaysia was in part an attempt to reduce the influence of the leftists. The effort to weaken the left-oriented faction of the PAP led to a split of the party in 1961, when a new party, the Barisan Sosialis (Malay for Socialist Front), was formed. This split caused great concern within the PAP, which had lost a significant number of members. Probably in order to rectify the situation, the government conducted the so-called "Operation Cold Store." On 3 February 1963, in an overnight sweep, security forces arrested 150 journalists, student leaders, labor activists, and opposition politicians. They were detained under the Internal Security Act (ISA), a law that dated back to colonial times and which allowed the government to arrest anyone without having to charge those arrested with a crime. In some cases the government even refused to admit to the arrests. Due to such harassment, the Barisan Sosialis, the only credible opposition party at the time, boycotted the 1968 general elections in protest against the tactics of the PAP. The PAP subsequently managed to capture all the seats in parliament in every election until the 1980s.

The departure of the British colonial authorities in 1963 was an important event in Singapore's history. Lee Kuan Yew was convinced that it would be best for Singapore to become part of a greater Malaysian Union and he therefore pushed for a referendum that would allow Singapore to unite with the Federation of Malaya, Sarawak and Sabah (North Borneo) to form the Malaysian Union. The only catch with the referendum was that the people of Singapore never had a chance to vote against a merger. All the referendum questions asked for an affirmation, and the attempt to add the possibility of rejection was denied (Trocki 2006). From the beginning, Singapore's short stint within the Malaysian Union was a rocky one. Political differences were so great that they were irreconcilable. The rulers of Singapore saw multi-racialism and meritocracy as the most important principle, while the Malaysian ruling elite favored greater emphasis on the Malay majority. The merger agreement, therefore, formalized two distinct political territories, with a non-interference agreement for either side. However, this was not feasible and attempts by Lee Kuan Yew to get involved in Malaysian politics in 1964 were not viewed favorably from Kuala Lumpur. Singapore, therefore, was forced into independence in the same year, an event that moved Lee Kuan Yew to tears on national television.

The race riots in the 1950s and 1960s also influenced the decisions of the newly elected ruling party (Quah 1990). They promoted the idea of so-called multiracialism, a peculiar form of multi-ethnic politics that promoted peaceful coexistence but also discouraged the development of a "melting pot," which would mean that people of different cultures, races, and religions were combined to form an integrated society. Instead, the idea was to divide the country into four different ethnic groups, or races, which were to live together according to strict quotas. In time, the government promoted ethnic-based self-help groups and the learning of one of four "mother-tongues" (Hill and Lian 1995). In the political arena, the conception of a multi-ethnic system obstructed the development of race-based parties. Furthermore, the assertion that political candidates were racist became an issue in a number of elections. In 1976, two opposition candidates, who had complained about discrimination against the Chinese educated, were accused of stirring up "communal and chauvinist emotions" (Shee 1978). In 1997, the PAP again accused a candidate of the opposition, Tang Liang Hong from the Workers' Party, of racist behavior when it asserted that Tang was an anti-Christian and a Chinese chauvinist.

Among the founders of modern Singapore, there was a strong sense of crisis, which placed the greatest priority on the survival of Singapore. Its geographical size, location, and ethnic heterogeneity were major sources of concern. This explains the leadership's emphasis on economic and security policies. While Singapore embarked on a dramatic economic transformation, it also focused heavily on its military defenses. In 1967, the government introduced the military draft, which had earlier been very controversial among the Chinese majority (Mauzy and Milne 2002). The military strategy was designed to deter attacks from unfriendly countries, as well as economic or political pressure from its neighbors (Huxley 2000). This was based on an ideology of "survivalism" propagated by a pragmatic leadership, with the focus on discipline and sacrifice (Chan 1971). The Singapore government not only built up one of the most potent militaries in the region, but also became actively involved in the development of regional organizations. For instance, it was a founding member of the Association of Southeast Asian Nations (ASEAN) in 1970 (Huxley 2000).

The threat against Singapore has become an important aspect of the legitimation strategy of the ruling elite. Oppositional behavior has often been characterized as a threat to the survival of the Singapore state. This sentiment was perhaps best expressed by S. Rajaratnam, a co-founder of the People's Action Party, who considered opposition to the ruling party "non-Communist subversion":

> Given a one-party government, the capacity of such a government to act far more independently than if it were harassed by an opposition and by proxies, is obvious. In the game of competitive interference pawns which can behave like bishops and castles and knights can in certain circumstances be extremely inconvenient and very irritating.
>
> (Rajaratnam 1975: 118)

This suggests that the leaders of the ruling elite were not willing to accept any challenges to their rule. During these early years of independence, Trocki (2006) notes, the PAP did everything it could to hinder any opposition party from challenging its rule. Legislation was passed that restricted whatever resources potential challengers could amass and the small size of Singapore ensured that alternative financial sources would not be readily available.

Since independence, the evocation of a national threat to the very existence of Singapore has played a prominent role in Singapore politics. The fear of being destroyed by outside forces has also mobilized the ruling elite to focus on economic development. The following section will show how the government was able to successfully develop the Singapore economy and what consequences this developmentalist strategy had on the regime and its challengers.

Economic modernization

There is no doubt that Singapore is one of the greatest economic success stories in the developing world. Lee Kuan Yew has indicated in the title of one of his books that Singapore has developed "from third world to first," and while this may not be the case in regard to its society, it certainly characterizes the economic transformation of the city-state. Singapore's development is matched only by that of the other Asian tigers, the other newly industrializing economies in Asia, South Korea, Taiwan, and the other case in this study, Hong Kong. High growth rates were accompanied by a high savings rate in the public and private sectors and a low inflation rate. Singapore's economy was transformed in the past 50 years from a trading center with a very small manufacturing sector to a business and financial service hub.

The beginning of the economic strategy can be traced to the creation of the Economic Development Board (EDB) in 1961, which was tasked with the goal of conceiving a developmental strategy. Economic development in Singapore was greatly influenced by historical circumstances and the determination of the leadership. Most significantly, it was the loss of the Malaysian hinterland, following the independence of Singapore in 1965, that increased the interest of the political leadership of focusing on a developmentalist strategy. The fact that Singapore lacked a powerful class of landlords, an entrenched aristocratic class, or a military gave the rulers the extraordinary opportunity to focus on developmental plans without any serious opposition (Lim et al. 1993). During its short stint as part of Malaysia, Singapore had focused on an import-substitution strategy, which had sought to strengthen local industry. After separation, largely because of Singapore's small size, the government saw the need to change gear and emphasize export substitution. Singapore's economy and market were just too small to offer any other alternatives (ibid. 1993).

Singapore's industrialization started in the late 1950s and early 1960s, 10 years later than Hong Kong's. The reasons for this were the political differences between the two trading colonies. In Hong Kong, industrialization was the outcome of historic events, as the two world wars and a relatively cheap workforce contributed significantly to the industrialization of the city-state. In contrast to Hong Kong, the Singaporean elite consciously promoted industrialization in the 1960s out of a sense of the city-state's vulnerability (Chiu et al.

1995). Despite the success of the industrialization strategy, Singapore's annual value of commerce always exceeded the combined incomes of the city-state's inhabitants. Trade therefore continued to be the engine that drove growth (Huff 1994).

Singapore's developmental strategy was and still is based on a combination of government-linked corporations and multinational corporations. After 1960, Singapore's impressive growth was based mainly on these two types of corporation (ibid.). This meant that local businesses were largely neglected. Small and medium-sized enterprises (SMEs) lost in significance and, due to their limited influence, were unable to oppose the government's strategies (Chalmers 1992). Furthermore, Huff (1999) has argued that there is general mistrust between the government and SMEs, as the EDB seems to be more indifferent toward local Singaporean businesses than toward multinational corporations. This development can be seen as a consequence of the power struggle between the English-educated elite and the Chinese-educated masses. Since most local entrepreneurs had been Chinese and China-oriented during colonial times, the new elite was intent on weakening this connection (Huff 1994).

Singapore, like no other country, has emphasized the importance of foreign investments. In 1980, for instance, 80 percent of the total investment originated from abroad (Bellows 1985), and between 1960 and 1994 Singapore had the highest investment ratio in the world (Huff 1999). Furthermore, in the 1990s, 70 percent of all manufacturing output came from foreign firms (Haas 1999). From the early days, the PAP leadership was convinced that "foreign capital was vital to the stability and prosperity of the small nation—indeed to its very survival" (Lim, et al. 1993: 103). The strategy was to attract companies that were considered a good fit with the existing developmental goals, and initial foreign investment was thus often subsidized by the government. Furthermore, the EDB maintained close personal contacts with foreign companies. It is therefore not surprising that Singapore offers multinational corporations very good conditions. Lack of corruption, political and financial stability, no restrictions on trade, a business-friendly government, an efficient bureaucracy and legal system, a well-developed infrastructure, the absence of an independent labor movement, low taxes, and a government that is known to adhere to its commitments are strong incentives for foreign companies to locate subsidiaries to Singapore (Huff 1999).

Apart from foreign-owned corporations, the government maintains control over large corporations that are linked to and, in some cases, even owned by the government. With the development of the Jurong Industrial Estate, the government showed that it was necessary not only to develop the infrastructure for industrialization but also to participate directly in industry. Singapore maintains investment corporations such as Temasek Holding, which serves the government in investing both in Singapore and abroad, and the Government of Singapore Investment Corporation, which manages foreign investments. Through Temasek, the Singapore government maintains controlling

shares in many large corporations. These corporations are all closely asso-
ciated with prominent PAP politicians, who often hold directorships in mul-
tiple corporations at the same time. For instance, as of May 2008, former MP
Wang Kai Yuen holds fourteen directorships in listed firms, including Comfort
DelGro, Cosco Corp, China Lifestyle Food and Beverages Group, and China
Aviation Oil (*ST* 29 April 2008).

By 1983 the ruling elite had developed, according to Linda Lim, into a
"separate 'class' with motivations and interests independent of, and more
than simply intermediary between, those of capital and labor" (Lim 1983:
761). Furthermore, as she claims, the rewards of this new class stem from the
share of profits of the state. Lim writes that "it comes from the power of
control over the vast assets of the state itself, and indirectly of the private
sector as well, and from the reflected glory of the very success the state has
created in the economy" (Lim 1983: 762).

Even though the oil crisis of 1973 slowed Singapore's growth, compared to
other countries during this period, Singapore's growth rate continued at an
impressive 8.7 percent (LePoer 1989). Furthermore, during the Asian financial
crisis of 1997, Singapore fared much better than other countries in the region
(Ngiam 2000). Until the world economic crisis, which started in late 2008,
Singapore's economy was still performing comparatively well. While the
effects of the world economic crisis can not yet be evaluated, economic slow-
downs and perceived shortcomings of the elite have in the past created
opportunities for oppositional groups to challenge the ruling elite. This will be
the focus of the next section.

The significance of J.B. Jeyaretnam's election victory in 1981

In the 1970s, many observers were of the opinion that the one-party dominance of the PAP was almost unbreakable (for instance, Chan 1976). However, socio-economic changes, higher education, and the growing complexity
of the society, among other factors, increasingly posed a challenge to the
ruling party. The PAP was well aware of the rising pressure in the 1970s and
considered renewing the leadership as a means to incorporate the younger
generation. Older members of the PAP were urged to retire, while new members, who were in their mid-thirties, spoke two or more languages, and tended
to be professionals, were recruited from outside the party (Shee 1978). These
changes, however, were not enough for the new middle class, which had
become increasingly sophisticated and was now demanding an opposition as
a check on the ruling party (Chan 1976). The PAP monopoly in parliament
was shattered in 1981, when the charismatic leader of the Workers' Party, J.B.
Jeyaretnam, was elected to parliament in the Anson by-election. The election
victory can be seen as the turning point in the development of opposition in
Singapore because it proved that the dominance of the ruling party could be
broken. It was "a threshold in the political development of Singapore"
(Hussin 2004: 137).

Even though this victory was the first visible sign of the opposition's success, it was preceded by the development of organized opposition in the 1970s. In June 1971, the Workers' Party (WP) was completely reorganized and a new executive body was elected (Workers' Party of Singapore 1971). Joshua Benjamin Jeyaretnam, or J.B.J. as he became popularly known, became the new secretary-general of the party. The Workers' Party was to him "little more than a convenient means of avoiding the bureaucratic hurdles of registering a new party" (Barr 2003: 306). The manifesto of the party was still very short and focused overwhelmingly on the economy and national interests, issues that were at the core of the PAP's agenda as well: "The Party intends to examine and assess the whole economic structure and in the light of this will institute a plan to further expand the programme of industrialization" (Workers' Party of Singapore 1971). A short paragraph was, however, devoted to the lack of civil rights in Singapore:

> The Party is aware that today in Singapore the individual enjoys none of the fundamental freedoms whatsoever under the law. We are committed to restoring to the individual what have been termed his inalienable rights, the freedom to speak his mind and the freedom of association, to exercise such rights within the framework of the law, as opposed to the present dictatorial and arbitrary policies of the present Government. We do not think it is necessary to curtail these freedoms in the supposed interests of the State.
>
> (ibid.)

It becomes clear that the Workers' Party agreed with the goals of the ruling party but distanced itself from the means by which these goals were achieved. A problem with this approach was, however, that the WP now needed to convince the people that its method would lead to the same success. Interestingly, the party opposes the ruling party's draconian policies only when this does not contradict the national interest, which in Singapore is defined by the ruling party.

The weakness of its argument motivated the Workers' Party to change its tactics. For instance, the 1976 party manifesto revealed a significant shift in regard to civil liberties. The party now emphasized that the lack of civil liberties was a question of the quality of life of Singaporeans, an important argument for the younger generation. The manifesto states: "We reiterate our belief in the concept of equality before the law and the freedom of every individual to exercise the rights with which he is endowed because he is a human being" (Workers' Party of Singapore 1976). Furthermore, the Workers' Party made it clear that civil liberties were part of the Singaporean constitution and needed to be restored. However, the party still did not state that the restoration of these "inalienable rights" would be in the interest of the country. Overall, the manifesto presents the reader with many sensible reform proposals aimed at greater social equitability and social justice. The call for greater democracy is made not simply in legal terms but also with a quote from Abraham Lincoln: "We believe that Government must be made accountable to the people and that the phrase 'Government of the people, for the people and by the people' is not mere cliché but a necessity" (ibid.). While the new manifesto and a new slogan, "Towards a Caring Society," increased popular interest in the Workers' Party, as evidenced in the election results, the opposition did not succeed in winning a seat in the 1976 general election or the 1977 and 1979 by-elections. However, the Workers' Party was the strongest opposition party, with 11.3 percent of the total vote in 1976 (Hussin 2004).

Jeyaretnam's slim by-election victory in 1981 came as a surprise to the ruling elite, which searched for reasons for the lost seat. There were many reasons for the shift in the opposition's fortunes after 1981. Most ostensibly, the prominent Devan Nair had resigned from the seat in the Anson constituency and the PAP had decided to nominate a relatively unknown "rich man's son," Pang Kim Hin (ibid.). Because of the growing dependence of the population on the state for services, the state's performance became the most important source of legitimacy. *The Straits Times*, for instance, considered housing issues the key factor (*ST* 28 Oct. 1981). Official opinion also connected Jeyaretnam's victory with the eviction of a thousand Anson residents and the overcrowding of the poorest electorate (Barr 2003). Barr (2003), however, thinks that the deeper reason for the victory of the opposition candidate was the disenchantment of the population. While the oil crisis of 1973 had led to only a mild recession, the government decided to introduce a modest wage policy, a decision that was reversed only in 1979. As long as the government was able to enhance economic and social development, it gained support, but when the economy suffered, a growing number of Singaporeans withdrew their support (Lim et al. 1993). This reflects the importance of performance for the legitimacy of the ruling elite in Singapore.

While the PAP attempted to regain its monopoly in parliament, the opposition continued to increase its influence. Lee Kuan Yew's 1983 proposal for a "Graduate Mother Scheme," which sought to promote an increase in the marriage and child bearing of higher-educated women in order to stem the declining birth rate, was an important reason for the victory of three additional opposition candidates in the 1984 election. This scheme had created widespread disapproval of the government because people felt that it impeded their individual choice (Ho 2003). At the same time, the popular vote of the PAP declined until 1991, when only 61 percent of Singapore's population voted for the PAP (Table 4.1).

This decline motivated the government to introduce a civil society[2] in the early 1990s (Brown and Jones 1995). The government wanted to reduce the need for increasing opposition representation, as well as to stimulate community participation in important social goals. In his famous 1991 speech, Minister for Trade and Industry Brigadier General George Yeo compared the state to a banyan tree that had left no space for other independent groups. Yeo argued that the tree had to be pruned in order to allow independent

Table 4.1 PAP Election results and elected members of the opposition in general elections

Election year	Vote for the PAP (%)	No. of elected opposition members
1959	54.1	7
1963	46.6	14
1968	84.4	0
1972	69.2	0
1976	72.4	0
1980	75.6	0
1984	62.9	3
1988	61.8	1
1991	61.0	4
1997	65.0	2
2001	75.3	2
2006	66.6	2

Source: www.singapore-elections.com

groups to develop. George Yeo added that the goal of civil society was the development of a Singapore identity:

> To create a sense of Singaporean-ness, citizens must do more things for them-selves and be less reliant on the state. Selectively, the state has to with-draw, so that more space between the family and the state can be freed up for civil society to grow and for intermediate organizations to develop. This is what we are trying to do now.
>
> (Yeo 2001)

However, the minister also made it clear that giving greater independence to social groups had to be done selectively. These groups should limit themselves to civic concerns and not lead to the development of interest groups, which might pressure the government for their own particularistic goals. Never-theless, this change in government policy provided new oppositional groups with a very narrow opening that developed into a political opportunity for the opposition. The effects of this shift in government policy will be discussed in more detail in Chapter 8.

In conclusion, it is important to note that the electoral losses of the ruling party, which can be attributed to perceived shortcomings of the regime, were a sign of expanding political opportunities. At first, economic problems were the greatest concern, but later, government elitism and a lack of willingness to allow alternative viewpoints provided these opportunities for the opposition. At the same time, the opposition has remained very weak. This is largely due to the institutions that allow Singapore's leaders to maintain their hegemony and that restrict oppositional groups which aim to remain within these institutional barriers.

The institutional structure

The institutional framework of modern Singapore shares a great deal with that of Hong Kong in the late 1960s and 1970s. The institutions are primarily geared so that the ruling party can stay in power. Furthermore, they also place restrictions on the kinds of goals and strategies of oppositional groups that are deemed legitimate. The ruling elite groups in Singapore have been able to institutionalize an intricate mix of control and incentives, which have significantly weakened potential challengers. In the following sections, these institutions will be examined in detail.

First, researchers have suggested that Singapore's political system can be characterized as a bureaucratic regime (Chan 1975; Bellows 1985). The regime maintains rigid developmental goals, which it tries to meet with the help of highly educated people. At the same time, the ruling party maintains a close fusion with the state, which can best be described as corporatist. This means that the recruitment of new decision makers occurs along lines of certain common beliefs. It is important to understand that Singapore is a heavily regulated state, with many rules and regulations that restrict oppositional groups from participating in the political process. When it comes to limits on oppositional behavior, the judiciary has played a particular role in Singapore. The repeated use of defamation lawsuits with the apparent goal of bankrupting opposition politicians has produced the specter of the state's use of the judicial system for the maintenance of the authoritarian state. The appearance of an independent judiciary, however, is also an important part of the legitimation strategy of the ruling elite, as are elections. In Singapore, elections are free, but heavily skewed in favor of the incumbent.

Singapore's bureaucratic regime

Similar to Hong Kong, Singapore's political system can be characterized as a bureaucratic or administrative regime, because the "*meaningful* political arena is shifting, or has shifted to the bureaucracy" (Chan 1975). In such a regime political decisions are made by a skilled, efficient bureaucracy with an emphasis on scientific management. At the same time, society is systematically depoliticized. Furthermore, in order to achieve efficiency, the legislature is regarded as subservient to the executive (Thio 1999). Bellows (1985: 56) agrees with Chan when he states that "Unquestionably, Singapore is an administrative state." However, he also notes that, despite the superior role of the bureaucracy, the ministers still have the last word in the decision-making process. Decisions are made by a very small, highly educated leadership.

Since independence, the bureaucracy in Singapore has become the tool of the ruling party. Upon independence, the rulers were of the opinion that the bureaucracy had two flaws: "the civil servants had a colonial mentality and were insensitive to the population at large; and they were hostile towards and afraid of the PAP" (Quah 1975: 325). The goal of the PAP in the initial years, therefore, was to create a bureaucracy that conformed ideologically to its own ideas and goals. Therefore the bureaucracy was "fully socialized in the developmentalist values" (Koh 1997: 120). From the beginning, the relationship between the PAP and the bureaucracy was very close. The political leadership sought to engender the support of the administrators by establishing a close working relationship, which included attempts to change the values of the bureaucrats so that they were similar to the PAP and a recruitment policy that sought to include a greater number of Chinese-educated intellectuals. This, then, formed the basis for the close cooperation between the political leadership and the bureaucracy (Chan 1976).

Natasha Hamilton-Hart (2000) argues that the bureaucracy in Singapore has only limited cohesion and is subordinate to the political elite. In her opinion, the state is less autonomous from the business sector, as there is an informal network that links governmental actors and members of the business elite to form the governing elite. The real power, therefore, rests with the ministers, who have been able to avert any political pressure coming from the bureaucracy (ibid.). Oftentimes, members of the private and the public sector in top positions tend to move from one institution to the other without much difficulty. Furthermore, the government aims to incorporate members of the private sector through directorships on government-linked corporations, or as directors of public-sector boards. Hamilton-Hart concludes that "the Singapore governing elite spans both public and private spheres, with the two sectors linked by shared interests, personal ties and overlapping career paths" (ibid.: 201). Good government, in this context, is only maintained through a system of informal norms that emphasize performance, efficiency, and effectiveness, which are, in turn, sustained by a network of trusted individuals who place great emphasis on achievements as the basis for the incorporation of individuals into the political elite.

In recent years, the image of the bureaucratic state has changed. Since the 1990s there has been a growing demand within the bureaucracy to augment the top-down approach so as to also allow for wider participation from lower ranks. Furthermore, bureaucrats increasingly consider themselves nonpartisan, which, it can be argued, has been reinforced by the return of elected opposition members to parliament. Koh argues that, among other reasons,[3] a more differentiated public that is increasingly politically aware has in recent years led to a "managerialist revolution" within the administrative state (Koh 1997). When, during the 2006 election, the PAP linked voting results to the upgrading of public housing estates, however, it raised doubts about the independence of the bureaucracy from the ruling party.

State corporatism in Singapore

While most researchers have understood Singapore as a prime example of a bureaucratic state, the city-state has recently also been characterized as a corporatist state (Chalmers 1992; Brown 1993; Wiarda 1996). Brown (1993: 16) argues that Singapore can no longer be understood only as an "administrative, bureaucratic, meritocratic or paternalist state, but must be conceived as shifting toward a form of consultative participatory politics which may best be denoted by the concept of corporatism." During the 1980s corporatism became an increasingly important method for Singapore's ruling party to counter the growing challenges from oppositional groups. In this context, corporatism is understood as

> a particular set of policies and institutional arrangements for structuring interest representation. Where such arrangements predominate, the state often charters or even creates interest groups, attempts to regulate their number, and give them the appearance of a quasi-representational monopoly along with special prerogatives.
>
> (Stepan 1978: 46)

Corporatism, therefore, may be regarded as an ideology that places the greatest emphasis on social unity, political order, and economic development (Chalmers 1992). For this the state attempts to "harness and control the new social and political forces to which modernization and industrialization give rise: emerging labor organizations, new businessmen, professionals and their associations, university students, and former peasants who have flocked to the cities in search for jobs" (Wiarda 1996: 84).

Since its ascent to power, the ruling party in Singapore has sought to incorporate different interests into the state apparatus. Perhaps the best example for this is the attempt to incorporate business and labor interests into a tripartite alliance. Barr (2000: 80) noted that by the early 1980s the relationship between the state and the labor movement was marked by "modest, but nevertheless real elements of inclusion." The tripartite alliance between the state, the labor unions and industry therefore provides a good example for Singapore's "hierarchical" corporatism, in which the state dominates. The PAP and the chief labor union organization, the National Trades Union Congress (NTUC), form an especially close relationship. It is not uncommon that the head of the union is also the chairman of the party. Furthermore, the union advertises the "benefits" of NTUC's symbiotic relationship on its website, which for instance, is an absence of strikes (Figure 4.1).

The goal of the labor union is not primarily to bargain for workers' rights but to support the development project, which makes it "proud that the workers, as much as employers, have contributed to the stability and prosperity of Singapore" (NTUC website 2007). The labor movement, therefore, represents an important part in the corporate structure of the bureaucratic state, and the disappearance of an independent labor movement contributes to the depoliticization of society. The close relationship between the government and the labor unions, furthermore, integrates potentially strong oppositional groups that could challenge the ruling elite. This has to be seen in contrast to Hong Kong, where, during the 1970s, the Hong Kong Professional Teachers' Union (HKPTU) repeatedly challenged the government and even forced it to make concessions.

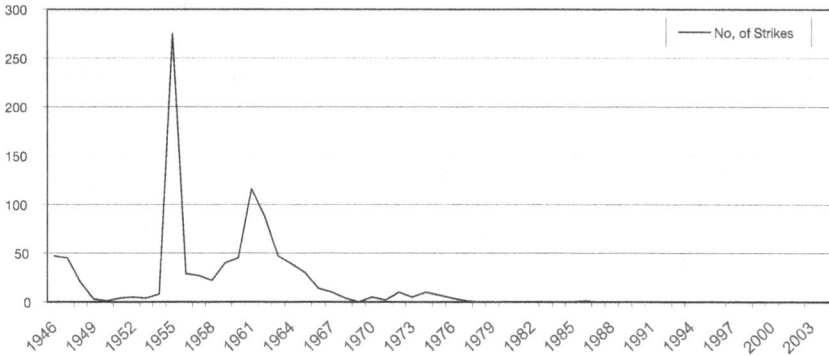

Figure 4.1 Strikes in Singapore
Source: Ministry of Manpower 2007.

An important element of Singapore's form of corporatism is the close connection between the state and the ruling People's Action Party, which has led to a synthesis between state and party in the dominant one-party system. The party has been able to form such a close relationship with the various organs of the state because it has dominated parliament ever since it was first elected in 1959. The PAP controls parliament and can thus enact any rule changes that it considers necessary. For this reason, Singapore has even been compared to the Communist regimes in the former Eastern Bloc, in which the political is more important than the economic (Huntington 1991). However, in Singapore the ideology of the ruling elite is not Communism but pragmatism and developmentalism, which stress the primary emphasis on the economy and technical leadership while denying the existence of politics and conflicts of interest. This has allowed the government to focus entirely on the economic development of the city-state. The economist Huff (1999) therefore concludes that Singapore is a corporate state run mainly by technocrats, which has led to the popular designation "Singapore Inc."

Finally, the most important aspect of the corporatist strategy is the co-option of the growing middle class into the political system. Modernization created a greater demand for political representation from the middle class, which led to a number of institutional innovations. While some of these have tried to skew the electoral process in favor of the ruling elite, others have tried to establish alternative feedback channels. The former will be discussed briefly in the section on elections in Singapore. The latter are founded on the need of an authoritarian regime to understand the wishes of the population and to reduce potential challenges to the ruling elite groups. The ruling elite groups have tried to inculcate in the population the idea that a form of communitarianism is preferable to liberal democracy. This argument has been used to stem rising demands for a more vocal opposition and checks and balances. The 1991 *White Paper on Shared Values* tried to institutionalize authoritarian "Asian values," which were meant to supersede supposedly negative Western values. While the government consulted the Feedback Unit and the Institute of Policy Studies to gauge the public view and made even some changes, interest in these values was muted. In the end, even though parliament approved of the Shared Values, it did not make them part of the constitution or give them any legal relevance (Mauzy and Milne 2002).

From the perspective of the Singaporean leadership, the return of the opposition in the 1980s was in part regarded as a sign that the existing feedback channels, the Citizens' Consultative Committees (CCCs), the Community Center Management Committees (CCMCs), Residents' Committees (RCs), Meet-the-People sessions, and the option for normal Singaporeans to become representatives on Parliamentary Select Committees, were inadequate (Quah and Quah 1989: 119). Thus the Feedback Unit was set up in 1985 under the aegis of the Ministry of Community Development, Youth and Sports to allow individual Singaporeans to voice their opinion on policies and their implementation. Rodan (1996) argues that the primary goal of the Feedback Unit is to channel dissent and dissatisfaction through institutions that the ruling elite controls. Another function of the Unit, which has raised skepticism about the government's true intentions, is its emphasis on explaining public policy (Chua 1995: 660). This created the impression that the government was interested less in the views of the public and more in creating acceptance for its policies.

While previous attempts to incorporate the public into these state-sponsored institutions have not been very successful, the government continues to improve these venues. For instance, in 2006 the Feedback Unit was renamed "Reach," which stands for "Reaching Everyone for Active Citizenry @ Home." The PAP has stated that the new institution "is going beyond gathering public feedback, to raising the level of public engagement and promoting active citizenry" (People's Action Party 2006). This latest attempt to improve communication between the people and the government goes beyond conducting dialog and tea sessions, and the traditional media "to convey key issues", to include modern technology such as SMS and internet blogs so as to be able to receive information from the increasing number of internet users in the country (Singapore Government 2006). This may be a difficult goal, because the growing number of internet authors value their independence from the government and therefore are not likely to be enticed to join a government-controlled platform. The government, furthermore, seems to believe that it can continue to co-opt members of the middle class without significantly relaxing the rules, which it deems necessary for the continuing stability of the city-state.

Laws and regulations—Singapore as a "fine city"

The co-optation of the rising middle class has not been sufficient to maintain the hegemony of the ruling elite. In order to control oppositional activity, the rulers have frequently made use of draconian legislation aimed mostly at potential challengers. There were many restrictive laws when Singapore was controlled by the British Empire. While in opposition, the People's Action Party had called for an end to laws such as the Emergency Regulations (which later became the Internal Security Act), which allowed for arrest without warrant. Once elected, the PAP retained these laws, amended them, and introduced similar new legislation. This was a crucial aspect of the party's strategy for achieving its dominant position in Singapore.

Today, Singapore is a country in which nearly every aspect of societal, political, and cultural life is controlled by laws and regulations. This is well expressed in the common statement "Singapore is a 'fine' city," meaning that there is a fine for nearly everything, even for not flushing a toilet. This sentence is so famous that it has become part of Singapore culture and is printed on T-shirts, cups, etc. When you travel with the subway, the MRT, you will notice the large prohibition signs, which, in contrast to many other places in the world, are already marked with the fine you will have to pay if you do not comply with the regulation. The sign displays the fines for smoking (S$1,000), for eating and drinking (S$500), and for the possession of flammable goods (S$5,000). Strangely, the last item on the sign, the possession of durians, does not carry a price tag. Symbolically, this may indicate an element of arbitrariness that persists in the Singapore legal system.

Since the need for economic growth has played a superior role, regulations have often served to enhance the economic position of Singapore. While social values are considered important, they are regarded as only secondary to the demands of the tourist industry. For example, while Singapore is a very conservative society and even the possession of pornographic material is forbidden, institutionalized prostitution has been officially sanctioned by the government, presumably to cater to the stream of tourists passing through Singapore. Similarly, despite considerable opposition from many Singaporeans, the government has decided to attract casinos to Singapore (Lim 2005). In order to "protect" society, the government has implemented control mechanisms. The sex trade is limited to the Geylang district, which potentially creates problems for married men who get caught there. Furthermore, in recent years the government has decided to install closed-circuit television cameras in the area (*Reuters* 24 Dec. 2005). The government's decision to allow casinos in Singapore is similarly accompanied by a control mechanism. Singaporeans planning to gamble in these casinos, unlike foreign tourists, will have to pay an entrance fee (*ST* 19 April 2005).

In the political arena, laws have sought to depoliticize the process as much as possible without losing the veneer of a parliamentary democracy. Table 4.2 is a non-exhaustive list of rules and regulations directly or indirectly regulating the ability of political actors or groups. Many of these regulations exist in other states, and are comparable to Hong Kong's laws discussed in the previous chapter.

Important restrictions on oppositional activity can be categorized into two types: the first restrict the organizational base of the group and the second target the ability of groups to pursue their goals and strategies. In the first category, the Societies Act (1967, amended 1988) requires that organizations of

Table 4.2 Selected laws restricting oppositional activity in Singapore

Law	Introduced	Major aspects
Films Act	1981	requires a license for importing, making, distributing or exhibiting films
Internal Security Act (ISA)	1960	arrest without warrant and detention without trial
Law of Defamation	1871	anything that could possibly be *interpreted* as defamatory is covered by this law
Miscellaneous Offences (Public Order And Nuisance) Act	1906	requires a license of any assembly or procession in a public space
Newspaper and Printing Presses Act (NPPA)	1974	requires a license for owning and using a printing press
Parliamentary Elections Act	1954	regulates the process of an election, for example sets rules about election advertisements, forbids exit polls and election surveys during election time
Public Entertainments and Meetings Act	1973	any public entertainment must be licensed by the government
Public Order (Preservation) Act	1958	allows for the declaration of any area to be in a state of danger to public order
Sedition Act	1948	any publication or words that "bring into hatred or contempt or to excite disaffection against the Government"
Societies Act	1967	organizations of 10 people or more must be registered; groups not registered as politically organizations may not act in a political manner
Undesirable Publications Act	1967	against publications that depict sex, violence or that are negative against religion or racist

ten or more people must be registered as a society. It has been used to prohibit groups that are deemed contrary to the national interest. The government has made use of the law to disallow the registration of religious organizations such as Jehovah's Witnesses, the Unification Church, and the Divine Light Mission (Mauzy 2006). It has also been applied to ban the gay rights group People Like Us. Its major impact on oppositional behavior, however, stems from a more recent innovation: a group registered under the Societies Act may only pursue political targets if it is explicitly registered as a political group. This happened to two groups, the Open Singapore Centre and Think Centre. The requirement restricted the groups' ability to receive funding because it disallowed financial support from foreign sources. It thus functions similarly to the Parliamentary Elections Act, which limits the fundraising of political parties.

Second, the ability of groups to pursue their goals and strategies is hampered by a number of laws such as the Law of Defamation, the Undesirable

Publications Act, Films Act, Newspaper and Printing Presses Act (NPPA), Public Entertainments and Meetings Act, and the Sedition Act. These laws motivate individuals to apply self-censorship in regard to sensitive topics. In cases of transgression, it is possible that they will have to pay severe fines or even be imprisoned. In particular, political expression has been heavily controlled. For example, while the arts have experienced increasing liberalization in recent years, political content is still largely avoided. A recent documentary film on Dr Chee Soon Juan was banned from a local film contest because it was considered a "party political film." Furthermore, most notably, the Law of Defamation has been used against opposition politicians, who were forced into bankruptcy as a result of severe fines awarded to the plaintiffs. Since bankrupts are not allowed to contest elections, this has also effectively weakened the organization of these groups.

An independent judiciary?

The PAP leaders consider an independent judiciary to be crucial for economic progress. They want Singapore to be regarded in contrast to arbitrary rule in neighboring countries. An independent judiciary is important for attracting foreign investment, because it guarantees security for investments (La Porta et al. 2000). For example, since the late 1980s the Singapore government has focused increasingly on the enforcement of intellectual property rights, which is an especially important concern for the entertainment and software industries (Uphoff 1991). This has become increasingly important as the country has moved from mass production to attracting high-tech companies. Furthermore, the high reputation of Singapore's legal system is an important reason for foreign companies locating their regional headquarters in Singapore (Greenless 2006). A biased judicial system would have greatly undermined the developmental plans of the government.

The government has been successful in promoting the image of an independent and impartial judiciary to the world business community. For example, the Heritage Foundation, which constantly rates Singapore as the second freest economy in the world (after Hong Kong), commented on Singapore's legal system:

> Singapore's investment laws are clear and fair. Foreign and domestic businesses are treated equally, there are no production or local content requirements, and nearly all sectors are open to 100 percent foreign ownership.
> ...
> The court system is very efficient and strongly protects private property.
>
> (Kane et al. 2007: 334)

Another example of this perception is reflected in the 1993 *World Competitiveness Report*, conducted by the World Economic Forum, which rated Singapore in first place for confidence in the judicial system (*ST* 26 Sept. 1993). Mauzy (2006: 56) has, furthermore, noted that that the judicial system in Singapore has received high international praise. The praise for Singapore's judicial system, such as in the case of the World Economic Forum, comes from opinion surveys conducted among business people (Seow 1997). The government has also been successful in making Singapore largely free of corruption, which is reflected in the annual *Corruption Perception Index* conducted by Transparency International. Thus, Mauzy and Milne (2002) argue that government officials, who include judges, know their limits and accept them (Mauzy and Milne 2002). Furthermore, it has been argued that, in comparison to Malaysia's judicial system, Singapore's is more independent because the courts have been able to state their constitutional goals more clearly (Seu 1992). Finally, the judiciary also considers itself to be a fair arbiter of justice. The new chief justice, Chan Sek Keong, promised in his welcome address to be determined "to uphold the rule of law and respect for the integrity of the law and a fair judicial process are also well known to the legal community" (Chan 2006; Chao 2007).

The regime has been intent on protecting the perception that Singapore's judiciary is independent. Even when someone merely suggests that the judiciary could be biased, the rulers have shown themselves bent on destroying the critic. The American economist Dr Christopher Lingle, who was on a scholarly visit to Singapore, had this very experience when he wrote in an article in the *International Herald Tribune* on 7 October 1994 that some unnamed "intolerant regime" in Asia relied "upon a compliant judiciary to bankrupt opposition politicians" (Lingle 1994). The Singapore government sued the *Tribune* and Dr Lingle and, during legal proceedings, attempted to prove that the economist could only have had Singapore in mind (Emmerson 1995). The message was clear: the ruling elite would not accept assertions that Singapore's judiciary could be biased in favor of the regime.

There have, however, been critics of the judiciary, who have largely focused on two areas: judicial appointments and the allegation that judges are compliant in regard to the law of defamation (Mauzy and Milne 2002). As Eugene Kheng-Boon Tan (2000) argues, Singapore's judicial system is marked by a dichotomy between two different law systems. Universalism or the universal applicability of the law, he argues, is an important feature of commercial law, while cultural relativism, or a communitarian-based understanding of law, is applied to civil rights or civil society. The combination of the British legal tradition with local values and a different legal tradition, Tan argues, entailed the formation of an indigenous, or autochthonous, legal system (Tan 2000). With a two-thirds majority in parliament, the PAP was able to quickly introduce changes to Singapore's legal system. In 1969, the jury system was abolished and cases are now heard by a single judge, and in 1994 the ability to appeal to the Privy Council was also rescinded.

Therefore, criticism of the use of defamation lawsuits against members of the opposition and the changes in the legal system, which gave power to a very small number of people, has led defendants of Singapore's regime to claim that this is a feature of a particularly Singaporean judicial system. While it became expedient for business reasons to maintain the British system, the authoritarian elements of Singapore's political system required greater flexibility in dealing with rising oppositional pressure. Constitutional lawyer Kevin Tan notes:

> What human rights groups and international non-governmental organisations criticise is our public law record, meaning things such as constitutional law, criminal law, anything involving the state. They are not concerned with the commercial areas, as our record is very good for dealing with these matters.
>
> *(ST* 25 Oct. 1997)

Jayasuriya (1996: 377) describes the legal system in East Asian countries, of which he considers Singapore to be a part, as a "managerial and technocratic device for the effective organization of the market and the state." The law is used to accomplish the developmental goals of the state. He describes this type of judicial system as "rule through law rather than the rule of law" (ibid.: 379). Dr Chee (2007) seems to agree with Jayasuriya's description of Singapore's legal system when he states that there is "rule by law instead of rule of law."

Worthington's research, furthermore, found that the Singaporean judiciary sees its own role in relation to the executive. He writes that "the judicial system has been hegemonized by a number of political and bureaucratic strategies, and interprets its role in terms of the overall goals of the political executive" (Worthington 2001: 133). Thio has also noted that "There is an explicit deference to executive concerns pertaining to public order and national development policy" (Thio 1999: 204). The judiciary is, however, not an institution that is controlled by the government, but a compromise between the need to have an esteemed judicial system and the goal of controlling a rising opposition (Worthington 2001). Worthington (2001), therefore, sees the independence of the judiciary as being contingent on its willingness to follow the wishes of the executive in political cases.

Elections and opposition in a Singaporean democracy

Democratic elections, which are largely free and secret, have played a pivotal role in contributing significantly to the legitimacy of the ruling elite. As in liberal democratic states, elections enable the PAP to assert the mandate of the people, as did Prime Minister Lee Hsien Loong after his first election victory in 2006: "We thank all of you for supporting me and my colleagues on my PAP team for electing me with a strong mandate, selecting us with a strong mandate" (quoted in *CNA* 7 May 2006). Elections, furthermore, serve as a barometer of how well the government is performing. It is, therefore, not surprising that the ruling party expends a great deal of effort during election campaigns.

In spite of their importance, elections in Singapore are skewed heavily in favor of the ruling party, virtually guaranteeing the party's re-election. Aside from the normal incumbency effect, the ruling party has resorted to a number of tactics to ensure its election victory. For instance, in recent elections the government has announced the election date only nine days before, which has limited the ability of opposition parties to campaign. The plurality voting system, furthermore, has placed constraints on the chances of opposition candidates being elected. Additionally, the government has frequently used the tactic of gerrymandering to increase support for members of the ruling party. Moreover, the introduction of group representation constituencies (GRCs),[4] through an amendment to the Parliamentary Elections Act in 1988, purportedly to guarantee an ethnic balance in parliament, has raised the bar for challengers to compete in elections because it requires a team of candidates to contest a single district. Despite the enormous challenges to opposition resources, a number of GRCs have been contested, but the opposition has never been able to secure a seat in these districts. GRCs were originally designed for three candidates but have progressively been enlarged in subsequent elections. Today, most of the seats in parliament are elected in multi-member districts with five or six candidates (in 2006, there were fourteen GRCs and nine single-member districts), which has not only increased the institutional hurdles for the opposition but also helped the government to retain seats, due to the incumbency factor. Last but not least, the government has been willing to employ almost any method, from cash handouts to threats, to convince the electorate. An example for the former is the "Progress Package," which gave S$2.6 billion to average Singaporeans, including top-ups to the Central Provident Fund, workfare bonuses, growth dividends in cash for all Singaporeans, and bonuses for national servicemen (Chin 2007). The latter can be illustrated with an example from 1997, when Prime Minister Goh Chok Tong warned the electorate that if they voted for the opposition their wards could become "slums" (Rodan 2004). In the 2006 election, the PAP again told the voters that those who lived in wards that voted for the PAP would come first in future upgrading projects for their housing estates (L. Lim 2006).

In addition to such attempts to manipulate the electoral process, there have also been a number of measures that seek to reduce the need to elect opposition members to parliament. First of all, in order to stem the increasing numbers of opposition politicians in parliament during the 1980s, the Non-Constituency Member of Parliament (NCMP) scheme was introduced in 1984. It was initially designed to give the top opposition losers a seat if fewer than three opposition members had won. This scheme aimed not only to fulfill the wishes of the people for opposition members in parliament, but also to weaken "the sentiment for *electing* more opposition members" (Mauzy and Milne 2002: 144). An NCMP could vote on all bills except funding bills, votes of no confidence, and constitutional amendments. The opposition parties initially opposed the scheme because they felt that NCMPs members might feel indebted to the government as they were selected by the government, and because the scheme was meant to weaken the opposition and thus maintain the status quo (Hussin 2004). Additionally, in 1990 the government introduced the Nominated Member of Parliament (NMP) scheme, which was yet another attempt to respond to the demand for alternative voices in parliament. Initially there were up to six NMPs, who were to be nominated for two years, after which they could be reappointed. In 1997, the government increased the number of NMPs to nine, again trying to co-opt dissenting voices into the institutional framework.

Finally, the introduction of the elected presidency in 1993 appeared at first to be a step toward greater democratization. The office was meant to check on the government and allow the people a greater voice in parliament. In reality, however, the PAP's goal was also to retain some power in case of an election eventually leading to victory for the opposition. In terms of legitimacy, the office had very little impact, because the criteria for running for president were set very high.[5] As a result, only established candidates are selected for the office. So it came as no surprise that in 1993 interest in the new office was very limited. Hussin Mutalib described the goal of the elected presidency as "one of many institutions and policies which have been introduced to contain and channel a better educated and more demanding electorate from pressuring the government to purchase political goodwill by dipping into the financial reserves" (Hussin 1997: 169).

Summary and outlook

In summary, this chapter has argued that the political structure in Singapore has, in recent years, provided more opportunities for opposition involvement. The government's successful economic policies and the capacity of the government to resort to a high degree of social control have, however, limited the ability of these oppositional groups to engage the state. The developments have created a situation in which a strong and powerful group of elites dominates a state where social movements can hardly flourish. The laws and regulations and the judiciary are skewed against any kind of political activism and protest. Furthermore, the existence of democratic elections and the use of feedback institutions have strengthened the ruling elite groups, because they have increased the regime's nominal legitimacy.

In the next chapter, Hong Kong's ruling elite groups will be analyzed. Similar to the Singaporean elite, which is the focus of Chapter 6, the Hong Kong elite was relatively strong and cohesive. However, unlike in Singapore, there was a division between expatriate administrators and local Chinese businessmen and between advocates of laissez-faire and social activists. Common values and goals, however, created enough common ground within the ruling elite. While this allowed social activists within the government to introduce lofty social programs aimed at fulfilling the demands of an increasingly assertive population, these programs were continuously underfunded, due to the prevailing emphasis on small government. Moreover, the political contention that was the result of unfulfilled promises was often not successfully contained through the co-optation of dissidents into the political process or the use of suppression against the most aggressive challengers.

5 Ruling elite groups in Hong Kong during the 1970s

Positive non-interventionism and the rise of contention

The previous two chapters have set the historical and institutional background in which political groups of the two city-states interact. In this chapter, we now turn to the ruling elite groups in colonial Hong Kong during the 1970s and early 1980s.

In 1972, ten officials from Hong Kong's Secretariat of Home Affairs went to Singapore to uncover the secrets behind the Southeast Asian city-state's economic and political development. Since Hong Kong at the time faced similar problems to Singapore, from overcrowding to rapid modernization, it comes as no surprise that Hong Kong's leaders considered emulating a system that had become politically stable, despite rapid growth, in a tremendously short period of time. The government officials' stated goal was to imitate certain features of Singapore's stable political environment. James So, then City District Commissioner of Kowloon, contended that "We feel that we could apply, with some modification, certain administrative methods in use here to suit Hong Kong" (quoted in *SCMP* 12 Jan. 1972). With this intention in mind, Hong Kong's ruling elite strategy developed in the same direction as that of Singapore, but, unlike in Singapore, administrators were unable to contain the rise of contentious politics.

While the ruling elite presented itself as a homogeneous block, there was a visible difference between those who advocated greater involvement in society and those who were opposed to restricting Hong Kong's free market. Because the governor, who was an advocate of the former, depended on the support of the business leaders, he had to balance between interventionism and laissez-faire. The incentive for these groups to continue this precarious relationship was the shared goal of economic growth, which depended on the status quo of the relationship between the political groups. At the same time, there was also a gap in the communication between different groups and an inability on the part of the government to monopolize its external communications. Within the ruling elite, a sense of superiority was widespread, especially among expatriates, which led to paternalistic dispositions. While, similarly to Singapore, the overall success of the government in developing the city-state added to its performance legitimacy, there were also significant differences in the extent of the success. In the last part of this chapter, we will turn our attention to the goals and tactics of the power-holders. The government emphasized social progress and, unlike in Singapore, used coercion sparingly and outside of the public eye. Instead, it tried to rely almost solely on co-opting the opposition into existing government channels. In times of intense conflict, the government also showed willingness to compromise.

Ruling elite groups in Hong Kong during the 1970s

On the one hand, there was the colonial administration, which was dominated by expatriates but gradually aimed toward localization. It has been argued that the civil servants, who were organized hierarchically under a small leadership, developed into the ruling elite (Huque et al. 1998). This power elite, however, lacked mediating institutions that could communicate with the familial structure of the Chinese elites (Lau 1981). The administration followed the pattern of a typical British colony, with a governor at the top, an Executive Council to assist the governor and a Legislative Council to provide advice. At the same time, the colonial government became increasingly autonomous from the motherland (Kuan 1979).

On the other hand, the city-state's administrators had to seek the support of the pro-British business elite, which preferred the continuation of authoritarian rule. They were mostly represented in the Legislative and Executive Councils of the city-state. Joseph S.Y. Cheng argues that power was concentrated in the colonial government and that the business community acted as the checks and balances (Cheng 1999). While, unlike in Singapore, there was an unmistakable separation between politics and economics, the government and the business groups shared the same goal: political stability and economic success. In spite of the disunity, the overall success of the Hong Kong government in achieving this goal contributed to the relative cohesiveness and strength within the ruling elite groups.

Organizational strength of ruling elite groups in colonial Hong Kong

Hong Kong's ruling elite groups can be regarded as relatively cohesive, even though they can be divided into the ruling bureaucrats and influential businesspeople, as well as into ethnic Chinese and expatriates. An analysis of their members shows that while there was a continuous increase in the number of government employees, the ethnic divisions were slowly disappearing. The hierarchical organization of the government, furthermore, ensured its cohesiveness and durability. The section on the leaders of the ruling elite argues that within the government there were mainly two types of leaders: strong advocates of laissez-faire and social activists. The two, however, agreed on the need for economic growth. The fact that members of the elite benefited from the regime created strong incentives for maintaining group cohesion. Finally, the lack of effective communication within the elite and from the elite to other groups did not have a strong adverse impact on group cohesion. However, it increased the willingness of outside actors to challenge the regime.

Members

The members of the ruling elite groups were mainly bureaucrats in the administrative state and also (influential) businessmen. At the beginning of the 1970s, the elite was still largely separated along ethnic lines into an expatriate (mostly) British elite and a Chinese elite. The British were mostly in charge of the government, while the Chinese were responsible for public peace. The latter group often led community organizations such as Kaifong associations, which were mutual aid organizations set up in 1949 with the help of the Secretariat of Chinese Affairs. However, once the colonial government initiated a process of localization after World War II and an increasing number of Chinese entered government, the old division started to erode. Even though they were at first only able to enter at the lower end of the hierarchy, they soon occupied important decision-making positions. Especially in the Legislative Council, the ethnic Chinese were increasingly making an impact.

The localization had the effect that the civil servants, except for those at the very top, were already "localized" in the 1970s. Table 5.1 shows the overall increase of the civil service and the degree of localization, which indicates that the 1970s was an era of continuously increasing government involvement in society. Government planning and execution as well as an increasingly complex bureaucracy required a growing number of government employees. Consequently, the government also became the largest employer in Hong Kong (Harris 1982).

The members of the civil service, furthermore, significantly contributed to the successful implementation of government policies. In practice, most bureaucrats were assigned to one ministry and became specialists in a particular field (Miners 1981). Since the heads of government departments were able to act with considerable discretion, they could effectively guide their subordinates. This also meant that they were able to recruit lower-level public employees without the need to refer them to consideration by the Public Services Commission (ibid.). Members of the bureaucracy were also not supposed to act independently, but were trained to comply with the policy directives of their superiors. The hierarchical structure thus ensured that government decisions could be efficiently implemented.

Table 5.1 Increase of Hong Kong civil service and localization

	Local	*Expatriates*	*% Local*	*% Expatriates*
January 1962	48,277	1,625	96.7	3.3
January 1968	71,057	1,879	97.4	2.6
January 1973	88,121	1,905	97.9	2.1
April 1977	105,769	2,616	97.6	2.4
April 1978	112,700	2,971	97.4	2.6
January 1980	124,950	3,064	97.6	2.4
April 1981	136,262	2,990	97.9	2.1

Source: Annual *Reports on the Public Service* and *Civil Service* and information from the Civil Service Branch (adapted from N.J. Miners 1981: 105).

Leaders

The leaders of the local ruling elite were mainly the heads of departments, of commissions, namely the senior civil servants, and leading members of the Legislative and Executive Councils. In terms of administration and governance, the administrative part of the government dominated. Paul Wilding argues that "Until the 1980s political power in Hong Kong was the unchallenged preserve of the Governor and a small group of key civil servants" (Wilding 1997: 247). The other actors rarely involved themselves directly in the politics of the city-state.

The leaders of the ruling elite were overwhelmingly expatriates, which is not surprising, because Hong Kong was still a colony. The localization of the government during the 1970s was much less recognizable in the top-level positions. It was often argued that there simply were not enough qualified Chinese to fill these positions. Moreover, for the business-dominated Chinese elite, an expatriate-dominated bureaucracy had the advantage that it made the government appear as if it was not biased in favor of any local group (Huque et al. 1998).

The leadership of the 1970s can be divided into two ideal-typical groups: on the one hand there were the activists, who were interested in introducing changes to social policy. The best example of this is Governor Murray MacLehose, who often pushed for greater involvement of the government in social affairs. On the other hand, there were the conservatives, who considered small government as the only choice for the city-state. Due to Hong Kong's focus on the economy, they had considerable influence. Finance Minister Sir Phillip Haddon-Cave can be seen as a representative of this traditional approach because he was someone who was a strong if not doctrinaire advocate of "laissez-faire" (Goodstadt 2005).

Arguably the most powerful figure within the ruling elite groups was the governor, who, through appointments, could influence every area of Hong Kong politics. For most of the 1970s, the charismatic Sir Murray MacLehose, who was appointed to Hong Kong in 1971, filled this position. He was of Scottish origin and spoke Mandarin. Upon arriving in Hong Kong, he first visited the slum areas of the city and was appalled by the living conditions of the people there. Under his rule, the government shifted toward greater social commitments. His priorities were housing, education, and social welfare, and after demands from pressure groups he also became a strong advocate of the fight against corruption. He established the Independent Commission Against Corruption (ICAC) in 1974. Nevertheless, as a pragmatist and realist, he insisted on Hong Kong's commitment to a free economy and rejected demands for greater democratization.

MacLehose was a very popular governor. While a governor was usually appointed for five years, popular governors, such as MacLehose, could have their terms extended several times. When he retired in 1982 he was the longest-serving governor in the colony's history, with ten years and six months in office (Miners 1981). It is therefore not surprising that the *Hong Kong*

Standard had nothing but praise for the governor one year before his retirement: "Sir Murray is a popular governor who graces many newspaper articles and much television news footage as he ambles here and attends special occasions there" (*Hong Kong Standard* 23 Dec. 1981). Even many critics of the government respected and even admired MacLehose. The governor's visionary emphasis on public housing contributed greatly to political stability in the 1970s (Wilding 1997). The impression that the government was interested in the concerns of the average citizen reduced the potential for conflict. Finally, an ownership scheme in public housing, which in principle if not in scope is similar to the public housing program in Singapore, was introduced in Hong Kong in 1976. This allowed Hong Kong citizens to have a stake in the city, tying the new middle class to the city-state (ibid.).

Next to the governor, the financial secretary was probably the second most powerful person in the city-state, even more than the chief secretary (Wilding 1997). This was due to the fact that the economy was the most important concern of the administration. From 1971 until 1981, Sir Phillip Haddon-Cave filled this position. As an advocate of the free market, he is well known for coining the phrase "positive non-interventionism," which meant that the government would only get involved in the economy if market forces failed. This, however, was already a change from previous policy. He was strongly criticized by members of the opposition because some believed he was controlled by business interests. For instance, Brook Bernacchi of the Reform Club said in 1979:

> Land prices are going up and up and Philip Haddon-Cave is just rubbing his hands together and saying: 'Ha! Ha! More revenue' … He cuts down on the already overdue housing programme that the Governor announced nearly 10 years ago, so that people on the waiting list for housing, small families, working families, middle class families, do not have a hope of getting into public housing in the foreseeable future.
>
> (quoted in *SCMP* 14 Nov. 1979)

Bernacchi juxtaposes and contrasts MacLehose and Haddon-Cave to show his support for social reforms. The failure of the government to fulfill its promise on public housing was one of the most important reasons for contention during the late 1970s and early 1980s.

Despite the differences between the two leadership styles, there was, however, enough common ground. The leaders agreed that the priority of the colony should be stability and prosperity. Economic growth, which was closely tied to a free market economy, was regarded as the most important method for achieving this goal.

Incentives: reasons for group cohesion

The most important incentives for individual members of the government were prestige and power, which, due to the colonial nature of the government, were structured along a rigid hierarchy. Because officials were appointed, government officials, and especially the higher-ranking secretaries, and judges were dependent on the grace of the governor. They, therefore, tried to fulfill their duties as officers of the British crown and not as representatives of the people. Furthermore, within the ruling elite there was a common interest in maintaining the present economic and political system from which everyone benefited. This included a special emphasis on stability. The power of the government was not based on "tame or even bullied unofficials though certainly the unofficials and government share more or less the same political assumptions" (Lowe 1980: 68).

The internal cohesion of the bureaucracy can, furthermore, be attributed to a set of values. Lui Ting Terry (1988) has identified three commonly accepted values within the administration: efficiency, neutrality, and hierarchical loyalty. She considered the first, efficiency, to be "of overriding importance to government officials in Hong Kong" (ibid.: 137). This had the result that the government paid most of its attention to the financial aspects of any program and also strove to be as economical as possible. As a consequence, the outcome of government policies was often neglected. Second, neutrality meant that members of the civil service were not allowed to participate in politics. Civil Service Regulation 523 prohibited bureaucrats from participating in public meetings, lobbying the government in their interest or distributing political publications. They could, however, unlike their Singaporean counterparts, participate in government unions. Third, the acceptance of the hierarchical structure supported by strict rules and regulations created an environment that discouraged criticism from within the bureaucracy.

In spite of the factors that contributed to cohesiveness within the government, there were also serious problems within the bureaucracy. For example, the government continuously faced a shortfall of qualified workers because salaries were much below those of the private sector—which is different from Singapore, where the government has, since 1994, pegged the salaries of top administrators to levels comparable to the private sector. The dire situation resulted in frequent labor union demands for higher wages. For example, in 1975 the Government Clerical Staff Association put up posters which urged government employees to fight for higher salaries (*Hong Kong Standard* 4 July 1975). In response to the labor shortage, the government attracted expatriates to work in these positions. While they received the same salary as their Chinese counterparts, they also received money for additional expenses, such as a housing allowance. This distinction between local employees and expatriates produced considerable discontent even though it did not create any serious fissures in the government, partly due to the common values (Lui 1988).

The major incentive for the business elite was the fact that Hong Kong had very few restrictions on business operations and free trade (Owen 1971). This created an environment that secured the support of the industrialists for the government. Eric Towner, paraphrasing the Deputy Director of Commerce Jim McGregor in 1973, writes:

Hongkong has a government that is not ashamed of the profit motive as the mainspring for economic advancement; it also believes that businessmen know better than bureaucrats how to run business.

(Towner 1973)

To show its support to the business interests, the government did not impose tariffs on the export or import of products and the whole administration was geared toward trade (Ngo 1999). Furthermore, in order to attract overseas investment, ownership by foreign companies was not restricted, and these companies were protected under the Hong Kong legal system as if they were local enterprises. While the government did not offer specific incentives to foreign companies, low tax rates were considered important in attracting capital.

Communication network

During the early days of the colony, communication between the members of the ruling elite was based mainly on interpersonal relationships. The growing complexity of the administrative state after World War II therefore resulted in serious problems of communication within the government, which impaired the ability of the government's policy-making process. For example, the Hong Kong government refused to publicize any economic statistics until the early 1970s. In the opinion of the government, statistics were expensive, it was impossible to produce accurate results, and they were contrary to the interests of the business community (Goodstadt 2006). Furthermore, "Statistics were seen as threatening [the Hong Kong Government's] freedom from London's control and its ability to limit political debate locally" (ibid.: 1). It was only in 1961 that the Hong Kong Government started to estimate the annual GDP and more than 10 years later, in 1973, it finally released these numbers to the public (ibid.). This change of policy reflected the general trend toward greater planning, which required the existence of sound economic data.

In the early 1970s, communication within the government was still very rudimentary. Goodstadt (1971) demonstrates the difficulties of inner-bureaucratic communication by showing that various government officials did not receive the correct information, which they needed to work effectively. For example, the director of the Government Information Service (GIS), Nigel Watt, was not sufficiently informed about his own government when he claimed that there had not been a census for 40 years, while there had been one in 1961, and a sample census in 1966.

Communication improved in the mid-1970s, when the government increasingly emphasized social policy to ameliorate the living conditions of the population and to maintain social stability. Following the McKinsey Report of 1973, the government attempted to streamline communication within the growing administration in order to remain effective in implementing policy outputs. The successes of the Hong Kong government can in part be attributed to these changes.

Aside from internal communication, it is also important to note how information and demands were channeled between the government and the business elite, and especially the Chinese elite. Lau (1982) claims that the communication channels between the bureaucratic polity and the Chinese elite were weak. The Chinese elite, however, played an important role in government-sponsored intermediate organizations (for example UMELCO), and their opinion was sought in various feedback mechanisms. Lau criticizes the inefficiency of the communication links "in bringing the opinion and desires of the bulk of the Chinese population to bear upon the decision makers in the bureaucracy" (Lau 1982: 122). This argument is based on a dichotomy of an expatriate government and a homogeneous Chinese society. However, in reality, the Chinese society was stratified into leaders, who not only were the recipients of government communication but also actively supported the regime, and the broad Chinese masses (the lower classes), which were, as in other societies, largely excluded from the decision-making process. The Chinese elite agreed with the British business elite that government intervention in the economy should be kept to a minimum. Any new law, according to the Legislative Councilor K.S. Lo, "generally represents a compromise between the government's and the unofficial (members') views. This activity behind the scenes is generally not known to the public" (quoted in Goodstadt 1971).

In order to secure communication links with the business class, the government asked important entrepreneurs for detailed reports on how a policy change would affect a respective business. Furthermore, through a network of advisory committees (which were consultative bodies attached to the civil service) and the Executive and Legislative Councils, the business community was able to influence the government. For this reason, the government considered it unnecessary to collect information about companies residing in Hong Kong. The influence of the business class on the policy-making process, therefore, is reflected not in any visible results but rather in what the government did not do (Miners 1996).

The ruling elite groups, however, were less effective in their message to oppositional groups and to the public. They had only limited control over newspapers, radio, and television. The owners of most media companies were members of the business class, so they rarely published articles that were adverse to business. The government, on the other hand, was not considered a sacred cow, and the newspapers, radio, and television increasingly reported on the flaws of the government during the 1970s. Therefore the senior bureaucrats preferred to allow the official Government Information Service (GIS) to speak for the administration (Harris 1982: 189). This lack of control weakened the government's ability to dominate the public discourse and also increased the ability of the opposition to put pressure on the government. The sometimes effective use of the media to achieve the goals of oppositional groups will be discussed in Chapter 7.

Cognitive perceptions and legitimacy

The slowly progressing decolonization process during the 1970s and 1980s influenced the perceptions of the administrators as well as the business elite.

Despite the localization of the government, colonial thinking continued to affect the ruling elite groups' leadership. Many in the expatriate class still perceived Western, and especially the British, tradition and culture as superior to the Chinese. The reluctance to allow Chinese to become the official language of the bureaucracy, the Urban Council, and especially the legal system, clearly reflects this sentiment. In the early 1970s it was still required to pass an English test to stand for Urban Council elections. In 1975, Chinese finally received equal status to English and only in 1989 was legislation enacted in both languages, still leaving many older laws untranslated. The two languages have, furthermore, fostered elitist structures, because fluency in English was a precondition of success in a highly competitive economy.

The leaders of the ethnic Chinese majority not only grudgingly accepted British rule but also actively supported it because they were the benefactors of the government's economic policies. The ruling elite groups, therefore, shared a sense of superiority versus the excluded members of society, who were not only the lower classes but also the increasingly vocal middle class. This had the result that the government was frequently willing to act as a paternal guardian of the lower echelons of society, a role that is often attributed to the Confucian ideal of ruling by good example. The sense of superiority and the need to act as a father figure for the masses had its origins in a peculiar form of government legitimacy, which depended both on positive non-interventionism in the economy and on the government's increasing focus on social programs, which were meant to maintain the stability of the colony.

A sense of superiority and self-confidence

The Hong Kong government considered itself superior to other actors in the political system. Bureaucrats regarded themselves as members of an expert bureaucracy, which ruled in a paternalistic and hierarchical manner over an inferior population. The Legislative Council, furthermore, perceived itself as the "Good, the Wise and the Rich" (Harris 1982: 186). In contrast to Singapore, Hong Kong completely lacked political actors comparable to the ministers of Singapore, to whom the bureaucracy was accountable. The Legislative Council did not have significant control over the activities of the bureaucracy.

Table 5.2 Cognitive image of the ruling elite groups in in Hong Kong during the 1970s

	Group strength	Emotions and policy disposition	Goals and tactics
Colonial Image	cohesive, strong	sense of superiority, sense of legitimacy, paternalism	focus on economic development, co-option and secret coercion

Furthermore, in most cases, the government did not allow challenges from other societal actors because it did not regard their participation as necessary. Changes to the administrative structure, furthermore, were only considered when they were absolutely necessary. The picture of the Hong Kong bureaucrat was that of a technocrat who was apolitical, introverted, and amoral (Lui 1988).

At the beginning of the colonial era, many expatriates shared a sense of superiority in regard to the Chinese, who were often seen as inferior and therefore were only important to the policy making of the government insofar as there was a need to maintain stability. As I have argued in Chapter 3, the government became increasingly localized and the interests of the Chinese majority became an integral part of policy making. At the same time, the government also progressively sought the opinion of these people even though it was reluctant to introduce democracy, which was, among other things, considered alien to the Chinese political culture. The lack of participation in Urban Council elections was seen as an indication of this.

Instead, the government considered the use of consultation as the best alternative to democracy. The preference for a system of consultation was voiced by the incoming Governor Murray MacLehose in his first speech before the Legislative Council, on 1 December 1971:

> It is a feature of Government in Hong Kong that it works through a series of advisory, consultative and constitutional bodies. Many of these do vital work, but it seems to me that the major burden falls on the Members of the Executive and Legislative Councils. Membership of UMELCO, Finance Committee, the Public Works Sub-Committee, the Establishment Sub-Committee all amount to a very great deal of work, much time in committee and perhaps even more in field work and preparation.
>
> (*Hong Kong Hansard* 1 December 1971: 224)

Emphasizing institutions such as the Legislative Council and UMELCO, MacLehose clearly shows his preference for government by consultation instead of greater participation. This is reinforced by the fact that he neglects to mention the only partially democratic institution, the Urban Council.

The ruling elite's perception of the role of opposition in the governing process was cogently presented in the eight principles of the debate on the presentation of the 1974–75 Estimates of Revenue and Expenditure, which Financial Secretary Philip Haddon-Cave delivered to the Legislative Council on 27 March 1974. The "imperial image" of the ruling elite groups in Hong Kong is represented in these principles. For example, the third principle deals with the involvement of oppositional groups or, in Haddon-Cave's words, "sectional groups." While he considers it important that these groups be allowed to express their opinion and that the government should listen to their concerns, this process should only be conducted through consultation. The Financial Secretary, furthermore, restricts the influence of pressure groups in the following way:

an obligation to listen does not necessarily carry an obligation to change our minds or modify our proposals, though we should always of course admit mistakes. We have such an obligation only if a sectional group can argue its case persuasively and demonstrate an identity of interest with the broad public interest (or, at least, an absence of conflict with the broad public interest).

(Hong Kong Hansard 27 March 1974: 724)

This argument severely restricts the potential influence oppositional groups are allowed to have on government policies. By leaving it unclear who defines the public interest, the government, in fact, restricts challenger groups in their ability to formulate alternatives. Furthermore, only if there is agreement between the government and pressure groups will there be a change in government policy. Consultation is therefore not a bidirectional process, but rather one in which the government dominates and defines the parameters. This is also reflected in his last principle, which attempts to balance government control with the principles of laissez-faire, of which he was the most important advocate:

there is a need for the Government to ensure first that the private and public sectors are in harmony and secondly that there are no constraints on, or imperfections in, the operation of the system which are detrimental to economic efficiency or to the legitimate interests of the individual.

(ibid.: 726)

The government is seen as a negotiator between the public and the private and as an institution that removes potential obstacles for the operation of business. At the same time, however, the economy should remain free.

Furthermore, his principles suggest that the government can find objective solutions to the city-state's challenges. Therefore, Haddon-Cave warns against subjective judgments in financial and economic matters. The assumption that an objective solution can be found rejects the notion of conflicting partisan interests. This has to be seen as an attempt to depoliticize this potentially very controversial debate on the budget. The idea that the best economic polices were no policies at all was, furthermore, echoed by many in the business community. For example, J.H. Bremridge, managing director of John Swire and Sons (HK) Ltd. and an Unofficial in the Legislative Council, stated in 1975:

I for one believe that the commercial success of Hongkong for many years has been materially helped by, if it is not only due to, the pragmatic realism of the Hongkong Government, and its declared intention not to interfere with commercial practices, nor especially with innovation, unless it is clearly right to do so.

(Bremridge 1975)

Bremridge's concurrence with the principle of "positive non-interventionism" has to be seen as a consensus among the business and political elites.

The ruling elite saw itself more as administrator than as policy maker. Since most of the decision makers were also bureaucrats, technical and pragmatic thinking tended to dominate. Furthermore, as bureaucrats, they tended to be conservative and careful about their actions (Wilding 1997). This, combined with Haddon-Cave's principles, shaped a government that was convinced of the rightfulness of its actions on the one hand and had a "touch of arrogance" on the other (ibid. 1997: 246). The discrepancy between the government's self-perception and the actual outcome resulted in the perception of bureaucrats as complacent, formalistic, legalistic, and inflexible.

Proxy paternalism and small government

The resistance to substantive democratic reforms alludes to the government's belief in the paternalistic guidance of a "good" government. In the 1970s many in the government rejected the notion that they were "paternalistic administrators, who know instinctively what is best for the public good" (Hong Kong Government 1974: 1). However, the claim that its purpose was to act in the best interest of the people provided the primary basis on which the rulers could justify the continuation of authoritarian rule. The primary task of the government was to uncover what the people wanted and develop suggestions based on that information. According to Governor Sir Murray MacLehose, who spoke to the members of the Legislative Council in 1975:

> Lacking, as is unavoidable, any electoral mandate, Members are required to try to think and plan and speak for the interests of the community as a whole as they see it, and not, as would be so much easier, for the narrow interests of a party, a group, a profession, an area or a class. But I believe it assists this general requirement if members are able to speak from as wide a spread as possible not only of professional experience, but also of social background.
>
> (*Hong Kong Hansard* 8 October 1975: 45)

The governor expected of the members of the Legislative Council that they would act in a non-partisan way and in the interest of the people. He tried to rectify the lack of an electoral mandate through the selection of individuals from different backgrounds, which created an institution that was at least supposedly representative of the interests of as many groups as possible. This reveals a certain level of idealism, which assumes that people from different groups can act as representatives of these groups merely because of their membership. Furthermore, MacLehose seems to ignore another important aspect of elections, namely that they serve as a check on the government. In MacLehose's conception of a representative government, politicians were supposed to act in the interest of the people and not represent any constituency or special interest. The lack of electoral representation, therefore, resulted in a paternalistic self-conception of the government.

The self-proclaimed paternalistic role of the government was organized through community leaders as proxies or through the Department of Home Affairs. Governor MacLehose explained this in 1974:

> The Government is not usually able to deal with the people directly, the contacts are usually made through the community leaders. Organized campaigns by the Government must have their assistance, and other matters such as site clearance by the Housing Department are often handled through the Department of Home Affairs in order to explain the situation to the people.
>
> (quoted in *SCMP* 5 March 1974)

The use of intermediate organizations shows that the government was mostly unwilling to involve directly itself in society and rather set basic guidelines to be executed by grassroots organizations.

Nevertheless, similar to Singapore, there were a number of public relations campaigns with which the government sought to actively influence the behavior of the people and inculcate certain values in the population. These campaigns focused on topics as diverse as the environment, violent crime, attracting recruits to the police, or registering voters for Urban Council elections. The significance of these campaigns was noted by Harris (1982: 187), who wrote that "A series of campaigns exhort citizens to good deeds and actions. In 1981, a campaign to remove litter from the streets had a decidedly Orwellian look." In contrast to Singapore, these campaigns, however, were notoriously underfunded.

The government's activist rhetoric coupled with a lack of sufficient resources is best illustrated by one of the most important campaigns of the Hong Kong Government in the 1970s: The Keep Hong Kong Clean Campaign. Officially launched in 1970, this campaign was one of the first in the city-state.[1] The campaign was able to attract 20,000 people as junior members after December 1972. In 1975, the government rated the campaign as "99 percent successful," which meant that 99 percent of the population knew about the campaign. According to the government in 1975, a total of HK$9 million was spent on the campaign, of which HK$3 million was used for direct advertisements. Assistant Director of Publicity G.S. Blundell praised the effort:

> In real terms I don't think it would be unfair to say that the equivalent amount of money that we spent is at least equal to Cathay Pacific or the Hongkong Tourist Association expenditure but all of it is spent in Hongkong for the benefit of the public.
>
> (quoted in *SCMP*, 26 June 1975)

This statement reveals two facets of the government's intention. The government attempted to work for the people (the paternalistic notion) and it had been very generous (the financial notion). This latter aspect was, however, seriously undermined when, in the following year, the head of the campaign, Dr Denny Huang, resigned, citing increasing government reluctance to provide financial support:

> The Government has changed from giving full support in the beginning to standing aside, watching with hands in the pockets. From 1975 on the Government no longer provided money for project under the campaign in the New Territories.
>
> (Huang 1976)

The government's frequent unwillingness to spend money on social projects such as publicity campaigns or public housing has to be seen in the context of the overall strategy of maintaining a small government. The government's ambitions thus often exceeded its own financial abilities, which provided opportunities for oppositional groups.

Performance legitimacy between success and failure

The Hong Kong government's perception of its legitimacy was largely based on the performance of the administrators. The largely successful ability to provide stability and prosperity bestowed upon the civil service the right to rule the city-state. After World War II, the idea that the Hong Kong Government was politically neutral, i.e. did not side with the Nationalists, while at the same time maintaining a clear distance from the Communists, strengthened government legitimacy. The sense of superiority and the need for paternalism provided sufficient justification for a class of administrators who believed in efficiency and neutrality. This was not negatively influenced by the fact that the government was a colonial regime, despite all the attendant legitimation problems. This perception influenced both the goals and strategies of the government as it transformed its role from a focus on public safety to activist intervention in the social sphere.

The government's legitimacy was, however, contingent on a number of factors. It depended to a large degree on the laissez-faire mentality, with few restrictions on business. This was premised on the idea that businessmen knew better how to run a business than did the government. A very good example of this can be found in a speech from 1973 by Sir Yuet-Keung Kan, the chairman of the Hong Kong Trade Development Council, and a member of the business elite:

> Hongkong's governmental system and indeed the Government's policies, have evolved naturally over the years in response to changing needs. But there have been no basic or drastic changes for the past 130 years and there is no pressure for changes in the future.
>
> (Kan 1973)

The government's legitimacy, therefore, rested on adjusting to the demands of the business elite. According to this opinion, drastic changes would have seriously undermined government legitimacy. The significant role of the government was to be supportive of businesses:

> The Government, for instance, itself provides or stimulates private enterprise to produce the services and infrastructure that all businesses and industry needs, to the great profit in the past of competitive British enterprise both from overseas and on the spot. It provides the assistance and encouragement necessary for successful economic and industrial development. It works hard and effectively in those sectors which, by their nature, must be its own preserve.
>
> (ibid.)

In the opinion of this tycoon, the government's role is solely that of a provider of infrastructure and services for businesses. Kan does not request financial assistance in the form of subsidies or tax relief for selected enterprises, which might give advantages to some businesses in favor over others.

Second, legitimacy was also the outcome of the government's increasing involvement in society. This started with an ambitious housing program in 1953 and increasingly expanded also to education and health. The housing program, for instance, not only helped many Hong Kongers to improve their housing conditions. It also gained the support of the business elite because improved living conditions for Hong Kong's workers enhanced the quality of work and also reduced the need to increase wages (Ho 1986). The change in the government's focus initially occurred merely as a reaction to deteriorating conditions, which seriously threatened the social peace of the colony. It was only in the 1970s that the government started to shift toward long-term planning and performance.

Finally, even though the colony lacked democratic representation, repression of oppositional groups was perceived to be illegitimate by large parts of society. The government could not openly arrest members of the opposition without serious repercussions. The revelation in 1980 of the existence of a secret committee to monitor and possibly control the opposition immediately led to strong condemnation of the government in the major newspapers. While the government initially justified its decision, it had to concede to the abolition of the committee in 1983. This example shows that repression had to be used sparingly.

Goals

Progressive goals: from status quo to improving society

The following presents an analysis of the slow transformation of Hong Kong politics from complete laissez-faire to some form of government intervention. The employment of the management consultants McKinsey and Company in

May of 1972 was perhaps the most important milestone in this transition, even though it did not lead to radical changes (Scott 1989). It signified a crucial development from colonial rule to rule based on good government. The goal of the consultants was to probe the processes within the administration and to determine ways of dealing with an increasingly complex government without sufficient numbers of experienced officials. The Colonial Secretary, Sir Hugh Norman-Walker, stated the purpose of the McKinsey inquiry in 1973:

> The overall objective was to diagnose the problems, to determine how Government's current management methods affected performance, and to see what could be done to change and improve them. Above all, the Consultants were seeking the most effective way of ensuring that our scant resources of particularly experienced manpower and skills were deployed to the best advantage.
>
> (*Hong Kong Hansard* 23 May 1973: 807)

The emphasis was placed on government efficiency, which meant "a smaller but highly powered central machine" with greater ability to plan the future development of the city-state's administration. Instead of the prevalent laissez-faire idea of the time, the government was moving in the direction of greater involvement in the overall development of society. This was seen in the government's "positive role for the initiation and formulation of policies and programmes, and for the monitoring, control and co-ordination of their implementation" (ibid.: 808).

The transformation of the role of the government from guardian of public order to direct involvement in the economy and in society entailed the need to hire more experts, which was a change toward greater technocratic rule. However, the limited number of experts in the government convinced the administrators that an efficient bureaucratic regime required a centralized implementation process.

> [A]n essential corollary of these proposals is to reaffirm and strengthen the authority and responsibility of Heads of Departments for the executive and effective operation of their departments, and for the formulation and implementation of departmental policies. At the same time, the departments will continue to contribute expert opinions and ideas to the process of policy formulation, amendment and revision at the Government level
>
> (ibid.: 808)

The highly centralized system was supposed to remove delays, because in the past everything had had to be channeled through the Colonial Secretary. The centralization of the process was also accompanied by greater standardization of processes (which involved the use of computers) and the delegation of powers to the high-level posts directly under the Colonial Secretary and the Financial Secretary (Miners 1981: 94). Another idea that was promoted was the recruitment of outside consultants on a permanent basis. (*SCMP* 11 Feb. 1973)

The most important implication of the McKinsey report was the realization that the government needed to place a high priority on long-term planning. The most important reason behind the introduction of social programs was the need to minimize the negative impact of bad living conditions. MacLehose, speaking about the housing situation, noted in 1972 that "The present housing inadequacies are a constant source of friction between the Government and the people, offending Hong Kong's humanity, civic pride, and political good sense" (Hong Kong Government 1973: 98). This statement is significant because it reveals two aspects of the government's goals. On the one hand, the government tried to eliminate the potential for social conflicts, either organized in social groups or disorganized in the form of riots. On the other hand, the governor stressed the need for greater involvement in society in order to improve the life of the people. MacLehose considered public housing a moral issue, which needed pragmatic decisions in the form of "political good sense." The quote shows that an important goal of the ruling elite groups was to improve society because, if successfully implemented, it would minimize the potential for contentious politics.

It has been argued that the "development in social policy had two problematic effects on political and social stability" (Wilding 1997: 251). According to Wilding, the emphasis on social policy first of all contributed to the undermining of the authoritarian regime because it stimulated social mobilization. Second, it generated satisfaction as well as dissatisfaction with the government. However, it is also possible to argue that the introduction of social programs preempted calls for fundamental change, as will be shown in Chapter 7. Furthermore, dissatisfaction with the government was the result of the government's inability to fulfill its promises. In contrast to Singapore, Hong Kong's social programs often missed their goals, which was mostly due to the prevailing emphasis on small government. Most of the social conflicts in the 1970s and afterwards can be attributed to the prevailing ideology of laissez-faire and not to the focus on social policy. Moreover, lack of government involvement, as in the case of the arrest of Peter Godber or the closure of the Shatin Lutheran School (see Chapter 7), often led to the strongest criticism from social activists.

Conservative goals: maintaining the status quo

During the colonial era, Hong Kong's rulers were primarily concerned with maintaining the status quo of an autonomous colony with a strong and efficient bureaucracy. They did not worry so much about strengthening or retaining the power of the ruling elite groups. The government even considered the introduction of limited democratization immediately after World War II. However, the plan to establish a municipal council[2] with thirty-two of forty-eight members elected through a limited franchise, conceived by Governor

Mark Young, failed in 1946, in part because of opposition from the business community, which feared that electoral politics could lead to social unrest (*Hong Kong Journal* 2005). Others even worried that democracy would "throw politics into Hong Kong's very grubby market place" (Harris 1982: 188). As has been discussed in Chapter 3, democratization was also rejected because the government was concerned about the apparent lack of participation in existing political institutions and worried about opposition from China.

The Hong Kong government argued that the city-state's dependence on foreign investments required the repression of internal conflicts in order to protect the confidence of these investors. A major concern was the possibility that contention could lead to violent riots. Only under stable circumstances could the colony provide the conditions necessary for economic prosperity (Rear 1971).

Furthermore, in order to ensure the steady and even economic development of the city-state, the government emphasized the need for an efficient administration, as well as continuity in its policies. Especially from the early 1970s, the government tried to increase the efficiency of the administration, which was supposed to broaden the acceptance of the rulers within the population. As has already been discussed, this had been the main reason for hiring the management consultants McKinsey and Company. In the early 1980s, the government again focused on the efficiency of the administration when it decided to reform the district administration. This was to be accomplished through District Management Committees (DMCs), in which senior departmental officers would meet and discuss policies in order to ensure responsive and coordinated administration at the grassroots level, following regionalization of the civil service. Second, the government planned the creation of district boards (DBs) in which officials and appointed unofficials would, together with directly elected district representatives, advise and scrutinize local services.

The tactics of Hong Kong's ruling elite groups

Co-option of the opposition and the willingness to compromise

Hong Kong's rulers sought to support the development of the economy, provide social services, and co-opt potential critics into government institutions. However, especially in regard to the latter two, the Hong Kong government often faced significant challenges. First of all, the government was often unable to achieve the targets of its ambitious social development plans, such as housing and education, because, as has been argued elsewhere, the government lacked enough funds to finance these plans. Second, the government was unable to co-opt large parts of the rising opposition movement into the government because of the lack of institutional channels for the newly developing groups. This created discontent that resulted in contentious politics that forced the government to deal with these challengers. However, instead of relying only on repression, the government sought to negotiate and find a compromise with oppositional groups. This can be exemplified by a discussion of the government's handling of the issue of corruption, as well as by its handling of the police force's opposition to the creation of the Independent Commission Against Corruption (ICAC) on 15 February 1974.

In the past, corruption was an accepted aspect of Hong Kong, the "fix-it" city, as it was commonly known. L.F. Goodstadt wrote in 1970 (21): "The people know a steady stream of cash flows into business and government circles to win friends and influence policies." In the same article, the writer noted a small change in the perception of corruption in the city-state. While Goodstadt asserts that this was the result of illegal immigrants from Communist China, whose officials were traditionally incorruptible, in hindsight it is probably more likely that the rising socio-economic conditions created an environment in which an increasing number of people, especially the more educated, became strong opponents of corruption. In 1970, however, Goodstadt still had to conclude that "The minority disgusted with their corrupt society get little general support" (ibid. 21).

Even in 1973, the government considered corruption less important than violent crime and the police were convinced that their own Anti-Corruption Office was able to deal with the problem satisfactorily. The *South China Morning Post* wrote: "The feeling in Government is believed to be that while a great deal of minor, low-level corruption exists in Hongkong there is none of the major corruption that is found in some Asian societies where the highest officials take bribes" (2 Feb. 1973). This did not mean, however, that the government was totally unconcerned with the situation. Denys Roberts, outgoing Attorney General and head of the Anti-Corruption Target Committee, again raised the issue in 1973, when he was appointed Colonial Secretary. He said: "I find it quite distasteful that there is as much corruption in Hongkong as there is" (*SCMP* 30 March 1973).

On 8 June, however, the issue of corruption took another turn, when Police Chief Superintendent Peter Fitzroy Godber, who was accused of corruption, was able to flee to Britain via Singapore. When news of his escape was confirmed on 11 June, it was met with strong criticism. The *South China Morning Post* called for an official commission of inquiry, which the government accepted when it announced the appointment of the Alastair Blair-Kerr Commission on 14 June. The issue of corruption subsequently mobilized large sections of society, which had already been very disenchanted with the government's attempts at fighting corruption. Student groups and community activists united with leftist groups to call for the return of Godber. A radical worker activist, Leung Chung-kwong of the *Daily Fighting Press*, told demonstrators: "We strongly believe that only with action will the Government bow to our legitimate demand of extraditing Godber" (*SCMP* 13 Aug. 1973). On 2 September 1973, about 2,000 people demonstrated for the return of the corrupt police official. The police ordered the demonstrators to disperse but angry protesters yelled insults at the officers. Finally, a number of protesters were arrested and threatened with prosecution.

The police were strongly opposed to the creation of an independent institution. Charles Sutcliffe, who was known for his reform of the police force, was also a strong opponent of outside investigators. However, the demand of many, even prestigious groups such as the Hong Kong Bar Association, was for a new anti-corruption department that ideally would be totally independent of the Hong Kong government. The police commissioner claimed that the Anti-Corruption Branch was already best equipped and that individuals would not want to work all their life in a department that fought against corruption:

> The investigation of corruption is not a pleasant job. ... none of my officers relish being posted to the Anti-Corruption Bureau. It's a job they have to do and they do it to the best of their ability and it all adds to their good training.
>
> (*SCMP* 19 March 1973)

Sutcliffe is unable to provide a good reason against the creation of an independent monitoring institution. Instead, the police commissioner was concerned about maintaining the self-sufficiency of the police force because the introduction of an independent agency would infringe upon its power.

Despite opposition from the police force, the Blair-Kerr commission "exposed the sort of decay that is unusual even by Asian standards and intolerable for a British colony" (Mangold 1975: 66). In response, the government and, most importantly, the governor established the Independent Commission Against Corruption (ICAC). While this new commission did not satisfy all of the government's critics (the head was still nominated by the governor and many of the officers were former policemen from the Anti-Corruption Branch), it proved to be a very important asset for the legitimacy of the regime because it enhanced the credibility of the government. When we see it in historical context, the ICAC represented radical reform toward a more modern society. Most importantly, in terms of tactics, the willingness to address the people's demands neutralized some of the criticism against the government. The protests against corruption had demonstrated the potential of cooperation between oppositional groups from all walks of life, which had been a serious challenge to the ruling elite.

While the Hong Kong government's readiness to compromise strengthened its rule, it also increased the willingness of oppositional groups to challenge the government. The ICAC was very successful in fighting corruption and received praise from many groups in Hong Kong. However, the aggressiveness with which the commission investigated corruption soon led to a significant decrease of morale within the police force and turned it, basically, into an oppositional group. Complaints against police misconduct increased dramatically. Mass arrests of rank-and-file policemen in 1977 increased the suspicion among average policemen that they were being singled out for punishment while higher-ranking officers were spared. In October of the same year, a group of discontented police officers petitioned the Commissioner of the Police, Brian Slevin, to put an end to the tactics of the ICAC. At an early meeting of the campaign one of the policemen voiced his anger: "They [ICAC officers] should conduct their inquiries in a lawful and justifiable manner and not use oppressive tactics against police officers" (quoted in *SCMP*, 27 Oct. 1977). Some police officers even suggested a strike, but this was quickly rejected by the majority of officers.

The protests against the ICAC reached a climax on 28 October, when 4,000 police officers staged a sit-in and some 120 officers attempted to storm the ICAC office. Despite the attempt of protest organizers to conduct a peaceful rally, a group of eight to ten officers and former officers started to riot inside the ICAC office. As a result, five ICAC officers were injured and a glass door was smashed. The protest organizers quickly condemned the actions of these renegade police officers, but the police commissioner was so concerned that he banned mass meetings of police officers on 3 November (*SCMP* 4 Nov. 1977). In an about turn, on 5 November 1977 the governor announced a partial amnesty of all police officers for alleged corruption prior to 1 January 1977, with the exception of those who were already under investigation. Murray MacLehose argued:

> We felt that such an announcement would greatly relieve the public service. We had envisaged doing this next spring. However, in view of recent events, and for all the difference a few months would make, I think it would be helpful if this was done immediately.
>
> (quoted in *Hong Kong Standard* 6 Nov. 1977)

The action was essentially meant to restore the morale of the police. Again, the government was willing to partially concede to the demands of the protesters.

This compromise by the government, however, also angered many who saw it as a failure to fulfill its promise of fighting corruption. For example, elected Urban Councilor Elsie Elliot charged that the amnesty should not have been given to all police officers. She argued instead that it should only have been granted to junior police officials: "I think the Government should treat corrupt senior officials as criminals for they use their junior officers to do the dirty work in collecting bribes" (quoted in *Hong Kong Standard* 6 Nov. 1977). While most police officers applauded the government's action, a number of them continued to campaign for an unconditional amnesty and even a complete break-up of the ICAC (Miners 1981). In response, in an emergency session on 7 November, the Legislative Council passed an amendment to the Police Force Ordinance, which allowed the dismissal of any police officer who refused to obey orders. MacLehose realized that the government's compromise had to be limited:

> The idea that pressure can achieve further concessions of this sort would result from a complete misconception of the mood of the Government

and the community. It would also ignore the true interests of at least 99 per cent of the Police Force itself. Needless to say it totally ignores the true interests of Hong Kong where the enforcement of law and order and the achievement of acceptable standards of honesty have made such strides in recent years. Concession to such demands under pressure would invite pressure on other issues.

(*Hong Kong Hansard* 1977: 158)

It is obvious that there is a contradiction between the willingness to concede to the demands from various groups and the ability of the government to contain contention. This is especially difficult for an unelected governor, who purports to speak in the public interest. For the government, there was a constant struggle to balance the interests of oppositional groups with those of the people of Hong Kong. The increasing challenges and the lack of democratic legitimation, therefore, forced the government to occasionally resort to more extreme tactics, such as coercion, in order to silence the empowered challengers.

Secretive control of dissent

Allegations of secret attempts to control and, if possible, coerce dissent date back to at least the beginning of the 1970s. In 1970, for example, the Hong Kong Bar Association focused public attention on the fact that the governor was able to allow any public official the right to intercept telephone calls and telegrams. "There is evidence that the powers are used frequently without reference to the governor or attorney-general and one wonders who decides when 'public interest' is involved" (quoted in Baird 1970a: 8). One person who claimed openly that she was monitored during the 1970s was activist and elected Urban Councilor Elsie Elliot (Tu 2003).

Rumors of various repressive tactics against potential dissent were voiced sporadically during the 1970s. An example of this kind of tactic is the following letter to the editor of the *South China Morning Post*:

In my own experience, when registering to vote a year ago, I was frankly and actively discouraged from doing so by the official who handled my case—a European, therefore presumably of some importance, who dismissed my attempts at democracy in Hongkong as a farce.

Secondly, a few days before the election was held I was the recipient of what I can only call a hate letter—directed not at me but at the whole idea of the Urban Council and urging me and other potential voters not to vote.

(Elias 1973)

The author asserts that government officials actively sought to undermine the only partially elected institution, the Urban Council. Even though this is the only such claim, the author still raises the issue of suppressing the development of democracy. While the lack of influence of the Urban Council probably hurt participation more, the author's concerns raise the possibility that there were other, more coercive methods of keeping turnout low.

Control of dissent seems to have become more important for the government toward the end of the 1970s. The rising opposition from increasingly assertive pressure groups increased the government's willingness to control this activity. First of all, in 1979 there were a number of arrests of peaceful protesters which raised serious concerns about human rights in Hong Kong. Second, the revelation in the early 1980s of a secret committee that was used to spy on and possibly even undermine certain pressure groups shows that the government was willing to use repression against dissent.

On 7 January 1979, seventy-eight boat people and social workers were arrested while in coaches on their way to the governor's residence. They were charged with breaking the Public Order Ordinance for unlawful assembly and were all released on bail of HK$200. The incident, which will be discussed in more detail in Chapter 7, raised the issue of government repression against oppositional groups. While many social activists protested at what they perceived to be a violation of human rights, pro-government voices considered the government's actions as a necessary tactic for guaranteeing the stability of the city-state. For example, the *South China Morning Post* wrote in its editorial:

> if society is to run smoothly and efficiently and in a way that permits the majority to go about their daily tasks, a degree of regulation and law is essential. ... In short, most would probably agree that the Government errs on the side of caution in imposing existing laws, rather than that it is over-rigid.
>
> (*SCMP* 28 Feb. 1979)

It was well known that the editors of the leading newspapers, and especially the *South China Morning Post*, were pro-government in their coverage and in their editorials. In this particular editorial, the paper justifies the government's tactics of arresting government critics. It argues that if an arrest would be in the interest of the "well-being and convenience of the majority," the government could say "No" to oppositional activity and resort to repression against the challengers (ibid.).

In 1978, the government decided to increase its control over the ever-increasing challenges from oppositional groups, when it set up the secret Standing Committee on Pressure Groups (SCOPG), supposedly to monitor the activities of the pressure groups. Only two years later, the British journalist Duncan Campbell revealed the existence of the committee in the British magazine the *New Statesman*, on 12 December 1980. Campbell asserted that any political group in Hong Kong had been subject to secret surveillance. He wrote that the committee:

> has the job of coordinating government surveillance of any protest or campaigning group and of mounting counter-attacks. Specifically, SCOPG

aims to undermine, co-opt or coerce any of eleven target groups, and others.

(Campbell 1980: 8)

The reason for the committee, according to Campbell, was the threat that these groups posed to government credibility. The fact that some oppositional groups had lobbied British MPs was highlighted. When the report was released, the government only admitted the existence of the committee but rejected the claim that it had any sinister motives. The real reason for the committee, according to government statements, was the ability to better listen to the demands of the pressure groups. Furthermore, the government attacked the *New Statesman* for inaccuracies and lies in the report, but did not sue the magazine for slander, as the Singapore government has repeatedly done against its critics.

Despite strong denials by government officials, Campbell's report was subsequently substantiated. Even though most of the SCOPG report was destroyed during the 1980s for "record management purposes" (*Hong Kong Hansard* 1995: 3595), Legislative Councilor Anna Wu was able to quote a short excerpt from the report in 1995:

Special Branch confirmed that while some pressure groups may be motivated more by self-interest than ultraism [*sic*], their activities have not generally been subversive and they do not seem to have had the effect of subverting the population so far. But SCOPG has been tasked with examining the pressure groups more critically and does not feel able to see the groups in such a favourable light. It is the potential of pressure groups which is disturbing the possibility of their developing into something more sinister or unleashing forces damaging to the whole community. The activities of pressure groups can encourage a widespread critical and argumentative attitude when knocking the Government is fashionable. In itself not a phenomenon to be afraid of, it nonetheless provides an ideal breeding ground for discontent and trouble-makers while there is always the danger that any group, no matter how innocent and well meaning initially, can be taken over by more unscrupulous elements. Whilst at present the conclusion must be that pressure groups are generally not subversive, the potential for subversion always exists.

(ibid.: 3596)

The report asserts that pressure groups have the potential not only to destroy the reputation of the government and thus foster a more critical population, which was considered to be the basis of social instability, but also to become the front for "sinister" groups. This excerpt does not give any indication of the consequences the government should draw from these findings but it is obvious that closer monitoring of oppositional groups was probably recommended. The SCOPG suggested that the mere existence of dissent warranted greater surveillance of pressure groups.

On 28 January 1981, after it had obtained eleven confidential reports, the *Hong Kong Standard* reported on a "Red List," which listed groups that were supposedly threatened by Communist infiltration. The three groups mentioned in the article were the Hong Kong Professional Teachers' Union (HKPTU), the Hong Kong Federation of Students (HKFS) and the Government School Non-Graduate Teachers Union (GSNTU). Again, the government was forced to justify the content of the reports. It claimed that those reports did not contain the official opinion of the government.

The government, however, never really admitted that it was using repression against the opposition. For instance, Denis Bray, in an interview with Lo Hsiu-hing, claimed "Our aim was to achieve stability. There was no guarantee for a revolution [in Hong Kong]. We had the stability that commanded the general support, not the stability of the police state" (quoted in Lo 2001: 36). This denial illustrates that the government's main goal was to minimize contentious politics without recourse to coercive tactics. However, it felt uncertain whether this stability could be maintained without greater control of the rising oppositional movement. The administrators were unsure of the direction of oppositional activism, which suggests uncertainty on behalf of the authoritarian ruler of the rightfulness of his rule. In conclusion, it is obvious that secretive coercion was counterproductive for the colonial regime when it was revealed. This tactic was used very sparingly in the 1970s and decreased even further in the 1980s. With the gradual introduction of greater democratization from the mid-1980s to the 1990s, the government almost completely abandoned repression and became more consultative as well as participatory.

Conclusion and outlook

This chapter has provided a detailed description of the ruling elite groups in Hong Kong during the 1970s, their perceptions, and their goals and tactics. While their members were diverse, communication was not always successful, and their leaders differed on the role of the state, the ruling elites formed a relatively cohesive and stable group because they shared the same goals. They valued most of all prosperity and stability, which, according to the conservatives, could be achieved only through laissez-faire, and according to the progressives, through an emphasis on social policy. The government, therefore, focused on social programs, which found support from both groups. At the same time, the government relied mostly on co-opting its challengers into the political system in order to reduce political contention. This included a propensity to compromise in the interests of stability, which, however, often led to greater challenges from oppositional groups. In contrast, the next chapter will show that Singapore's ruling elite has hardly ever been willing to compromise with any challenger. This means that the Singaporean rulers have been more inclined to use repression of oppositional groups in addition to co-option.

Hong Kong's rulers shared with their Singaporean counterparts the perception that they were the most qualified to govern the city-state. This resulted in a general understanding that the role of the government was that of a paternalistic guardian. This may have been influenced by the rulers' understanding of traditional Chinese culture, but it was mostly the outcome of colonial rule, which places the government in a position of absolute power. Notions of superiority and an ability to govern in the interests of the population gave the rulers a tremendous sense of legitimacy. The Singapore case will show that this "colonial image" is even more evident in the independent city-state. It is perhaps ironic that Singapore's rulers were able to maintain many of the colonial structures and incorporate them into a modern nation-state.

6 Ruling elite groups in Singapore
Strength through cohesion

Singapore's ruling elite is much more homogeneous, internally cohesive, and more effective in executing its plans than Hong Kong's. Singapore's state is particularly strong, which enables the government to defuse pressure from opposition groups and thus contain any kind of contention. It therefore enables the ruling elite groups to implement unpopular measures that they deem important for the long-term future of Singapore. According to Worthington, the Westminster political system in place in Singapore allows for very strong governments in between elections. Ideally, the system is based on the mutual trust between different political parties and between the government and the electorate (Worthington 2003). In the case of Singapore, however, the highly centralized institutional network has enabled the government to monopolize power in a very small group of people, which can be considered the core of the ruling elite groups. This chapter will demonstrate how Singapore's elite maintains cohesion and what tactics and goals it pursues in order to maintain its rule over the small city-state.

Ruling elite groups in Singapore

The ruling elite groups in Singapore include the ministers, the ruling party, the bureaucracy and government-linked-corporations. Writing in 1978, Peter Chen considered Singapore's power structure to be "formed by a cohesive power elite which is made up of the political elite, the bureaucrats and the select professional elite" (Chen 1978: 9). The latter group includes only those professionals that share the ideologies, objectives, and interests of the political elite. There is no doubt that the use of co-optation plays an important role in integrating the various interests. Chan Heng Chee offers a different reason for the unity within the elite: "The amazing elite cohesion of the present PAP leadership, must to a great extent be attributed to their experience in fighting and maneuvering against common enemies, first the colonial authorities, but more so in the intra-party struggle" (Chan 1975: 301). A technocratic ideology, in part as a reaction against threats from external and internal enemies, furthermore, has strengthened the cohesiveness of the political elite and avoided political cleavages.

Overall, Singapore's elite groups are hierarchically organized groups, similar to Hong Kong. Every group within the elite manifests its own hierarchy and each is tightly organized. At the top is the leadership, which Ross Worthington has labeled the power elite. However, the lower echelons of the Singapore elite are also significant because their existence and choices, their tactics and goals guarantee the survival of the system. To a large degree, the leaders of the elite groups have been able to organize their members using a discourse of meritocracy and certain shared values that are aimed at creating the impression that everyone is capable of becoming a member of the inner circle.

Since Singapore closely resembles an administrative state, the bureaucracy constitutes the basis of Singapore's political regime. The various government departments are organized according to modern management practices. In his unique study of the Economic Development Board (EDB), Edgar H. Schein (1996) concluded that the organization was a "close-knit community" in which most of the officers are able to get to know each other through team work in projects, committee meetings, etc. For Schein, it was a mystery how an organization which promoted the achievements of individuals could at the same time promote team work in an environment that was seemingly free of boundaries. His conclusion was that Singapore had developed a particularly Singaporean management culture that is neither Asian nor Western. This, however, fails to solve the "mystery" satisfactorily. Group behavior should not be understood as necessarily synonymous with conformity. An environment that promotes individual achievements has the potential to motivate group members, because they all stand in competition with each other. At the same time, the members of the group need the help of each other to achieve their goals. This is rooted in the EDB's culture of a high-morale organization with a shared vision of a successful economy. Informal rituals, awards to stipulate performance, and the high regard for private matters (such as friendship and weddings) support the organization (ibid.). While Schein's analysis focused on the EDB, it can be assumed that similar aspects also play a role in other departments and in government-linked corporations.

Another important constituent element of the regime is the ruling political party, the People's Action Party. The party itself is a representation of the elite as a whole. Organized as a cadre party with four types of cadres, it is dominated by an autonomous and autocratic Central Election Committee (CEC). This and the strict hierarchical organization have earned it the classification of a Leninist party (Peebles and Wilson 2002: 30). The rest of the party machine has very little influence over the decisions that are made by the CEC. Compared to other one-party dominated states, the party has a relatively small bureaucracy. According to Mauzy and Milne (2002: 42) this is due to Singapore's size and the ruling elite's belief that participation should be channeled through parapolitical grassroots organizations.

Ever since the People's Action Party (PAP) was elected to office in 1959, the English-educated elite has tried to monopolize power in Singapore (Chua 1995). Lee Kuan Yew and his lieutenants profited greatly from their education in Great Britain, where they had been influenced by the Labour Party and the Fabian socialist thought that permeated the party at the time. These early leaders were convinced that the government should play an active role in the economy and provide public housing and medical care (Peebles and Wilson 2002: 30). Most significantly, in contrast to Hong Kong, we can detect a tight integration of the greatest part of the business elite into the ruling elite through networks of government-linked corporations.

Organizational strength

Singapore's ruling elite groups are very cohesive. This is surprising because Singapore's increasingly complex bureaucracy has in recent years experienced a rapid increase in members. Most of these members of the ruling elite closely follow the wishes of the leaders. Technocrats dominate the leadership and there has been a strong centralization of power in the hands of very few. Consequently, there are no known factions within the government today (Chan 1989). A small number of leaders have successfully dominated government-linked corporations, the military, and the labor movement. The incentives for the members lie with the managerialist organization of the bureaucracy and the prestige awarded to members of the ruling party. Finally, perhaps the greatest strength comes from the ability to monopolize the means of communication. The ruling elite groups not only control their internal communication but also the media. This has only been challenged recently, with the proliferation of the internet.

Members

The members of the ruling elite groups can largely be categorized into members of the ruling People's Action Party, employees within government agencies,[1] supporters of the regime, and, to a certain degree, employees in government-linked corporations. This list of members shows that in Singapore a large part of the population is directly linked to the government. For the leaders of the ruling elite, this has meant that they can rely on a large section of the populace to follow and implement decisions rather than participate in active politics.

As Chapter 4 has shown, Singapore has many features of a bureaucratic regime. It is therefore not surprising that during the 1990s, a time of budget surpluses, the number of government employees rose steadily (Figure 6.1). As in Hong Kong, these government employees are not allowed to take part in politics. In contrast to Hong Kong, however, Singapore government employees are even forbidden to form or join a union (U.S. Department of State 2006). This, of course, reduces the potential of organized dissent, which, for example, occurred in Hong Kong during the 1970s when policemen protested against overly harsh treatment due to anti-corruption measures (Chapter 5). The 2008/09 budget shows that in the ministries almost half of all government employees (46 percent) work for the Ministry of Education. Second is the

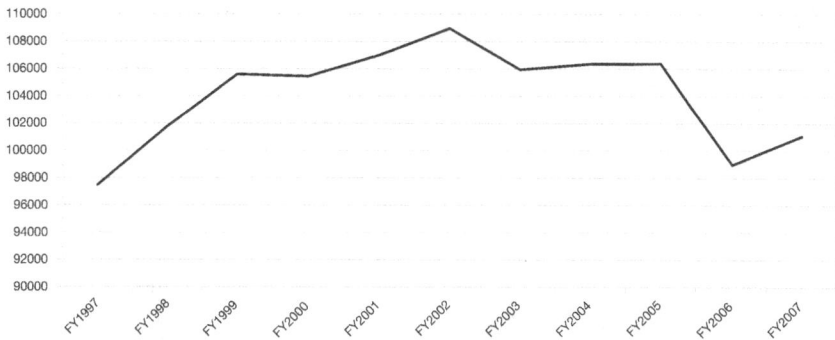

Figure 6.1 Increase of government employees in Singapore betwen 1997 and 2007
Source: Singapore Government 2009a.

Ministry of Home Affairs with 21 percent of employees, and third is the Ministry of National Development with 6.6 percent (Singapore Government 2009a) (Table 6.1).

These numbers show that Singapore's ruling elite emphasizes education, national defense, and economic survival. Education is particularly important because it not only supports economic development but also enables the rulers to influence the people at a young age. National defense also serves the goals of the rulers, because through national service and various other activities they are able to communicate their values and goals. It is intended to unite the people behind the goal of national and economic survival.

Besides the bureaucracy, there is also the ruling party, the People's Action Party (PAP). It boasts a membership of 15,000, which is large in comparison to Singapore's other political parties. While the number of cadres is considered "privileged information," the party revealed in 1998 that there were more than 1,000 cadre members (Koh 1998). It has a youth wing, called Young PAP, which was set up in 1986, and a women's wing, set up in 1989. For every election the PAP selects around twenty new members to run for political office.

It is important to note that the PAP is not a party with mass membership or a complex party structure (Mauzy and Milne 2002). It serves more as a cohesive support organization for the party leadership, which reigns supreme. The elite has tried to maintain the cohesiveness of the party by constantly urging its members to remain united behind the party's pragmatic ideology of national survival. In an interpretation of the speech of Prime Minister Lee Kuan Yew on the PAP's twenty-fifth anniversary, Chan Heng Chee (1989: 74) considers the party's strategy to "Give clear signals: don't confuse the people" and to be "A reminder to the party not to form cliques and indulge in factionalism."

Despite the party's election victories, the lack of a credible alternative makes it difficult to assess the support for the ruling party. In recent elections, the PAP has increasingly become concerned with younger voters, which suggests a generational shift. The typical PAP supporter, therefore, is on average

Table 6.1 Number of government employees in Singapore's ministries

	FY 2007
Presidential Councils	8
Public Service Commission	10
Cabinet Office	11
Parliament	46
Civil List	53
Auditor-General's Office	104
Attorney-General's Chambers	253
Prime Minister's Office	483
Judicature	537
Ministry of Law	733
Ministry of Foreign Affairs	1,149
Ministry of Health	1,162
Ministry of Defence	1,525
Ministry of Manpower	1,701
Ministry of Trade and Industry	2,607
Ministry of Information, Communications and the Arts	2,684
Ministry of Finance	2,906
Ministry of the Environment and Water Resources	3,485
Ministry of Transport	3,547
Ministry of Community Development, Youth and Sports	3,760
Ministry of National Development	6,673
Ministry of Home Affairs	20,994
Ministry of Education	46,666
Total	**101,082**

Source: adapted from Singapore Government 2009a: 46

probably older and more conservative than opposition supporters. This is due to the fact that the younger population have not experienced the rapid changes during the 1960s and are accustomed to political stability. The older generation, but especially regime supporters, continue to emphasize the numerous national threats that Singapore supposedly continues to face. They often base their support on the party's economic achievements over the past 50 years (see, for instance, Chow 2006). Many regime supporters point out that Singapore's leaders have committed themselves to the future of Singapore, because they act in the interest of the nation. For these people, support for the government is based on performance, achievements, and lack of corruption.

Leaders

The leaders of the ruling elite groups are mostly the ministers of parliament (who perform the same function as the heads of departments in Hong Kong but are part of the ruling party) as well as members of the PAP Central Election Committee. In this system, the ministers are the top power holders, with the Prime Minister holding the highest position. The absence of a powerful independent business elite is notable. The dominance of government-linked corporations and multinational corporations has restricted the development of a business class with divergent interests.

In the past, Lee Kuan Yew and his closest advisers have monopolized power, which enabled them to deal successfully with the problems of the 1960s and 1970s (Regnier 1987: 233). This changed with the slow transfer of power to a new generation of leaders. Bellows argues that the younger leaders are no longer able to monopolize power as much as the older were able to do (Bellows 1985: 55). While there has been some decentralization in the system, the government's ability to change course fairly rapidly suggests that power still remains in the hands of very few.

The smoothness of the power transfer, furthermore, has to be seen within this context, where younger leaders are allowed to take a leading role in politics, while guaranteeing some influence for the elders. There are still questions as to how much influence former Prime Minister Lee Kuan Yew still wields in government. Since he vacated the position of Prime Minister, he has changed his position twice, first to Senior Minister and presently to Minister Mentor. Both of these positions were newly created to allow for a power transfer to a younger generation without the need for the older prime ministers to retire. When former Prime Minister Goh Chok Tong relinquished his seat to the son of Lee Kuan Yew in 2004, he also became Senior Minister.

Since 1959, when the PAP was elected to power, an overwhelming majority of the leaders have been highly educated. The leadership favors a modern technological state and focuses on economic development. This has also influenced the recruitment of new leaders, as Chan Heng Chee makes clear:

> In Singapore, the consequence of coming to power of intellectual politicians in 1959 is the tendency to favor well-educated and highly trained men especially since the emphasis in recent years has been economic development and the establishment of a modern technological state after the model of a Western state.
>
> (Chan 2000: 122)

The leaders of the first generation were able to enshrine this emphasis on academic excellence in the present political system. An appraisal of the current ministers of parliament shows that they are all highly educated and all but one hold degrees from overseas universities.

Furthermore, the age of the current political leadership reveals the influences of developmentalism on the ideology of the ruling elite. The youngest minister, Dr Vivian Balakrishnan, was born in 1961 and the majority of ministers were born between 1954 and 1959. The oldest is Lee Kuan Yew, who was born in 1923, and another member of the old guard is Prof. S. Jayakumar, born in 1939. All ministers were born before Singapore became independent, which is significant, because all of them have experienced the tremendous changes of the 1960s and 1970s.

Another significant characteristic of the leaders is that five of the eighteen ministers have had careers in the military. The close connection between the military and the Singapore government is also evident in the city-state's budget. Nearly half (49 percent) of the total budgeted government expenditures for 2006 were allocated for security and external relations, of which 81 percent was for defense, which was also the single largest item in the budget (Singapore Government 2006). The present prime minister, furthermore, is a very good example of this relationship. Lee Hsien Loong's military career started in 1971, when he joined the Singapore Armed Forces (SAF). He managed to become the first Director of the Joint Operations and Plans Directorate. When he left the SAF to enter politics in 1984, he was the youngest Brigadier-General.

Aside from the government–military relationship, the Singapore core elite is also closely linked to the economy. For instance, until October 2009 Lee Hsien Loong's wife Ho Ching is the chief executive of Singapore's state investment holding company, Temasek, which not only has large stakes in Singapore's government-linked corporations but also has been credited as one of the city-state's major economic drivers. The minister without portfolio, Lim Boon Heng, who is chairman of the People's Action Party and was concurrently, until the end of 2006, Secretary-General of the National Trades Union Congress (NTUC), represents another very important link between the economy and the government. The close link between the PAP and the labor unions allows the government to exert control over the relationship between employees and employers. In effect, this has resulted in a lack of strikes since 1986, when there was a minor strike. This close relationship has, to a certain degree, enabled the leadership to steer the economy. With the labor movement tamed, unpopular measures such as wage cuts or reductions in employers' contributions to the Central Provident Fund (CPF) can easily be implemented when they are considered necessary for economic success.

Incentives: reasons for group cohesion

The ruling elite is marked by extraordinary group cohesiveness. While there have been individuals who were forced to rescind power, today there are no known factions within the government (Chan 1989). Due to the opaqueness of the Singapore government, it is not possible to provide a comprehensive explanation of the incentives for individual members. There are a number of indicators, however, which help us to better understand some of the factors that contribute to this cohesion.

First of all, Singapore's rulers are the world's best-paid leaders, even compared to much larger countries such as the United States of America or Australia. While in 2000 the Singapore prime minister earned S$1,958,000 (US$1,100,000) a year, the US president only earned US$200,000 and the Australian Prime Minister only US$137,060.[2] Even after perks and other allowances (which the Singaporean prime minister does not get), other government leaders earn much less than their Singaporean counterparts. Table 6.2 shows the monthly and annual salaries of top government officials and their ranking in comparison to the private sector.

The government has justified these salaries by claiming that they prevent corruption and provide sufficient incentives to attract highly qualified candidates. The White Paper propagating benchmarks for ministers and senior public officials stated that public officials have to make many sacrifices. "But the financial sacrifice is the simplest to minimize, by paying realistic salaries comparable to what potential Ministers can earn in the private sector" (Singapore Government 1994: 2). Other members of the civil service also earn salaries that are comparable to the private sector.

However, financial incentives can not fully explain the cohesion of the ruling elite. The achievements of the government fill the members, who have been selected according to meritocratic principles, with pride. In this context, it should be noted that reputation plays an important role for individual members of the Singapore government (Huff 1999). This has contributed significantly to an elite consensus, which is based on the effective implementation of government policies. The negative side of this tendency has, however, been the development of elitism, which has been accompanied by an unwillingness to expose potential weaknesses. Schein (1996) notes that the EDB tries to maintain a perfect image of the organization and does not easily accept criticism. As this has a central focus in the perception of the elite, it will be discussed in detail in a later section.

Because membership in the People's Action Party is not necessary and not even a guarantee for becoming a member of the ruling elite, the incentives for joining the party need to be analyzed. At least officially, membership in the party, unlike in Communist regimes, cannot guarantee better employment perspectives. Furthermore, party members are unpaid volunteers[3] who cannot expect to be rewarded with a candidacy (Mauzy and Milne 2002). So what are the reasons for joining the party? One long-time party member, Mah Guan Lin, the assistant director of the PAP headquarters in New Upper Changi Road, said in 1998: "We join because we know this is a good system that we want to protect. Through our dialogue with MPs, we understand

Table 6.2 Ranking of ministers' pay among top private sector earners (2007 figures)

Grade	Monthly Salary (S$)	Annual Salary (S$)	Ranking
President	104,840	3,187,100	90
Prime Minister	101,680	3,091,200	102
Senior Minister	100,110	3,043,300	108
Minister Mentor	100,100	3,043,300	108
Deputy Prime Minister	80,670	350,000	166

Source: adapted from Singapore Government 2007

things better and get a chance to find out more, that's the only advantage" (quoted in Koh 1998). For some members the reason for joining the party, however, has some prestige. Once members have become cadres of the party they get the right to vote for the party leadership every two years, which means they really have become members of the elite (ibid.).

In order to understand the kind of prestige that party membership provides, it is important to consider the party's rigid imagery. With a particular style of clothing, songs, and other rituals the party tries to create the impression that it is a distinguished group of people which acts solely in the interest of the nation. The party members are motivated to propagate the party's vision, which is manifested in their pledge. Table 6.3 demonstrates how the text is very similar to that of the national pledge, which was written by S. Rajaratnam in 1966 and polished by Lee Kuan Yew.

The similarity is probably intended to suggest that the PAP is a "national party," meaning that it always acts in the interests of the country. While the nation is supposed to stand united, the People's Action Party similarly needs to maintain unity. In the PAP pledge, the term "united" is equated with strength, which is needed to build a "vibrant, just and equal society." While the Singapore pledge emphasizes democracy, justice, and equality, the party's pledge extols the merits of meritocracy. It is unclear, however, what is meant by the term "all" in the PAP pledge. The term could refer to "society" or to each individual "citizen." The pledge finally establishes the importance of the PAP as the gatekeeper of Singapore's economic success.

During election campaigns, at the National Day Parade, and at other festive events, members of the party wear a white uniform, which stands for purity and integrity. According to Dr Lee Boon Yang, Minister for Information, Communications and the Arts, the uniform is a symbol of the PAP ideology. People who want to join the party need to demonstrate by their appearance that they want to follow the principles of the party. The PAP prides itself on not being a populist party but on acting in the interests of the people. Furthermore, the decision to join the PAP is equated with willingness to serve the nation, a claim that permeates much of the PAP's official propaganda. This raises the

Table 6.3 Comparison of the PAP pledge and the Singapore National Pledge

The PAP Party Pledge	The Singapore National Pledge
We, the members of the PAP, pledge ourselves to build a strong united Party, to create a vibrant, just and equal society, through achieving excellence by all, so that every citizen, regardless of race, language or religion, can enjoy a full and happy life.	We, the citizens of Singapore, pledge ourselves as one united people, regardless of race, language or religion, to build a democratic society based on justice and equality so as to achieve happiness, prosperity and progress for our nation.

Sources: PAP 2009, Rajaratnam 1966

party beyond the role of a partisan arbiter of particularistic goals, to a national institution whose primary interest is the representation of the people.

Communication network

In order to enhance the sense of community within the government, the role of both internal and external communication is of central importance. The example of the Economic Development Board (EDB), which can be seen as representative of the Singapore government, also provides ample evidence for this. A crucial element of the communication strategy is the use of corporate forms of communication. For instance, the EDB has an in-house publication that publicizes the achievements of special employees and marriages between employees. Publications like these create a sense of belonging to the institution and enhance its ability to increase output, because important achievements are highlighted.

Since 1954 the ruling People's Action Party has also maintained its own party publication, *Petir*. The magazine is published regularly, features commercial advertisements, and has been available on the internet since September 2004. The publication not only aims to rally party members behind the leadership and maintain cohesion but also attempts to communicate the party platform to the media (Gomez 2001). The majority of its articles are in English, while some are also in Chinese, Malay and Tamil. In 2006, the party added a "'PAP Policy Forum,' to provide new platforms for everyone to voice their views and concerns" (Gan 2006). This suggests that the party wants to increase the ability of party members to comment on party issues. Prior to this change, articles reflected mostly the views of the inner circle of the PAP, and ordinary members were rarely able to contribute to the magazine's content. This change will, however, mean very little as long as editorial selection continues to be controlled by the Publicity and Publications Committee.

Finally, unlike Hong Kong, Singapore's ruling elite controls nearly all of the major external means of communication. The leading English-language newspaper, the pro-government *Straits Times*, is owned by the Singapore Press Holdings (SPH), which is closely linked to the government. The other major media company, MediaCorp, a government-linked corporation, has a monopoly over freely available terrestrial television stations and owns the only freely distributed daily tabloid, *Today*. There are virtually no alternative voices in Singapore's media landscape, which means that the government possesses a strong ability to control the masses. Prominent party members have, furthermore, published autobiographies, monographs, and other commemorative books, which are widely available in Singapore bookstores. This stands in contrast to the opposition, which has difficulty getting its books and magazines published. The PAP has also used the mainstream media to broadcast documentaries which are biased in favor of the ruling elite.

Cognitive attribution and perceptions: the "colonial image"

The following will discuss three different aspects of the cognitive perceptions and the resulting behavior patterns of the members of the ruling elite groups (Table 6.4). The historical developments and the institutions summarized in Chapter 4 provide the basis for how Singapore's elite sees the world around it.

In terms of self-perception, the successful economic and social transformation of Singapore has generated a great sense of self-confidence within the ruling elite groups. People who succeed during their life often feel pride in their accomplishments. In a group setting this often translates to collective pride, especially when there is a strong sense of belonging to the group. These sentiments consequently become part of the values and norms of the ruling elite groups and are enshrined in the inner group culture. After some time, this becomes transformed into a self-perception of superiority, which is reflected in the elitism of the ruling class. The feeling that the ruling elite is the best to rule the country leads to the idea that it should guide the people for their own good. This will be described as the paternalist dispositions of the government. Finally, the impression that it is especially qualified to improve the lives of the people generates a great sense of legitimacy. While this legitimacy draws its major resource from the impression that the ruling elite has successfully managed the economy and averted a number of national crises, it also needs to be sustained through periodic elections.

A sense of superiority

Over the years, Singapore's leaders have developed a strong sense of superiority. While members of the ruling elite often mention the fear of national destruction, they also consider themselves capable of protecting the nation against all threats. The successful implementation of government programs has led to elitism within the ruling elite groups because it has proved to them that only they, the most capable, were qualified to lead well (Schein 1996; Mauzy and Milne 2002). Due to the extraordinary emphasis on excellence and efficiency, the ruling elite often denies to itself the possibility of making mistakes. This has also led to a great aversion to criticism, which is often framed in terms of personal attacks against the leadership (Schein 1996).

Table 6.4 Cognitive image of ruling elite groups in Singapore

	Group strength	*Emotions and policy disposition*	*Goals and tactic*
Strong Colonial Image	cohesive, strong	sense of superiority, paternalistic dispositions, sense of legitimacy	Developmentalist goals and a mix of co-option and overt coercion

The ruling elite considers meritocracy to be an important characteristic of the Singapore state. The emphasis on a meritocratic society exemplifies the conviction that only a few people are truly capable of leading. This has developed into the conception of Singapore as a technocracy in which decisions are based on scientific answers (Vennewald 1994a). The Singapore leadership has become convinced that technology and natural science provide the best answers for societal ills (Mauzy and Milne 2002). Some in the leadership, most notably Lee Kuan Yew, have, furthermore, become convinced of the idea that intelligence is 80 percent inherited, which led to a failed attempt to institutionalize eugenics in the proposed Graduate Mother Scheme of 1983. (It failed because it was opposed by a majority of Singaporeans). For this reason, the Singapore educational system places great emphasis on "hard" science in favor of "soft" social science. Leadership renewal is, to a large extent, based on exams, foreign experience, etc. The apparent success of this approach has even spurred Singapore's leaders to declare the city-state a developmental model for other countries and an alternative to liberal democracy (Lam 1999).

Many of the government programs reveal this sense of superiority. The Central Provident Fund (CPF), for example, allows the government to control to a certain degree the savings and investments of the population. The principle behind the scheme is that "government knows best—and knows better than the people themselves how they should spend their money" (Lim et al. 1993: 120). Members of the Singapore elite tend to believe that the ruling party's solutions are the best for Singapore and that they are therefore indispensable. Prime Minister Lee Kuan Yew best expressed this perception in 1971:

> The main burden of present planning and implementation rests on the shoulders of some 300 key persons ... . Singapore is a meritocracy. Together they are a close knit and coordinated hard core. If all the 300 were to crash in one Jumbo jet, then Singapore will disintegrate.
>
> (quoted in Han et al. 1998: 315)

As a consequence, the leaders of the old guard, and in particular Lee Kuan Yew, have been unwilling to reduce their influence. In the role of Minister Mentor, Lee Kuan Yew probably still wields considerable power today. Political scientist Hussin Mutalib suggests that the main task of the Minister Mentor is to maintain continuity, when he argues that "the idea of having a Minister Mentor in the form of SM Lee in the cabinet is to try to give a guiding hand, overall, in its holistic perspective, in all and every important aspect of governance in Singapore" (quoted in Yip 2004). Lee Kuan Yew, therefore, is hardly willing to concede all of his power to the younger generation. The core of the ruling elite group believe that Singapore would collapse if they were to disappear.

This self-perception of the ruling elite groups as particularly qualified to rule the country in the interests of the people consequently also excludes the possibility of contestation by other political groups, which are necessarily inferior and thus potentially a threat to the very survival of the Singapore state. This sense of superiority is especially apparent when it is challenged, because criticizing government decisions is problematic. Recently, a column by the popular internet blogger "mrbrown" (Lee Kin Mun) in the newspaper *Today* was canceled after he wrote a satire of the ruling party's practice of postponing the disclosure of problems, such as price increases, until after the election and giving cash benefits before. The press secretary to the Minister for Information, Communications and the Arts, Krishnasamy Bhavani, wrote a scathing reply in the same paper:

> mr brown's views on all these issues distort the truth. They are polemics dressed up as analysis, blaming the Government for all that he is unhappy with. He offers no alternatives or solutions. His piece is calculated to encourage cynicism and despondency, which can only make things worse, not better, for those he professes to sympathise with.
>
> (Bhavani 2006)

Bhavani attempts to place mrbrown in a bad light when he alleges that the "analysis" of the author cannot be trusted. In reality, the article in question was not an analysis but rather a cleverly worded satire. Furthermore, Bhavani seems either not to know or to ignore the fact that the true identity of the author is well known in Singapore.

This letter demonstrates three main government responses to criticism. First of all, Bhavani asserts that the author of the original article is misrepresenting the truth. To make her point, she asserts that Singaporeans should have been aware of the price increases prior to the election. What mrbrown had asserted, however, was not the fact that the news was known, i.e. published a year before, but that these facts were not mentioned during the election campaign. The "truth" that Bhavani tries to assert is that the PAP is not political. The timing of the news has therefore nothing to do with the election. Using this reasoning, she can discard all of mrbrown's criticism as mere polemics.

Bhavani's second assertion accuses the author of not providing an alternative. She thus argues that any criticism must be accompanied by policy alternatives. When, however, oppositional members propose alternatives, the government usually publicly rejects them. Criticism that does not come from within the ruling elite groups is generally dismissed as unproductive.

Finally, Bhavani tries to discredit the writer of the column. She asserts that the article should meet "higher standards" and should not be written under a pseudonym. Furthermore, she writes:

> If a columnist presents himself as a non-political observer, while exploiting his access to the mass media to undermine the Government's standing with the electorate, then he is no longer a constructive critic, but a partisan player in politics.
>
> (ibid.)

This statement alleges that mrbrown is biased and does not offer constructive criticism. Bhavani not only disparages the columnist but also alleges that partisanship is destructive to Singapore.

This has led some to assert that the PAP style of governance is arrogant. For example, opposition leader Chiam See Tong of the Singapore Democratic Alliance said in response to PAP criticism of the Workers' Party manifesto: "The PAP's arrogant behaviour is like that of a school master rebuking a primary school pupil. It is surely not for the PAP to say that it is right and that the WP is wrong" (Singapore Democratic Alliance 2006). This impression is based mainly on the comments of a number of members of the ruling elite. For instance, PAP Member of Parliament Wee Siew Kim asserted in 2006 that "a well educated university graduate who works for a multinational company should not be bemoaning about the Government and get on with the challenges in life" (Wee 2006). This attitude has been widely criticized in chat rooms, internet forums, and blogs. Many are angry about the lack of compassion and understanding for the concerns of ordinary Singaporeans. These arguments create the impression among many Singaporeans that the government does not care about ordinary problems such as joblessness or the increasing divide between rich and poor.

Paternalistic dispositions

The ruling elite groups have also been convinced that the population needs a benevolent leader, similar to what Confucius propagated in his teachings. Since the government sees itself as a role model for the rest of Singapore, it often speaks to the people in a high moral tone, telling them how to behave (Mauzy and Milne 2002). The ruling elite groups in Singapore are convinced that, because of the inferiority of the rest of the population, the government should be for the people and not by the people. As Jose and Doran (1997: 477) have noted: "Central to the PAP strategy of governance has been its deliberate posture of a liberating 'father' of the previously immature 'child' of colonial domination." Lee Hsien Loong emphasized this point in his Mandarin version of the 2006 National Day Rally Speech:

> We are part of the Singapore family, and must support one another to achieve our goals. For its part, the Government will do its best to look after every Singaporean, and ensure that everyone can share in the nation's prosperity.
>
> (Lee 2006a)

In this speech, the Prime Minister consciously evokes the Confucian emphasis on family values. This statement implies that the government and the people have distinct roles. The former is responsible for policy making and the latter for working hard so that Singapore's future will be bright.

The government seems convinced that a top-down process is the solution for all problems. In 2002, for instance, the government called on the people to be more creative (Tan 2002). This goal was supposed to be achieved without significant reduction of social control. However, many Singaporeans found that this call for creativity had significant limits. Political, social, and racial topics were considered taboo and were often stopped by the censors of the Media Development Authority (MDA). A similar approach has been used to strengthen the national identity of Singaporeans. The government commissioned two reports that were aimed at understanding the reasons for the apparent lack of national identity.[4] In the end, it considered exhortations as the best way of achieving its goal. For instance, the Remaking Singapore Committee report suggested that the government should promote the use of national symbols to engender a stronger sense of belonging (Remaking Singapore Committee 2003).

Whenever there are social problems, the government actively urges the population to improve its behavior. When there was a tremendous increase in the size of the population, the government called on the people to have fewer babies. The government attempted to achieve its goal by means of financial disincentives. When the situation changed and projections showed that Singaporeans were not procreating enough to replenish the population, the government changed its position and promoted procreation (Saw 1990). Initially, Lee Kuan Yew, who believes in eugenics, also thought that it would be preferable to promote child rearing only among the higher educated. This was, however, strongly rejected by Singaporeans and the proposal was soon withdrawn (Lee 2000). Furthermore, the government has not been successful in convincing increasingly higher-educated women to have children. The population trend, which is comparable to that in other advanced countries, has continued unabated (Saw 1999).

Despite lack of success in some of its programs, the government constantly devises new ways of improving the behavior of the Singaporean population. This becomes most evident in annual campaigns that are targeted at the perceived shortcomings of Singaporeans. For instance, the government started a "Keep Singapore Clean and Green" campaign in 1968 in order to convince Singaporeans to protect the environment. Only recently, Peh Shing Huei (2006) wrote in the *Straits Times* that the campaign was "a social-engineering attempt to turn Singaporeans from unwashed descendants of migrant stock to clean, civilised urban citizens." This shows that Singaporeans are well aware of the paternalistic character of the government, and many criticize the government for that. In the same article, Peh also makes it clear that the campaign has not been successful. He attributes Singapore's cleanliness to efficient street cleaners and heavy fines, and not to environmental understanding.

According to Chua (1995: 67), paternalism has two consequences: when the subordinate behaves well it is rewarded and when it misbehaves it is punished. The latter, furthermore, suggests that there is mistrust in the obedience of the subject once the ruler is no longer present. In Singapore, these two modes have played a crucial role in the decision-making process. An example of this can be found in another public relations campaign, called the Total Defense Campaign, which was introduced in 1984 and has been held on a yearly basis since. The campaign, which is also the city-state's official defense plan, was modeled on the experiences of Switzerland and Sweden. Furthermore, it also incorporates ideas from the "Asian values" discourse (Jones 1997). The official website states the goals of the campaign to be as follows:

> There are two reasons why we adopted it. First, as a young nation with a small population, we cannot afford to maintain a regular armed forces. Thus, we need to involve every Singaporean to multiply our defence capability. Second, the nature of modern warfare has changed. Wars are no longer limited to the battlefield. Instead, potential aggressors can strike in less obvious, non-military ways.
>
> (NEXUS 2008)

The concept of Total Defense comprises not only military defense and civil defense but also concepts such as "economic defense," "social defense" and "psychological defense." Economic defense is an attempt instituted by the elite to strengthen the economic system, which emphasizes flexibility for employers and rejects labor activism. The goal of ethnic and religious harmony, also known as multiracialism and multireligiosity, is behind the concept of social defense. The concept of psychological defense refers to the attempt to build a national identity, which is an ongoing project of the Singapore government. It is an effort to develop "the collective will of Singaporeans" (Jones 1997: 293). As a whole, these three concepts reflect the mistrust of the rulers toward the Singaporean population. The Total Defense website lists the threats that Singapore faces:

> Potential aggressors and threats can appear in less obvious and non-conventional ways (e.g., destroying social cohesion by exploiting differences in race, language, religion, culture, social or economic class; weakening national resilience by using psychological warfare to play on the people's fears and apprehensions; or waging economic warfare through economic boycotts, trade sanctions or acts of sabotage to bring down the economy).
>
> (Singapore Government 2009b)

While this list discounts a wide range of topics which could be used by oppositional groups, the call for unity that is also part of Total Defense aims to delegitimize oppositional politics. It is probably not a coincidence that the concept was introduced during a year in which the opposition was able to secure three seats and the ruling party experienced the greatest slide in electoral support in its history.

The number of campaigns in Singapore's history has made some individuals insensitive to the exhortations of the government. Therefore, the government has tried to make these campaigns more sophisticated. Today, they make use of computer games, fictional characters, famous singers, etc. to attract the young, entertainment-conscious element of the population. For instance, to increase the effect of the Total Defense Campaign of 2005, the government developed a game with five fictional online pets called Berryl, Ms Enxor Tyndall, Horag, Ms Kellin and Rorie in which players could earn points by solving puzzles related to the campaign (*ST* 4 Feb. 2005). Due to a lack of empirical data, it is impossible to know whether this change of approach can satisfactorily achieve its goals. However, it seems unlikely that the use of online technology can be as successful as traditional methods, because the internet offers a much wider spectrum of potential entertainment and information.

A sense of legitimacy and the fear of survival

The sense of legitimacy of the ruling elite groups strengthens their resolve to govern and to control other groups. In Singapore, this legitimacy is born out of the need to have rational, pragmatic leaders in the face of numerous potential national crises. The ruling PAP sees itself as the only party capable of protecting Singapore from the abyss, and this strengthens its legitimacy. While there is no doubt that the threat is used as a political weapon against the regime's opposition, there are clear indications that this fear is real. It is an important aspect of the perceptions of the ruling regime and its environment.

Since the turbulent years between World War II and the 1960s, nearly every problem has been framed as a potential crisis to the Singaporean state: Communism, oppositional politics, race relations, scarce resources, etc. Even today, the government continues to emphasize the need for unity in the face of serious threats. Emphasizing a crisis alone, however, does not contribute to legitimacy. Moreover, crises could potentially threaten the survival of the regime. The legitimacy is the outcome of the successful management of the myriad challenges that the country faces (Hill and Lian 1995; Ortmann 2009).

Similar to Hong Kong, the Singaporean state's legitimacy is primarily based on performance. The extraordinary ability of the government to provide housing, eliminate crime and corruption, promote economic growth, and create stability, among others, gives it the right to rule. In all these areas, Singapore has succeeded better than most countries.

Because the effectiveness of government policies can never be guaranteed, the ruling PAP has tried to enhance its legitimacy. The claim to rule in the interests of the people requires the existence of free elections, which are designed to give the PAP a democratic mandate. Election victories in the 1960s and 1970s were successful in this regard, but when the opposition returned to parliament, the PAP saw this as more than merely a problem; it considered it a legitimacy crisis. In order to regain an absolute electoral majority, the party has continuously fought to eliminate the opposition. It has not shied away from introducing measures that threaten to undermine the fairness of elections (for instance the GRCs, see Chapter 4). Furthermore, it has even violated the principle of merit of the bureaucratic regime by threatening the electorate that it should either vote for the PAP or face the possibility of not receiving housing upgrades (Pang 1998). This presents a significant shift for a political regime that emphasized technocratic decision-making. Another example of increasing politicization during election campaigns is the vilification of opposition members. During the 2006 election, for instance, the PAP's campaign focused mainly on the failure of Workers' Party candidate James Gomez to submit an application form for minority candidates, despite his claim that he had done so. The government asserted that this raised serious questions about the opposition member's character, even though he had apologized for his mistake (Tong 2006). P.N. Balji, a media consultant, argued that "The PAP's handling of the James Gomez affair just does not fit in with what is now accepted by many as the Prime Minister's inclusive style of politics" (Balji 2006). While the regime still enjoys significant support, tactics such as these threaten to undermine its legitimacy.

Finally, the government has repeatedly stressed in public that the majority of Singaporeans accept the country's political system. This is explicitly directed at foreign critics, who have pointed to its shortcomings in terms of civil liberties. For instance, in a reply to *Liberal International*'s condemnation of the arrest of Dr Chee Soon Juan, the government stated:

> Ultimately, whether or not Singapore laws have been applied fairly to Dr Chee, and what is legitimate or otherwise, should be judged by Singaporeans, not by foreigners who have no stake in our future or who disagree with us simply because we do not subscribe to their notions of justice and democracy.
>
> (Yap 2006)

The Singaporean leadership's conception of its legitimacy is thus also based on the notion that Singapore has a unique Asian or Singaporean identity that is distinct from that of other countries. This nationalist argumentation considers election victories and the lack of public protest as clear signs of public support that the government has earned due to its superior economic performance.

The goals of the ruling elite groups

It's the economy, stupid

The most important goal for the Singaporean leaders since independence has been the development of the city-state into a prosperous nation in order to secure national survival. All other goals have to be seen in the context of this grand strategy. Since Singapore has limited space and a small population, the leaders were convinced that economic growth depended on its only resource, the population. A meritocracy, which would give equal chances to everyone, was therefore seen as the best option for achieving this goal. Another aspect of this approach is the Singaporean leadership's insistence on the pragmatic, supposedly nonpolitical nature of its policy-making decisions, even if this sometimes involves unpopular choices. An example of an unpopular choice, which was made in order to ensure economic growth, is the 2005 decision to attract casino operators to build euphemistically named Integrated Resorts (IRs). Religious groups and social activists warned of the negative social consequences and the possibility that these casinos would attract money laundering and organized crime. However, the government's need to support economic growth has outweighed public opposition and even opposition from within the ranks of the ruling elite groups.[5] Lim Hng Kiang, Minister for Trade and Industry, articulated the government's reasoning in 2005:

> Opportunity is knocking on our door. We can take full advantage of this opportunity, but only if we are prepared to act boldly. It is in this context that the Government decided to proceed with the two IRs.
>
> (*Singapore Hansard* 18 April 2005)

The government promises itself an "incremental" annual GDP, which is estimated to exceed $1.5 billion and a total "incremental" employment of about 35,000 jobs from the construction of these casinos. Members of the opposition have charged that these will likely be mostly low-paying service jobs and that many may also go to foreigners.

The ruling elite's goal of delivering economic growth is also reflected in the attempt to display a perfect image of Singapore. For example, to accomplish this, the media have corrected previously published online articles without comment, a practice that is reminiscent of the Department of Truth in the fictional world of *1984*. In an online Channel NewsAsia report on 11 January 2007 on the results of the Institute of Policy Studies' annual conference, the first version reported that "123,000 jobs were created last year and economists estimate some 70 percent of these jobs went to foreigners." This report was later changed to read: "Manpower Ministry data shows that 124,000 jobs were created last year and 45 percent of these jobs went to foreigners" (Forss 2007). According to Jeffrey Yen, a blogger, the journalist said that the first number was the estimate of the IPS, but that this number was not exact (Yen 2007). This example shows that the government is intent on maintaining the image of positive economic development, which is its most important goal.

A second goal was and still is social development, which is considered to be supportive of the first goal, economic development. The first step was elimination of the bad living conditions of many Singaporeans, which was achieved by means of a successful public housing program, which has also allowed many Singaporeans to buy their own homes, so that today Singapore is the largest home-owning country in the world. Furthermore, the elimination of racist behavior in the form of communalism, which led to major race riots in the 1950 and 1960s, was also a priority for the government.

Part of social development has been the attempt to instill a set of core values into the population in order to influence the moral behavior of the people. This was the result of the "Asian values" discourse, which attributed to "Asians" certain unique cultural values such as filial piety, harmony, or group behavior (Emmerson 1995). Lee Kuan Yew even argued that these different values were part of the neurological development of Asians and therefore inborn (Zakaria 1994). The government argued that the Confucian ethics were similar to other Asian moral ethics and that they stood in clear contrast to the Western system, which was supposedly marked by decadence, violence, or social decay (Kim 1997). In the dichotomy between West and East, the ruling elite in Singapore was clearly influenced by its perception of the United States as the paradigmatic model of the West.

In an effort to inculcate or, from the perspective of Lee Kuan Yew, resurrect these values, the government introduced the Religious Knowledge Programme into schools in 1984, to counter the "westernization" of the young population, which was perceived to be a great threat for the future of the city-state. Of course, this "westernization" merely reflected the process of modernization. The plan to introduce religious education was, however, abandoned after only six years because interest in Confucianism was low and because it threatened the concept of multiracialism. It was replaced in 1989 by the "Civics/Ethics Moral Education Program" (Hicks 2003).

The government was made to rethink its strategy, and decided to develop national values that could be accepted across all religions. Thus, in 1988, the government conceived the so-called "Shared Values," which were formulated in cooperation with the Feedback Unit so as to legitimate them as consensual. These values, as published in the White Paper on Shared Values in 1991, are:

1. Nation before community and society before self
2. Family as the basic unit of society
3. Community support and respect for the individual
4. Consensus, not conflict
5. Racial and religious harmony. (Singapore Government 1991)

These five values represent the societal goals of the ruling elite groups. Each value stresses the need of the community over the individual. Individual rights are thus placed below the needs of the society. The original formulation of the fourth value, "consensus, not contention," makes it clear that one of the government's goals is the elimination of political contention. The decisions on the future of Singapore are better left in the hands of the ruling elite. This shows that progressive goals in Singapore closely overlap with conservative goals, which are discussed in the following section.

Consolidating power

The goal of economic success and social development, in the eyes of the rulers, is closely related to the near monopoly of power in the hands of the PAP government. Power and good government in Singapore are closely related, and the leadership has therefore made regime survival a national goal. Since the leaders are the most educated and sophisticated, there is no one who could possibly challenge the power of the regime. It is, therefore, not power per se that Singaporean leaders strive for; it is, rather, the ability to help the people to provide the best solutions for the future. Maintaining power has therefore become a priority for the ruling elite. The argumentation behind this thinking will be analyzed more closely in this section.

The ruling party, the PAP, has gone to great lengths to create a negative impression of the opposition. The opposition is often seen as yet another threat to the survival of the nation. Opposition parties are characterized as unqualified, irresponsible, and unsuitable for the survival of a strong Singapore. For example, prior to the 2006 election, Prime Minister Lee Hsien Loong suggested that more members of the opposition in parliament would be a waste of resources:

> What is the opposition's job? It's not to help the PAP do a better job ... because if they help the PAP do a better job, you're going to vote for me again and they're going to be out of a job for a long time. So their job is to make life miserable for me.
>
> Right now we have Low Thia Khiang, Chiam See Tong, Steve Chia. We can deal with them. Suppose you had 10, 15, 20 opposition members in Parliament. Instead of spending my time thinking what is the right policy for Singapore, I'm going to spend all my time thinking what's the right way to fix them, to buy my supporters' votes, how can I solve this week's problem and forget about next year's challenges?
>
> (quoted in Tong and Ramesh 2006)

The disadvantage of a plural system, according to Lee, is that the government's efforts would be wasted in political conflicts. It then could not focus on the formulation of well-planned policies for the long-term development of Singapore. The prime minister thus argues that because the government is already capable of making the right decisions, a checks-and-balances system is unnecessary.

The opposition has, furthermore, been accused of being a threat to potential investors, who value Singapore's political stability. Christopher de Souza, who was elected as a member of parliament for Holland-Bukit Timah GRC in a walkover, expressed this sentiment a few days before the 2006 election:

> We need to have political stability and incorruptibility in governance in order to have a strong and competitive economy. Two purposes can be achieved by your one vote. One, give PM Lee Hsien Loong a strong

mandate so the PAP government will be in a good position to launch Singapore into the future. Two, give yourself a good local representative who will be able to voice your concerns and those of your constituency in a constructive manner in Parliament.

(quoted in Ng 2006)

A similar argument was put forward by Prime Minister Goh Chok Tong before the 1996 election. He even suggested that it is the government's task not to allow a member of the opposition to win the election: "Our job is to ensure that the wrong people don't get into Parliament. So don't just think that you feel sorry for this fellow and vote him in" (quoted in *ST* 21 Dec. 1996).

Finally, members of the ruling elite have occasionally made proposals to further restrict Singapore's democratic system. Sensing the increasing divide between younger and older voters, Lee Kuan Yew once proposed that older Singaporeans between 30 and 60 should get two votes, one more than those below 30 (Tor 2006). Lee Kuan Yew asserts that "good government" and not democracy is the most important goal of the elite and that "no Singaporean leader can afford to put political theory above the practical need of stability and orderly progress" (quoted in Han et al. 1998: 147). Even if these undisguised attempts to limit democracy have not yet been implemented, it still shows that the preservation of power constitutes one of the ruling elite groups' most important goals.

Tactics

Moderate tactics: developmentalism and co-option

The Singapore government has been careful about the implementation of its progressive goals of economic growth and social stability. This appears logical, but in many countries the government makes promises but fails to achieve its goals. However, Singapore's leaders have never promised something they could not achieve, which has been expressed in the realism and pragmatism of government officials. While the rapid economic development has already been the focus of Chapter 4, the achievement of social peace (i.e. the opposite of conflict) will be the focus of this section. This has been accomplished not merely through the use of repression of dissent, which will be part of the next section, but has been the outcome of the implementation of successful social programs, such as housing and education. Furthermore, it is also the result of the successful co-option of potential critics into the political system.

The moderate tactics can best be exemplified by Singapore's public housing program, which has been one of the world's most successful. As has already been noted, its success has given the government significant legitimacy. The housing program is especially significant because of its transformative character and its ability to enhance social peace. Only one year after the PAP was elected to office, the Housing and Development Act of 1960, which created the Housing and Development Board (HDB), was passed. Its first target was the colonial-era slums and ethnic enclaves. In less than three years 21,000 flats were built, and by 1965 there were 54,000 apartments, exceeding the target of the HDB's First Five-Year Building Program by 4,000 units. As of the fiscal year 2007/08, around 82 percent of the population lives in HDB estates (Housing and Development Board 2008). Moreover, in 1990 the government introduced the so-called "upgrading" program for public housing, which allows occupants to improve their apartments at an affordable price and on a cost-sharing basis.

The Singapore government started the housing program with aggressive land acquisition in the name of "national development." The leaders of the ruling elites claimed that the acquisition of land well below the market value was important for improving the material conditions of the population (Chua 1997). Before public housing was introduced, the city was overcrowded, with many people living in substandard conditions, and the population welcomed the construction of the new housing estates. Even today, no one in Singapore would criticize the government for this decision. Most of the apartments in public housing are, unlike in Hong Kong, leased to the occupants for 99 years. However, public housing should not be understood as a lifetime commitment, as residents are permitted to sell their apartments and move to better housing estates (resale policy).

Since its early days, the HDB has been credited not only with the eradication of the dismal living conditions of pre-independence times but also with achieving the highest homeownership in the world. A record 92 percent of the total population (which includes those in private estates) own their own home (Singapore Department of Statistics 2005). This has been accomplished in part through a government-sponsored home ownership scheme which enables prospective buyers to get an apartment at an affordable price. Of those living in public housing, 93 percent have purchased an apartment (ibid.). The public housing program has, furthermore, enabled the government to use social engineering. Ethnic quotas were established for each housing estate in order to eliminate the concentration of ethnic groups in particular areas. Furthermore, the government makes it easier for families rather than single-person households to get public housing, it is an attempt to foster the development of ordinary families.[6]

The successful implementation of public housing has also enhanced the legitimacy of the ruling elite groups. Chua Beng Huat notes that "For the PAP government, continuing support for public housing is, like economic development, one plank of its legitimacy to rule" (Chua 1997: 125). The HDB, therefore, has contributed indirectly to stability, has created employment possibilities for the building sector, has integrated the various ethnic groups, and has helped with nation-building through raising awareness of Singapore in other countries in Asia and Africa (Quah 1980). It should also be pointed out that the HDB ownership scheme has given those Singaporeans who are homeowners a material stake in the country. This has had the consequence that "Opportunities for home ownership and financial gain have engendered a strong ideological consensus between the PAP government and the electorate" (Chua 1997: 132).

The program also reduces the potential for class conflict, because the government-controlled quotas avoid the development of ghetto districts. Except for a wealthy minority, most Singaporeans live in HDB estates and, as a consequence, most Singaporeans share a similar standard of living (Phang 2007).

The success of the HDB and other similar government institutions can be attributed mainly to four factors. First of all, Singapore's small size has been key to the government's ability to control and to monitor the development of public housing. Second, the political leadership has shown determination in its support for public housing and has been willing to invest in the housing market, while not worrying about the free market economy. For public housing, the government has expropriated land for the project, which was an intrusion into the property market. Third, the HDB has been designed as an effective organization, similar to the Economic Development Board discussed earlier. Last but not least, the population and the opposition have largely endorsed and supported these projects. Public housing as well as many other aspects of Singapore life, such as meritocracy, multiracialism, or the CPF system are almost unanimously credited for Singapore's successful transformation. As these measures are considered achievements of the ruling PAP government, they have contributed to the legitimacy of the ruling elite groups.

The government has, furthermore, tried to draw comparisons with other countries in order to emphasize its success. For this purpose, the media often broadcast Singapore's excellent performance in surveys such as Transparency International's *Corruption Perception Index (CPI)*. In regard to the housing program, Goh Chok Tong remarked:

> Compare yourself with your counterparts in other countries and see how well you have done. If you are a technician or a teacher, compare yourself with technicians or teachers elsewhere. If you are a taxi driver, compare yourself with taxi drivers in Thailand, Taiwan, London, or anywhere else in the world. How many own their homes? How many of them own shares? You are ahead of them.
>
> (Goh 1994)

By highlighting the differences between the homeownership and stock ownership rates in Singapore and other countries, the prime minister argues that the ruling elite's policies have been successfully implemented. In his opinion, the success of a program relies upon the ruling party's rigorous planning. Also implied in this statement is that liberal democratic countries such as Great Britain or Taiwan have not been able to perform as well as Singapore.

Housing, of course, also has the function of co-opting potential critics. The government's strategy has been to co-opt almost all of its critics into the state and state-sponsored organizations. This has been a very successful strategy, which has effectively depoliticized the population and has significantly weakened the opposition (Chua 1997). As argued in Chapter 4, this includes community leaders, the Feedback Unit, nominated members of parliament, the Institute of Policy Studies and many other institutions. The next section will show that, despite the government's ability to co-opt large segments of the population into the state apparatus, the ruling elite has felt the need to resort to more extreme tactics, such as the repression of dissent, in order to strengthen its power.

Extreme tactics: selective repression of dissent

Even though Singapore's leaders sometimes resort to repression, the city-state's political system is often characterized as "soft-authoritarian," which means that the ruling party prefers to use persuasion rather than coercion (Roy 1994; Neher 1999). This impression comes from a comparison with other "strong" authoritarian and totalitarian regimes. In Singapore, the rulers have not resorted to violence against their critics, as have other authoritarian and totalitarian regimes. There has never been anything comparable to the Kwangju massacre in South Korea, the so-called 228 Incident in Taiwan, or the Tiananmen massacre in China. However, it is also wrong to assume that the regime has used only persuasion to co-opt its critics. From the beginning, the rulers of Singapore have wisely used the laws and the judiciary to elim-inate dissent. Repression in Singapore has just been more sophisticated and better planned than in other authoritarian regimes. It has still created a level of fear in the population (see Chapter 8), which, as Jones (1997) argues, is the result of a calculated strategy of the ruling elite designed to "achieve a government determined rational consensus."

This section will highlight four different areas in which the government has resorted to extreme tactics as defined in Chapter 2. First, the government has threatened voters with the risk of losing the right to upgrade their housing estate if they vote for the opposition. Second, the government has threatened legal residents and other foreigners with expulsion or has denied their visas. Third, the government maintains a law that allows it to arrest anyone without a warrant or trial. Last, the government has effectively used personal attacks and defamation lawsuits to silence and even bankrupt outspoken members of the opposition.

Starting with the 1997 election, the government has threatened to neglect public housing estates in opposition-ruled districts. Increasing its support in the 1997 election, the ruling party considered the linking of housing upgrades with the vote a crucial success factor: "By linking the priority of upgrading to electoral support, we focus the minds of voters on the link between upgrading and the people whose policies make it possible. This has the desired result" (quoted in Pang 1998). The linking of repairs of public housing (known as "upgrading") with votes has been justified on the basis of the need to provide services for the constituents of the ruling party. In Singapore, where the ruling elite groups have rejected "vote buying" and have emphasized a merit-based system, such favoritism seems oddly out of place.

For the nearly 20 percent of Singapore's population who are not Singaporean citizens, the government has, furthermore, used the threat of expulsion to restrict the ability of foreigners to get involved in politics. Legal residents risk having their resident status or their visa revoked. For instance, in 2004 a pilot of Malaysian nationality, by the name of Ryan Goh, was accused of insti- gating union action when pilots were retrenched or had to accept pay cuts even though Singapore Airlines (SIA) had announced a healthy profit margin. The members of the Airline Pilots Association sacked its leadership for their inaction. The government, which considers peaceful labor relations of the greatest importance, regarded this act of defiance as a threat to the interests of Singapore. Home Affairs Minister Wong Kan Seng thus publicly called Goh an "undesirable immigrant," and subsequently had the pilot's permanent resident status revoked (Wong 2005).

A similar tactic has also been employed to keep undesired individuals from entering the country. This drew international attention prior to the World Bank–International Monetary Fund conference in 2006, when the Singapore government prohibited a large number of civil society activists from entering the country. This was the first time in the history of these meetings that there were no demonstrations close to the conference. The government claimed that it was trying to avoid violence during the meeting, but it denied entry even to those activists whom the World Bank had cleared. After the strongly worded censure of the World Bank, the government finally allowed twenty-two of the activists to enter. The actions of the Singapore government, however, had already resulted in negative media coverage. The reason for the government's reluctance to allow protests was probably aimed at Singaporeans, who should not see that others could demonstrate freely. Ironically, a handful of Singa- porean activists used the conference to stage their own protest, which resulted in more negative publicity.

The most infamous law against political opposition, however, is the Internal Security Act (ISA), which enables the arrest of anyone without warrant and denies judicial review. In an earlier form, it was enacted as the Emergency Regulations during colonial times in 1948, and it became law in 1960. It has been officially justified in the fight against Communists and, more recently, against terrorists. The law was applied against left-wing political opposition during Operation Cold Store in February 1963 and again in 1966, as well as in 1987 during the so-called "Marxist Conspiracy" against Catholic activists and members of the Workers' Party. Furthermore, Chia Thye Poh, Singapore's longest-serving political prisoner, who was confined on Sentosa from 1966 until 1989 was arrested under the ISA and never received a trial. The most infamous section of the law provides for "preventive detention" in the interests of national security or for the maintenance of public order. It also gives the government extensive control over all political organizations, publications, exhibitions, and public entertainment (Tan 2000). Even though the ISA is rarely used today, its existence hangs like a sword of Damocles over members of the opposition and the public who might want to oppose the government. The threat of the ISA therefore functions as a psychological restraint on individuals who are potentially willing to voice their opinion in public or even join opposition parties.

The most aggressive tactic against dissent has been the use of personal attacks and defamation lawsuits against both internal and external critics. Repeatedly, members of the ruling elite have sued opposition members for slander and subsequently exacted exorbitant sums from them after court proceedings. This has raised serious concerns with human rights organizations. In some cases, the ruling elite has even bankrupted particularly vocal opposition members. The government's use of the media and defamation suits has created a sense of fear within the opposition. Perhaps the most notorious case of the use of defamation lawsuits against the opposition occurred during the 1997 election. Leading members of the PAP had called opposition candidate Tang Liang Hong an anti-Christian, Chinese chauvinist. The reason for this accusation was a speech in 1994 in which Tang had asserted that the cabinet was dominated by Christians and English-educated members. However, considering that Tang's daughter is a Christian, the ruling elite's attack appeared somewhat exaggerated (*ST* 27 Dec. 27 1996). To Tang Liang Hong, it was a personal attack on his character and he filed a police report in which he accused the PAP leaders of criminal conspiracy and lying. In response, he was sued by the PAP leadership for defamation. As a result of this affair, Tang Liang Hong had to flee to Australia and the judge awarded the prime minister and his colleagues S$7.175 million in damages for defamation, which was later reduced to S$3.63 million (*ST* 13 Nov. 1997). Tang was declared a bankrupt in 1998 and charged with thirty-three counts of tax evasion, and there is a warrant outstanding for his arrest. Defamation lawsuits and personal attacks have also been successful in marginalizing other outspoken members of the opposition, like Francis Seow (1988), Jufrie Mahmood (1991), J.B. Jeyeratnam (1997), Dr Chee Soon Juan (2001) and James Gomez (2006).

Conclusion and outlook

The focus of this chapter was the organizational strength, the perceptions, and the goals and tactics of the ruling elite groups in Singapore. Most studies of Singapore politics have focused on the ruling elite, and not without reason. The ruling elite groups form a very cohesive group, whose core leadership has been able to monopolize power. The lack of factions (not to speak of splits), strong incentives ranging from high salaries to honors, and effective communication both within the elite and to the population through the monopolization of the media have contributed to the overall strength of the ruling elite. In light of the economic successes, it is perhaps not surprising that the elites consider themselves superior to other political actors and the population. The result of this sense of superiority has been elitism and strong paternalist dispositions. The government considers its role to be as the guardian of a helpless population. Finally, the government's performance has led to a considerable degree of legitimacy.

The goals and tactics of the ruling elite reveal that their primary objective is the economic development of the country. Much of the government's efforts have been based on its most important goal, economic growth. However, due to shortcomings in the strategy, there was a resurgence of opposition. For a regime that considers only itself to be capable of solving the country's problems, this was a very unwelcome development. Since the country needed the PAP in power, the leaders had to conceive of ways to maintain power. They cleverly balanced co-option of moderate opposition members into the political system and coercion of more radical members. This tactic has been very successful, as Chapter 8 will show.

Before we discuss Singapore's opposition, we will again turn our attention to Hong Kong. The 1970s was an important turning point for oppositional groups in the former British colony, which were increasingly willing to challenge the regime. As a consequence, they were able to enhance their ability to influence government policies. Furthermore, the opposition increasingly considered it to be its duty to act as a check on an undemocratic government. While Hong Kong's government also tried to contain this rising contention, it was not as successful as its counterpart in Singapore. The next chapter shows that the inability of the government to fulfill the expectations of many Hong Kongers often resulted in collective action, which towards the end of the 1970s involved coalitions of political groups. Nevertheless, there was still no significant pressure for democratization, because the opposition was moderate and willing to limit its own expectations to institutional reform and nothing more.

7 Oppositional groups in Hong Kong
The right to protest

This chapter focuses on the composition of oppositional groups in Hong Kong mostly during the 1970s, their social identity image, and their goals and tactics. It shows that the perceptions of oppositional groups were such that they considered the government to be detached from their concerns and rarely willing to listen to public opinion. A prevailing sense of political powerlessness crippled any attempt at launching a pro-democracy movement before 1984 (Sing 1999). Many groups demanded comprehensive reforms, but they did not challenge the political system. While some outspoken but marginalized Singaporean members of the opposition have advocated revolutionary goals, as the next chapter will show, Hong Kong's opposition tended to be very modest: its goals ranged from merely reforms of existing policies to increasing electoral representation in the Urban and Legislative Council. However, similar to the Singapore Democratic Party (SDP) in recent years, Hong Kong's oppositional groups during the 1970s were increasingly willing to go beyond institutionalized tactics. There was a growing number of people willing to demonstrate publicly for change, and toward the end of the 1970s there were protesters who were even willing to break the law in order to get their message out.

Oppositional groups in Hong Kong

In the 1970s, the mushrooming opposition movement in Hong Kong was oriented against a colonial regime whose bureaucracy was increasingly localized but still dominated by English career bureaucrats. The opposition movement, which was separated along ethnic lines, also gradually lost that distinction during this time. While the Reform Club of Hong Kong, a political quasi-party, was founded as two ethnic groups in 1949, in the 1970s there was only one Reform Club. In 1952, elections were introduced and three years later another group, the Civic Association, was founded. Since these groups vied for electoral office, they can be regarded as rudimentary political parties. David Baird, for example, wrote in 1970 that "The Reform Club and the Civic Association are the nearest thing to an opposition Hongkong's anachronistic system of government can lay claim to" (Baird 1970b). However, since they were able to contest only Urban Council elections, they were very limited in scope. In 1977, a survey conducted by the Reform Club found that a mere 60 percent of the respondents had ever heard of the Reform Club and even fewer, namely 47 percent, knew of the Civic Association (Reform Club 1977).

The 1970s also saw the rise of pressure groups, which increasingly became active in the oppositional movement. Before the 1970s, political groups in Hong Kong had mirrored the different political factions on the mainland. The labor movement, for example, was split into a pro-Nationalist and pro-Communist faction. These groups tended to spend very little time on oppositional politics because they did not consider it necessary to introduce any reforms into the colonial government. Instead, they were largely anti-colonial and nationalist, and focused on welfare services (Turner et al. 1980). While at the outset of the 1970s Chinese nationalism still played an important role in oppositional politics, the end of the Cultural Revolution in 1976 marked a shift toward social activism, and a steadily increasing number of political groups became interested in reforms to Hong Kong's political system.

The rising oppositional movement, however, failed to generate a strong demand for greater democratization. Joseph Y.S. Cheng summarizes some of the most important arguments when he writes that "spectacular economic growth and the development of social services offered by the public sector severely weakened the community's demand for political awareness and participation; and the government's aggressive 'administrative absorption' and expansion of the consultative network also soften such demands from activists" (Cheng 1999: 9). The government's successful management of the demands and problems that developed during the 1970s, therefore, contributes significantly to an explanation of the weakness of oppositional groups. However, the government's failure to fulfill some of its promises, and its aloofness, created opportunities for oppositional groups to challenge the regime.

Organizational strength

In the 1970s, Hong Kong's oppositional movement greatly increased its organizational strength. There was a significant growth in membership and a greater willingness to participate in collective action. Initially, oppositional groups were very fragmented, but during the 1970s there was an increasing willingness to cooperate on certain issues, which also increased the groups' strength. This section will describe who the members of oppositional groups were, who led them, what reasons there were for joining a pressure group or other political group, and how communication worked within the groups and with the population at large.

Members

The 1970s proved to be not only a period of rapidly growing pressure group activity but also an era in which the number of people who became members of political groups dramatically increased. The growth occurred primarily within the new rising middle class, which was increasingly demanding political changes. Furthermore, it extended to the labor movement, which experienced tremendous growth rates in terms of membership in the period between 1968 and 1978. While in 1968 only 13.5 percent of the population were members of a trade union, this number had risen to 25 percent by 1976. Most of the new unions during this era were founded by employees in the civil and community services field (Levin and Jao 1988). The most impressive example of this is the Hong Kong Professional Teachers Union (HKPTU), which was able to more than double its members between its founding in 1973 and 1980 (see Figure 7.1).

The large membership numbers, however, did not necessarily translate into greater group strength. The labor movement, for instance, was split into three conflicting factions: the Nationalists (close to the Kuomintang), the Communists, and the newly developing, largely independent unions of professionals. The membership growth rates were the largest in the latter group and among the Communists, while the membership of the Nationalists stagnated. The student movement, furthermore, was also split between Nationalists and Reformists. When the Nationalists lost their interest in China, after the end of the Cultural Revolution, and the Reformists had become part of the rising social movements, the student movement lost its strength (Leung 2000).

While ethnic cleavages slowly disappeared during this time, some groups were still mainly dominated by either the Chinese or the expatriate British. For example, during the 1970s expatriates dominated the Conservancy Association, two-thirds of its members being foreign born. The environmental group had only 400 members in 1973 and 500 in 1976. Other reasons for the groups' relatively small sizes may have been the low priority of environmental issues during this period and the fact that most members were rich individuals or powerful corporations.[1] As a result, the groups often appeared biased in favor of large corporations and economic concerns.

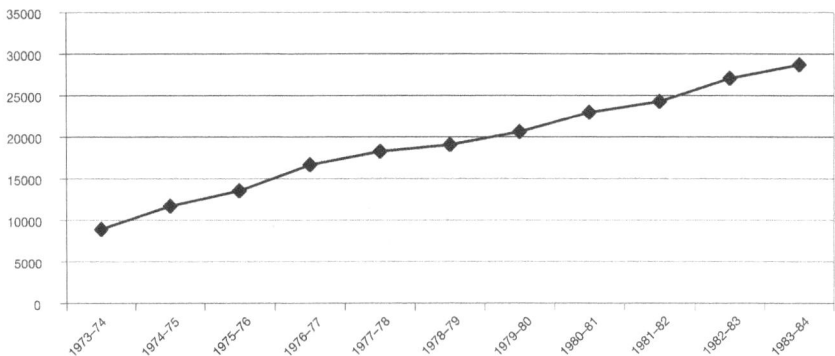

Figure 7.1 Increase of the member of the Hong Kong Professional Teachers' Union (1975–1984)
Source: HKPTU Flyer 1984

Table 7.1 Prominent oppositional groups in Hong Kong during the 1970s

Name	Founded	Members (Year)	Description
Hong Kong Federation of Trade Unions (FTU)	1948	145,500 (1974)	pro-Communist labor federation
Reform Club of Hong Kong	1949	30,400 (1975)	Quasi political party, moderate
Hong Kong Civic Association	1954	10,000 (1975)	Quasi political party, conservative
Hong Kong Christian Industrial Committee	1966	unknown	labor group, moderate
Conservancy Association	1968	400 (1973), 500 (1976)	nature group
Society for Community Organization (SoCO)	1971	9 hardcore (1974)	social group
Education Action Group	1972	60 (1976)	educational group
Hong Kong Professional Teachers' Union	1973	*See Illustration 7.1*	labor union, progressive
Hong Kong Observers Ltd.	1975	ca. 50	discussion group, moderate
Heritage Society	1977	unknown	heritage preservation group, dissolved 1983
Hong Kong Belongers Association Ltd.	1978	unknown	representation of Hong Kong people

Sources: Various newspaper articles from *South China Morning Post* and *Hong Kong Standard* between 1970 and 1982, Interview with Joseph S.Y. Cheng

Oppositional groups were often internally heterogeneous and unable to formulate common objectives. Even worse, the lack of a common basis also led to disagreements and infighting within some of these groups. For instance, in 1974 the Reform Club experienced a number of high-profile resignations. Dr P.C. Wong stated his reasons for resigning: "We wanted to resign because we felt that we were redundant in the Club. Our existence seemed to have been neglected—we were not even notified of its executive meeting." (quoted in *SCMP* 20 March 1974). In response, the Reform Club demanded that those who had resigned should also vacate their seats on the Urban Council. A spokesman for the party said: "It is the general ruling of any political party that it is the duty and obligation of a member to vacate his councillorship when he wishes to resign from the party" (quoted in *SCMP* 28 March 28 1974). Probably due its large membership base, the Reform Club seemed to have been unable to maintain group cohesion.

Finally, even though oppositional groups in the 1970s would unite for single-issue causes, these coalitions usually broke up once the issue was resolved (Lam 2004). Because oppositional groups had a shared experience of being rejected, they could easily form alliances (Lui 1999). These ad hoc associations proved successful in campaigns against rent hikes, public transportation fare increases, etc. and posed a greater challenge to the government because they proved that pressure groups and residents' associations could unite to press for certain issues. However, only after 1984 was there significant consolidation between individual groups, some of which became political parties.

Overall, it can be said that the increasing membership base during the 1970s provided the organizational potential for the development of protest movements in Hong Kong after 1984. The era can therefore be seen as an educational phase, which allowed oppositional groups to organize a more sophisticated challenge to the government once political opportunities developed.

Leaders

Since there were so many groups in Hong Kong in the 1970s, it is impossible to even attempt to generalize about their leaders. However, among the leading groups, it is perhaps most intriguing that at least two of their leaders were accused of a dictatorial style. One reason for this may have been the lack of a representative government, which forced groups to act in a uniform manner against an overbearing government. Oppositional groups, which were often internally split, wanted to speak with one voice and there was therefore a tendency for them to become merely political vehicles for very active individuals.

One leader who was accused of being a dictator and "running a one-man club" was Brook Bernacchi, the head of the Reform Club. This criticism was voiced by Ma Man-fai, a co-founder of the Reform Club, in the context of the resignations described above. Bernacchi denied the allegation and blamed the government for the difficulties of his political group:

> The Government has done all it can to discourage the formation of political parties. Consequently, members of the public—including Mr. Tsin and Dr. Wong—do not understand things like party loyalty.
>
> (*SCMP* 20 March 1974)

It is interesting to note that Bernacchi considered the Reform Club to be a political party. The chairman of this group, who from 1952 until 1981 served as an elected member of the Urban Council, demanded partisanship from other members, while he was unable to maintain anything close to party unity.

Another leading figure of the oppositional movement of the 1970s was Szeto Wah, chairman of the Hong Kong Professional Teachers' Union from 1974 until 1990. Like Bernacchi, he was also described as a strongman by one of his associates:

> A dictatorial leader ... In most meetings he monopolises the talking, with detail of his plan, strategies well-sorted out before his colleagues start to comprehend the basic outline.
>
> (quoted in do Rosario 1981)

Szeto Wah rejected participation in Urban Council elections and instead chose to criticize the government strongly. "He is a man with strong political convictions but he makes no noise nor clamour for idealistic goals" (do Rosario 1981). According to do Rosario, he even became one of "the most influential persons in Hongkong's political scene since mid-70s" (ibid.). He was certainly able to motivate the base of his group, as the increasing membership numbers show.

Other prominent leaders of oppositional groups of the 1970s were Dr L.K. Ding of the Christian Industrial Committee, Hilton Cheong-leen of the Civic Association, David Russell of the Heritage Society, and Judy Butler of the Education Action Group. There were also leaders who frequently changed political groups, such as Tsin Sai-nin, or were opposed to belonging to any group, such as Elsie Elliot. They were leaders because they were able to get elected to the Urban Council and/or get their views published in the newspapers. However, the personalization of politics during the 1970s also contributed to a lack of cohesion within the opposition.

Incentives: why did members join?

There were many incentives for joining an oppositional group in the 1970s. For example, nearly all political groups in Hong Kong offered their members social services and other activities. Most importantly, these clubs, unions, and associations provided their members with an important network in a city in which social services from the government were still in their infancy. For example, Brook Bernacchi, chairman of the Reform Club, said in 1988:

> I should be the last one to pretend that all individual members have joined purely because they are interested in politics. People join for many reasons. For instance, an unlicensed hawker may join the club in the hope that he may get some sort of protection from it. I hope some of them believe in the objectives of the club.
>
> (quoted in Lau 1988)

One of the major assets for members of the Reform Club was its legal services. Members with legal problems could get free advice from lawyers and other experts who were not necessarily members of the club. This played an important role, because in the early 1970s the language of the judicial system was still restricted to English, which many people did not understand. The Reform Club also provided other services, such as welfare and health care, at significantly reduced rates. In 1988, the club even became involved in an illegal gambling scandal at one of its branch offices.[2] These activities, however, also reveal that, of the club's 30,400 members in 1975, only a small minority took part in politics, and there is no way to ascertain how many people actually believed in the objectives of the club.

Membership in the traditional unions was also to a large extent motivated by the fact that these groups delivered services that fulfilled needs outside of the workplace, such the welfare of its members. These included many recreational activities, which were effective in attracting new members (Levin and Jao 1988). According to Turner et al. (1980) labor unions during this time acted as "friendly societies," which pursued trade union functions only under pressure from their members. In this regard, the traditional trade unions resembled the Kaifong organizations, which were neighborhood organizations that looked after the people within a certain territory.

The newer labor unions, in contrast, resembled the Western labor unions, which were primarily interested in protecting workers' rights. However, as the Hong Kong Professional Teachers' Association (HKPTA) shows, these newer unions also provided many essential social services for their members. The group offered interest groups and courses, a kindergarten group, insurances, full pay for maternity leave, paid sick leave, book sales, library services for primary students, dental care and so on. This is a very broad spectrum of services that targeted a large segment of the population. Furthermore, it suggests that a group like the HKPTA was able to raise significant financial resources.

Despite large membership numbers, pressure groups were mostly fragmented. Since the incentives for joining a group were largely nonpolitical, group leaders could not necessarily rely on their membership base for political causes. Consequently, oppositional groups could only be mobilized for truly salient issues.

Communication network

Oppositional groups in Hong Kong were able to rely on a number of means to communicate their opinions. First of all, they were free to print and distribute their own publications without government restrictions. Second, they had access to a relatively free press. While there were allegations of bias in the media, the press was frequently willing to give considerable space to the opposition. Sometimes, the media even considered itself to be part of the opposition (see Chapter 3).

Most pressure groups usually maintained their own papers, magazines, or newsletters with which they targeted the members of their group and sometimes tried to reach out to the public. For example, in 1984, the Hong Kong Professional Teachers' Union had ten different publications: *PTU News* (bi-weekly), *School and Family* (monthly), *The Young* (monthly), *Infant Education* (quarterly), *Mathematics* (quarterly), *Pulse* (monthly), *Sales News* (twice or three times a year), *Travel News* (twice or three times a year), *Summer Vacation Programmes* (once a year) and *PTU News Extract* (bi-weekly for English speaking members). These publications were mainly targeted at the membership base and ensured group cohesion. Their topics, however, were rarely of a political nature.

It was more difficult for opposition groups to make use of newspapers and television, which were alleged to be biased in favor of big business and the government. There were allegations that Hong Kong journalists heavily self-censored their reporting. In 1979, the chairperson of the Hong Kong Journalists' Association (HKJA), Vickie Barrett, accused the conservative publishers of the city-state's newspapers of "what is wrong with Hongkong's Press" (Barrett 1979). She claimed that the publishers were conspiring with the government and business owners against the interests of the people:

> Would it be too cynical to suggest that there is a collusion between the Government, business and the newspaper owners?—three categories that often overlap. Would it be too cynical to suggest that in Hongkong, freedom of the Press means "freedom to suppress"?
>
> (Ibid.)

In her speech, which was supposed to be delivered before the Rotary Club of Hong Kong but was instead printed in the *Hong Kong Standard*, she used words like "smug," "self-serving," and "docile" to describe her perception of the press. She claimed that oftentimes there was very little critical reporting in the press. The reasons for this misery, she asserted, could mainly be found in the lack of training of prospective journalists and the very low salaries that they earned.

Despite this bias in the press, newspapers frequently printed the opinions of members of the opposition. For instance the Hong Kong Observers had a regular column in the *South China Morning Post* and Elsie Elliot published her often-critical comments in all major English-language newspapers. These articles were highly valued by the newspapers, which were desperate for content. Even though many of these articles were very critical of the government, there appears to have been very little direct censorship. The heterogeneous nature of the media, furthermore, made it impossible for anyone to dominate the political discourse. The generally accepted value of freedom of the press and speech allowed oppositional groups to communicate efficiently with each other and with outside sympathizers.

Many of the campaigns against the government were specifically designed to achieve significant coverage in the press. Oppositional groups often held news conferences and released press statements to get their views heard, which were subsequently published in many of Hong Kong's newspapers. Furthermore, the use of demonstrations, which will be discussed later, was in part intended to garner the attention of the press. If the press had failed to report on these evens, oppositional groups would probably have been much less effective.

Finally, it is noteworthy that Hong Kong's press also saw itself as an "oppositional group". For instance, the chairperson of the HKJA, Vickie Barrett (1979), considered the press an important part of Hong Kong politics despite its bias: "I am not here to tell you that the local media are totally corrupt and emasculated." She singles out the *Hong Kong Standard*, which she thinks is a "tough campaigner," for particular praise. This shows that newspapers were not simply a source of information but played a part in oppositional politics. Furthermore, in the opinion of the HKJA, the lack of formalized political opposition endowed the press with the role of providing an opposition. Thus, Emily Lau (1986: 422) argued that "Since the colony does not have formalized political opposition to the government, the news media have sometimes acted as a quasi-opposition."

The "imperial image" and conflicts in Hong Kong

Oppositional groups in Hong Kong valued stability and economic prosperity as much as did their Singaporean counterparts. This desire of the rising middle class superseded all other aspirations. In this context, the demand for greater democratization hinged on the question as to whether the increase of elected members would enhance the stability of the city-state. The inability of oppositional groups to participate in the political system, however, also fostered a deep sense of powerlessness (Table 7.2).

What distinguished Hong Kong's oppositional groups from those in Singapore was the widespread perception that the government was not fulfilling its promises or was often even acting against the interests of society, possibly even conspiring with the business elite. This perception led to a deep-seated anger within the aggrieved groups that was often voiced in public. Many individuals were willing to join demonstrations and sit-ins, sign petitions or participate in other public protests. Some were even willing to break the law in order to advocate their concerns. While these protesters were often called "troublemakers," this did not significantly influence the strategies of the opposition. On the contrary, by the end of the 1970s people were more willing to participate in activity that was directed against the government.

It should be noted that members of the opposition considered their tactics necessary to guarantee stability and prosperity in the future. Control in the hands of a few administrators was seen as a threat to this goal. Opposition members, therefore, justified their tactics, even if they were non-institutionalized, with reference to the long-term stability of the city-state.

Desire for stability and prosperity and a sense of powerlessness

For most oppositional groups, political stability[3] and increasing prosperity were considered the most pressing issues. The political groups and many

Table 7.2 Cognitive image of oppositional groups in Hong Kong during the 1970s

	Group strength	Emotions and policy disposition	Goals and tactics
(Weakening) Imperial Image	split, weak	desire for stability and prosperity, sense of discontent, sense of rightfulness to challenge the government	reform-oriented, willingness to use non-institutionalized tactics

pressure groups saw it as their goal to function as a counterweight to the government. For example, the press releases of the Reform Club during the year 1974 place an emphasis on stabilizing inflation. In February, the group wrote: "The Reform Club is astonished that the Financial Secretary, Mr Haddon-Cave, has not suggested any measures to tackle the current serious inflation in Hong Kong" (Reform Club 1975). The HKPTU, which was one of the most active groups in the 1970s, also stated as its main goal the development of a stable and wealthy society. In 1984, Szeto Wah wrote to his members and to prospective new members:

> At the eve of this history-making change, it is more important than ever that we should strive to strengthen and expand our unity and solidarity so that we may continue to protect the labour rights of our members, promote the healthy development of education, and, in co-operation with all members of the public who are well-intentioned about the future of Hong Kong, contribute towards its *prosperity*, and *stability*.
>
> (HKPTU Flyer 1984, emphasis added)

Democratic rights such as labor rights and the promotion of education are framed in the context of stability and prosperity. The basis of these rights is a stable society, but these rights are also needed to maintain stability.

While the opposition expressed the need for stability, there was also a sense of powerlessness, which was a result of the overbearing government and the very limited institutionalization of oppositional politics in weak institutions such as the Urban Council (see Chapters 3 and 5). This feeling was expressed in 1972 when a group of young activists tried to register a pig for Urban Council elections in order to protest the lack of influence of the elected Councilors (*SCMP* 12 Dec. 1972). When the opposition wanted to achieve a goal, they were very keenly aware of their limited influence within the government and therefore opted to rely on techniques that were designed to exert outside pressure on the government. In cases in which there was widespread discontent, opposition members considered it necessary to employ as many methods as necessary to achieve their goals.

A sense of discontent

The increasing number of protests in the 1970s reveals a deep-seated sense of discontent, which was often, but certainly not always, targeted at the government. The government's failure to fulfill its promises and the resulting inadequacies of public services often fueled the dissatisfaction of the activists. Many disputes that started as small grievances escalated when members of oppositional groups thought that the government had become involved on the wrong side. From the viewpoint of the pressure groups, it was their task to alert the government to become aware of these deficiencies, and to pressure it to act in favor of the people of Hong Kong. The perceived inertia of the government and lack of transparency in the decision-making process often led to disappointment and anger.

Oppositional groups called for greater involvement of the government in the economy and in society. Whether it was helping industry, fighting pornography, eliminating corruption, or improving public housing and education, oppositional groups felt that the government could do more about these issues. History shows that the Hong Kong government often felt the need to respond to public pressure. While the government increasingly became involved in the economy and in society, in some cases it was also seen to be intervening on the "wrong" side. The government was obviously not able to satisfy all the needs of the different groups. The increasing complexity of the political system and rising social problems therefore produced an increasingly aggressive opposition movement. This stands in contrast to Singapore, where the government has always considered control of the economy and of society to be important priorities.

In the following, a number of exemplary cases will be discussed that vividly demonstrate the importance of this emotional response to government action or inaction. The government's plan to provide adequate housing for the city's residents was one of the most important reasons for the outbreak of group conflict. In 1977, 40 percent of Hong Kong residents lived in public housing administered by the Housing Authority. Criticism, however, was targeted at the living conditions in public housing, the inability of the government to meet public housing targets, and the occasional rent increases. For example, the residents of the Shekkipmei housing estate were told in March of 1977 that they would have to accept a rent increase of between HK$8 and HK$25 on what were considered to be already expensive apartments. They charged that this was an attempt to get more money from the working class for new public housing. The rent increase finally caused 600 residents to threaten not to pay the next month's rent. Shekkipmei Housing Estate Residents' Committee chairman Li Yue-man accused the government of neglecting the estate: "We are very angry that the government had the heart to increase rent despite the deplorable conditions our converted flats are in" (quoted in *HK Standard* 1977). In an article in the *Hong Kong Standard* (14 Sep. 1977), the Tenants' Committee of the Shekkipmei Redeveloped Blocks, furthermore, asserted that "This [rental] policy will create unstability and all sorts of negative and sad consequences." The residents charged that it was the political system that kept them poor, so that the rich could continue to live a comfortable life. Public housing, the tenants asserted, was the responsibility of the government.

Furthermore, discontent was not limited to the people in these public housing estates. The residents could find support from popular Urban Councilors such as Elsie Elliot and Tsin Sai-nin, who demanded that the government should listen to the residents' demands and lower the rents. The Education Action Group also became involved in the dispute over rent increases, when it was announced that schools and kindergartens would also have to pay significantly higher rents, forcing some of the schools to close.

Another area for discontent was the government's inability to provide adequate education for the rapidly increasing population. The Precious Blood Golden Jubilee School incident of 1978/79, in which a great number of teachers and students accused the school administration of financial improprieties, while the Education Department supported the school leadership, may be the most prominent example. The government was unable to resolve this crisis and thus decided to close the school. Szeto Wah, chairman of the Hong Kong Professional Teachers' Union, voiced his anger when he raised the potential of repression in response to the government's closing of the school. In a speech summarized in the *South China Morning Post*, the union leader warned about coercion by the government if the people were unwilling to stand up against the crackdown. While the paper did not quote Wah's speech at length, it is clear that the union leader felt strong anger, which was directed at the government's inaction. The use of strong, emotional terms such as "fascist" and "repression" merely hints at the extent of the union leader's sentiment (*SCMP* 19 May 1978).

Anger was also the result when the government acted without informing the public about impending changes. For example, a group of angry parents and students protested against the planned destruction of Shatin Lutheran Primary School without the provision of an adequate replacement. The parents petitioned the government, including Governor Murray MacLehose, who was in London at the time, and acting Governor Denys Roberts, to intervene in the dispute. The government promised to provide answers to the parents' demands but nothing happened. The parents even prevented Assistant Director of Education A.G. Reeve from leaving a meeting until he had signed a pledge that he would give them a reply by 13 July. The Education Department, however, refused to respond, claiming that since the protesters had petitioned the Governor, they could not make a decision. Discontent turned into anger, when 200 to 230 parents and students stormed the Government Secretariat on 14 July, bringing in banners. A representative for the parents, Ng Chan Sin-fong, showed his disapproval of the government's behavior: "We feel we are being cheated because the Education Department still has not answered our demands" (quoted in Li 1978). The government finally caved in to the parents' appeals on 25 July and promised to leave the school open until February and find an adequate replacement by that time. This event shows that a lot of anger was directed at the government when it did not act in the interest of some wronged segment of the population. Furthermore, the fact that the government gave in to the demands of the protesters legitimized future protests against the government.

The duty to confront the government

The right and even duty of oppositional groups to oppose the government came from their self-appointed role as protectors of society. The government's failure to address many of the most pressing issues served as motivation for many of the activists. Even though most of the challenges to the government during the 1970s came from pressure groups, they did not regard themselves as "interest groups" or groups biased in favor of a single constituency. Instead, they maintained that they constituted an important part of society because their task was to pressure the government in the interests of the people. The lack of democracy and the inability of the government always to work in the best interests of the people legitimated the use of contentious politics against the government. The Hong Kong Observers made this clear in their mission statement:

> we came to the conclusion that it was important for people in Hongkong, which has an unelected, unrepresentative Government, to voice their feelings over issues, to condemn the many injustices in our midst, to criticise policies that are perceived to be wrong and, wherever possible, to offer alternative courses of action. In short, we decided to be a pressure group.
>
> (Hong Kong Observers 1983: 1)

Because Hong Kong lacked democracy, the Observers considered it their duty to act as a watchdog over the government. They could claim this even though they were not popularly elected and, as a group of educated members of the middle class, could not really represent the opinion of the people. This conception of the role of pressure groups was echoed by a large majority of oppositional groups. For example, the chairman of the Education Action Group (EAG), Han Men-ho, thought that the purpose of pressure groups was to "help voice the grievances of the common citizens, reflect their views, influence the government, and bring about policy changes" (quoted in *HK Standard* 1982).

The elected members of the only partially democratic institution the Urban Council also considered it their duty to check on the government. For instance, the chairman of the Reform Club, Brook Bernacchi, said in 1973: "The duty of the Opposition is to oppose. The Reform Club strongly supports the wishes, the wants and needs of Hongkong citizens" (quoted in *SCMP*, 16 Feb. 1973). Bernacchi demanded the right to act as if he were a member of the opposition in Hong Kong's political system. He was, however, merely a member of the Urban Council and could not even hope to participate in either the legislature or the executive. The fact that he was elected by a portion of the Hong Kong population (even if it was a minuscule minority), however, invested him, in his opinion, with the right and even the duty to oppose government legislation that he considered unjust. Since the government did not always succeed in fulfilling the demands of the population, groups such as residents' associations, nature groups, labor groups, etc. considered it their right and even duty to fight for the interests of their members as if this was also in the interest of society.

Goals

Reform is necessary and sufficient

The goals of oppositional groups in the 1970s were moderate and tended to be reform oriented. Lam Wai-man argues that activists were "ready to make fundamental demands of the government" (Lam 2004: 182), but they hardly ever demanded fundamental change that questioned the political regime. Particularly when they asked for greater participation, these groups were willing to negotiate. They largely accepted their inferior position, because they were often successful in pressuring the government to accept their demands.

The oldest institution in Hong Kong by which demands for political reform were expressed was the Urban Council. Since the council's jurisdiction was very limited, the parties and individual candidates contesting Urban Council elections tended to promote issues dealing directly with the administration of urban affairs. The Reform Club manifesto of 1970, for example, focused on five main issues: rent control, better social welfare, Urban Council control of medical services, compulsory primary education, and the concentration of all housing matters in one department (Baird 1970b). Four of the Reform Club's proposals dealt with changes to current policies, while only one dealt with institutional changes. Faced with a significant housing crisis, the last demand was actually a call for the colonial government to create a housing department, which was realized in 1973 with the creation of the Hong Kong Housing Authority.

The Reform Club, which was the earliest group constantly to ask for greater democratization did not, however, demand revolutionary change. In its 1975 platform, the Reform Club stated its demand for constitutional reform in the following way:

> a. The Legislative Council must be reformed so that people from all walks of lives will have at least some form of representation in the law making body. The Reform Club suggests the creation of at least two seats in the said Council.
>
> b. However, if for reasons which the Government of Hong Kong has no control over, elected representation to the Legislative Council is at present not possible, then the Urban Council must be reformed ... .
>
> (Reform Club 1975)

The Reform Club's phrasing reveals an important aspect of the goals of oppositional groups during the 1970s. Due to its powerlessness, it has to argue moderately for some constitutional change. It also signals a willingness to compromise to some degree on issues that might appear fundamental to the group's influence. The Reform Club recognizes the widespread perception that the Hong Kong government is dependent on external factors. As I have mentioned elsewhere, the government often claimed that the Chinese government was strongly opposed to greater democratization.

The goals of other Urban Councilors were equally reform oriented. For example, in 1978 a number of elected Urban Councilors complained in an open letter to the British government about the city's undemocratic political system and demanded political reforms:

> We have some simple proposals, and even these are adjustable. They are:
> 1. A Legislature of which one third is directly elected, one third appointed, and one third indirectly elected by professionals, as in our neighbouring Portuguese Colony, Macau.
> 2. A gradual phasing out of appointed members on the Urban Council at the rate of four every two years.
> 3. An expanded franchise to include all long-term adult residents of Hongkong.
> 4. Expansion of Urban Council jurisdiction to include housing, education, social welfare, town planning, etc. ...
>
> (Elliot, Huang and Tsin 1978)

This letter represented perhaps the strongest demand for greater democratization during the 1970s. The independent councilors, who wrote this letter, stressed that democratic reforms were necessary but needed to be introduced progressively. While the Reform Club had demanded only two directly elected members to the Legislative Council in 1975, only three years later these Urban Councilors asked for one third of the Legislative Council to be elected. It is noteworthy that they considered the option of letting professionals elect one third of this institution, which is somewhat similar to the functional constituencies of the modern Legislative Council.[4] Similarly to the Reform Club's proposal, this open letter clearly states that the proposals were flexible and open to negotiation.

While constitutional reform was on the agenda of many political groups, most pressure groups that arose in the 1970s were more interested in influencing specific government policy. They did not advocate fundamental changes to the political order. A good example of this is the Hong Kong Observers Ltd., which were founded in 1975 by a group of young liberal professionals. The Hong Kong Observers considered themselves a pressure group because they were interested in influencing government decisions. In 1976, the group declared that its objective was to "work for the betterment of Hongkong's political and social atmosphere" (Hong Kong Observers 1976). The group's goals were:

(a) To promote and organise interest and activities to participate in the governance of Hongkong.
(b) To press and solicit the Government of Hongkong to be responsive to the needs of the people of Hongkong.

(c) To organise research of issues of public interest affecting Hongkong.
(d) To promote community welfare.

(Hong Kong Observers 1983: 1)

The group's goals reveal a certain degree of elitism, because there is an intention to educate the public and the government on the public will. They considered it their role to be a negotiator between these two groups. Their articles feature well-researched rebuttals of government policies. The Observers' articles tend to be very long and detailed, which obviously limited their influence to an educated elite.

The articles produced by the Hong Kong Observers did not challenge the political system but, rather, identified specific problems and shortcomings which required changes in policy. Derek Davies criticized the Observers in 1983:

There is no express theoretical or ideological position. That is there is no *political* position. ... If this is the basis of, even the first glimmerings of Hong Kong party politics, as yet it shows a failure to grasp that the essential of politics is systematic partisanship.

(Davies 1983: 106)

The group resembles many of the opposition parties in Singapore, whose goals are also the idealistic improvement of society. Partisanship is rejected because it cannot promote the welfare of the people as a whole. Due to the elitist orientation of the group as educator and as provider of constructive criticism, its influence remained very limited. The demise of the Hong Kong Observers after the introduction of democratic reforms in the 1980s occurred because those members who were interested in politics either joined political parties or focused their interests on their careers (Interview with Joseph S.Y. Cheng 2006).

The lack of a revolutionary vision

Oppositional groups in Hong Kong during the 1970s lacked a truly revolutionary vision. The only "revolutionary" goal that was frequently mentioned during this time was the demand for greater participation. Democracy, however, was not regarded as an institutional framework for representing as many individuals as possible, but rather as a panacea for all societal ills. In 1975, an anonymous writer used the example of Great Britain to explain why the Hong Kong government should not worry about instability. The author, moreover, considered democracy as a guarantee for the continuation of the city-state's stability:

A fundamental principle of government is that it will govern as effectively as it is answerable to the people. If there is no orderly means available whereby the people can throw the undesirable people out, there is no way of ensuring that government will seriously tackle problems of corruption and the like. To entrust oneself to government is naiveté.

(A Concerned Resident 1975)

The "concerned citizen" considered representative government as a solution to the problems of the authoritarian rule of the colonial regime.

The calls for greater representation ranged from increasing the franchise for the Urban Council, to an elected Legislative Council. The goal of many in the opposition was the improvement of their ability to communicate with the government. While the government repeatedly bemoaned the lack of communication between the people and the government, opposition groups were equally convinced of this problem. David Russell, president of the Hong Kong Heritage Society, agreed with this viewpoint when he announced that his group would take part in the 1979 Urban Council elections:

> From our past experience, we find a communication gap between the Government and the people. ... We hope to bridge this gap by sponsoring candidates in Urban Council elections.

(quoted in *The Star* 1978)

The impression that the problem of Hong Kong's political system was due to a lack of communication between the government and the people was widespread.

Calls for the introduction of greater democracy in the colony were often driven by the desire to create a more stable society. Many of these government critics assumed that greater representation of the public would lead to a more stable and prosperous society. These groups regarded the West as a model of political development because democratization had led to extremely stable countries. For example, an anonymous writer with the pseudonym Honi Soit wrote in the *Hong Kong Standard* in 1979 in response to the arrest of unlawful protesters:

> Why is the question of public assembly and peaceful petition for redress of grievances such a threatening issue for administrations everywhere, and that in Hongkong in particular?
>
> The answer is fairly obvious. In a modern world in which there is an increasing desire for popular involvement in government; in a world where the only stable and progressive administrations are those that permit the people to elect their representatives to govern them, the Hongkong Government has adamantly refused to move with the times—has defied the people's right to have any say in the way they are governed.

(Honi Soit 1979)

The government should introduce elections in order to increase social stability. In this letter, democracy is the only option for a stable modern society. By aligning modernity and stability with democratic rights, oppositional groups and individuals tried to use the prevalent discourse on stability and prosperity to propagate their goal. This, however, also meant that the opposition during this time did not actively fight for democratic rights.

Tactics

The oppositional groups of the 1970s were largely excluded from the policy-making process. As a consequence, they were forced to rely mostly on non-institutionalized tactics to achieve their goals. There were numerous protests, sit-ins, poster campaigns etc. to press the issues of a particular group. Institutional tactics were largely limited to the filing of petitions and the possibility of being elected to the Urban Council or nominated to another government institution. The latter tactic was, however, open to only a very few in the opposition. The use of newspapers, furthermore, can be considered a quasi-institutionalized tactic, because it was welcomed by the government.

Despite the emphasis on non-institutional tactics, the late 1970s and early 1980s already showed a trend toward the increasing institutionalization of oppositional politics. In his study of neighborhood mobilization between 1966 and 1985, Ma Fook-Tong (1986) compared the use of non-institutional and institutional means by activists in the area of housing. While in the 1970s demonstrations, sit-ins and similar activities dominated, the use of participation in institutional politics became more common after the institutional reforms of the early 1980s.

Institutionalized tactics

For oppositional groups, institutionalized tactics were the election or nomination of leading members to government bodies, the use of petitions and articles in newspapers to enhance the interests of the group. The government encouraged these attempts because it considered this a way to understand public opinion.

After elected members were introduced into the Urban Council, members of the opposition considered this municipal institution an important asset in their efforts to influence the government. Despite the tremendous short-comings of the institution, it provided prospective candidates with a channel for communicating their grievances with the government. The council's influence was limited to urban affairs, but until 1972 it also provided a platform for criticism of the government. Aside from issues relating to the jurisdiction of the Council, members often spoke about issues much broader in scope. While the government may have considered the Urban Council as meddling in its affairs, the introduction of limits on the content of its debates in 1972 forced criticism to other venues. There were, of course, election campaigns, but the lack of influence of the councilors once they were elected led to many of the campaign promises sounding hollow. Therefore, Urban Councilors such as Elsie Elliot continued to voice their criticism in the newspapers.

In 1973, the government tried to satisfy its critics by nominating an elected member of the Urban Council to the Legislative Council, Hilton Cheong-leen, the chairman of the Civic Association and Vice Chairman of the Urban Council, was selected for this appointment. Cheong-leen was a relatively moderate critic of the government who, however, considered it his task to repeatedly question the government while he was part of the Legislative Council. He asked questions about government proposals or voiced his own opinion on important issues in nearly every session. Quite often he also asked follow-up questions if he was not satisfied with the answer. Urban Councilors considered the appointment of one of their own as great progress. In 1976, the government decided to enlarge the Legislative Council, which increased the chances of an elected Urban Councilor becoming part of this esteemed institution. On 1 September of the same year, following the wishes of elected Urban Councilors, Henry Hu, Vice Chairman of the Reform Club, was appointed to the LegCo. This time the Governor had carefully chosen someone from the liberal camp, while avoiding one of the more outspoken personalities such as Brook Bernacchi or Elsie Elliot.

The lack of influence of the oppositional groups resulted in frustration among the more active members. The limited franchise and the unwillingness of the government to increase the number of elected offices motivated the Reform Club in 1979 to threaten a boycott of the Urban Council elections. In 1981, they followed up on their threat and refused to contest the elections. The prominent leader of the party, Brook Bernacchi, vacated his seat, saying: "How can one purport to represent nearly six million people in Hong Kong when you have been elected by only 6,000 voters?" (Chan 1981). His decision marked a temporary repudiation of the Reform Club's use of institutionalized tactics. In the following election, the party returned to institutional politics, but it slowly declined in political significance afterwards.

Members of pressure groups also tried to get involved in institutional politics, for instance through Urban Council elections. In 1978, a British Member of Parliament advised the Heritage Society to enter institutional politics and contest Urban Council elections in order to preserve the old Kowloon Canton railway terminal. The MP was of the opinion that this tactic would be more effective. But before the elections in 1979, the government had already demolished the old train station, leaving only the clock tower behind. This example suggests that institutionalized tactics were not very effective in the 1970s. In the 1980s pressure groups began to adopt more institutional forms of mobilization, because the government introduced significant institutional changes which allowed these groups to have greater influence over government policies (Castells et al. 1990).

Non-institutionalized tactics

While the government successfully co-opted groups like the Reform Club or the Civic Association, "most of the pressure groups were active mainly outside formal institutional politics" (Lui and Chiu 1999: 152). Agreeing with Lui, Ma Fook-tong (1986), who analyzed mobilization in public housing, claims that non-institutional forms dominated for most of the years during the late 1960s and the 1970s. Because of the 1966/67 riots, non-institutionalized tactics were generally considered disruptive to the social stability of Hong Kong. The 1970s, however, saw a continuous increase in street demonstrations (both registered and unregistered), sit-ins, boycotts, and other acts of civil disobedience. What distinguished these events from the riots of the 1960s was the fact that these protests were peaceful, organized, and in most cases permitted or at least tolerated by the government. The political groups were able to increase their influence by continuously pushing the boundaries of what was legally possible or even what was tolerated. The 1970s was an era in which, as Lam Wai-man (2004) observes, oppositional groups increasingly used overt tactics. These tactics provided them with the necessary press coverage, which had the potential of influencing the government. The following examples of campaigns in which non-institutionalized tactics dominated will demonstrate how the oppositional movement was able to increase its influence over the government.

First of all, non-institutionalized strategies played an important role in the white-collar labor movement. While the economy thrived, unfair salaries became an important aspect of contention in the thriving city-port. Increasing wealth brought about greater demands for higher or merely reasonable salaries and there was an increase in white-collar labor activity between 1974 and 1981 (Leung and Chiu 1991). In 1970 female nurses protested for equal pay for men and women. They conducted meetings, put up posters, petitioned the Legislative Council, the Executive Council and the British parliament. On 6 October 1971, 300 off-duty nurses marched to the Government House to make their demands known. They were aided by positive coverage in the newspapers, and the government caved in to the protesters' demands on 11 October. This protest was significant because it was the first labor demonstration by civil servants from any part of the government, and thus served as an example for future cases (Lam 2004).

The territory-wide strike of certificated teachers on 4 April 1973, over a 15 percent cut in their salary, also led to a change of tactics. While the protesting nurses had been off-duty, the teachers decided to conduct strikes. The government staunchly opposed the sit-in strike, which was timed to coincide with important examinations, because the teachers disrupted the educational system. A day after the strike, the Deputy Director of Education, Charles Lowe, declared that the teachers had miscalculated "if they imagined that the tactics employed against pupils yesterday could cause the Government to reconsider its stand" (quoted in *SCMP* 5 April 1973). The government accused the teachers of using the students for their own purposes and claimed that some of the striking teachers had threatened the students so that they would not come to school. In response, the teachers asserted that some principals had forced students to attend class or face automatic disqualification. The strike led to the formation of the most powerful union in Hong Kong history, the Hong Kong Professional Teachers' Union, with Szeto Wah, one of the strike leaders, at its head. At the time, Wah was accused by the conservative *South China Morning Post* of being a Communist sympathizer. The paper wrote "in one dramatic move (familiar to those versed in united front activities of the communists), a massive rally of teachers was held and at this meeting Mr Szeto Wah emerged as the overall leader" (*SCMP* 5 April 1973).

Despite the initial refusal by the Education Department and negative press reports in the mainstream media, the government appointed a commission headed by Legislative Councilor T.K. Ann that looked into the Education Department's handling of the case. Finally, in 1975, the commission's report sharply criticized the government and placed the greatest blame on a failure of communication. In the eyes of the activists, and especially the students, this event demonstrated that overt protest and other non-institutionalized tactics could be successful against unfair practices.

Willingness to confront the government directly was repeated in the 1977/78 campaign against corruption within the administration of the Precious Blood Golden Jubilee school. The activities of the school board led to a student sit-in, a massive protest with 4,000 people participating, and a hunger strike of 52 individuals for 48 hours. Because of its support for the school administration, the Education Department also became a target of this dispute. After a long battle between dissenting teachers and the school administration, the government relented and created two schools, one of which continued to employ the dissenting teachers. The government, however, refused to accept full responsibility and blamed both parties for the dispute.

There was also a readiness to use non-institutionalized tactics to protest against price increases in public services such as housing or telephone services. The activists were willing to threaten a collective refusal to pay unless the government rescinded the price increases. While public housing price increases were always controversial, a 1975 decision to grant the Hong Kong Telephone Company a 30 percent increase in phone rates met with significant opposition. Great losses in the operations of the company had motivated the government's decision. In this case, respected Urban Councilor and long-time critic of the government Elsie Elliot called for a boycott of the telephone rate increase:

> We must refuse to pay the 30 per cent increase, and demand the nationalization of public enterprises. Why has the Telephone Advisory Committee not spoken to the public, and why does the Telephone Company refuse to reveal its accounts to the public? Surely there must be inefficiency and dubious things in the company.
>
> (quoted in *HK Standard* 27 Jan. 1975)

Elliot's accusation focuses on lack of transparency and inefficiency in the telephone company. She is of the opinion that nationalization is the best solution to the problem. This was, however, very unlikely to happen, because it would have been a radical departure for a government that insisted on a free market.

The rate increase resulted in numerous colony-wide protests that drew the support of a large segment of the population, including even many conservative groups. On 26 January 1975, 2,000 people, including students, Urban Councilors, and workers staged an orderly rally against the phone rate increases. Many groups, including the Hong Kong Professional Teachers' Union supported the protests. Dr L.K Ding, director of the Christian Industrial Committee (CIC) declared: "If the Government succeeds in getting the 30 per cent passed in Legco, I suggest that all Unofficial Members should resign to apologise for failing to stop the Government" (quoted in *HK Standard*, 27 Jan. 1975). The labor activist expected the members of the Legislative Council to act in the interests of the people even though they were nominated by the Governor. The government set up a Commission of Inquiry that even included members of the pressure groups and that concluded, among other things, that the Hong Kong Telephone Company should set up governmental controls over the utilities. The report, however, failed to resolve whether the public should share the burden of the financial mismanagement (Lam 2004).

By the end of the 1970s, protests had become an accepted part of Hong Kong politics. Since 1977, boat people who lived in the Yaumati typhoon shelter in squalid conditions,[5] had conducted nine public processions and six public meetings, which were all unlicensed under the Public Order Ordinance. On 7 January 1979, sixty-seven boat people and eleven activists (one Italian parish priest, four students, five social workers and a doctor) were arrested while they were traveling in coaches on their way to protest in front of the Governor's residence. Subsequently, they were charged with breaking the Public Order Ordinance for "unlawful assembly." While the magistrate judge absolutely discharged the boat people, the social activists were all placed on good behavior bonds of HK$300 for 18 months, and thus received a criminal record. The arrests led to calls for more civil liberties and the abolition of the Public Order Ordinance. On 12 February, about 250 students protested against the arrests, and two more students were arrested when they refused to put down a banner supporting the Yaumati boat people.

In response to these arrests, around 100 people demonstrated on 27 April 1979 against what they perceived to be the end of democracy. The protesters handed out pamphlets arguing against the Public Order Ordinance and shouted "We have to unite to fight for human rights" When they arrived in front of the court house, in which the social activists were sentenced, they placed a wreath at the front door with the inscription: "Democracy is dead!" The protesters never questioned whether there had ever been democracy in Hong Kong.

Why did Hong Kong's oppositional groups increasingly resort to non-institutionalized tactics? It was certainly important that there was an absence of institutionalization of the opposition. Another reason was the ability of oppositional groups to make use of a free press, which enabled them to influence government policies and consequently increase their power. By the end of the 1970s, social movements and pressure groups were an accepted feature of the Hong Kong political scene. The attempt to control this rising movement, for example through the Standing Committee on Pressure Groups (SCOPG), failed because there was a "consolidation of social protest through pressure group politics" (Lui 1999: 152).

While pressure group politics had become a central feature of the political system, democratization had not occurred. This lack of democratization was due not only to the reluctance of the ruling elite groups to increase representation, but also to a lack of pressure from below. Oppositional groups were more interested in narrow and short-term goals. The occasional call for greater democratization was open to negotiation. If there had been one thing all oppositional groups could unite for, it would have been the stability and continuing prosperity of the city-state. And the government was more than capable of guaranteeing this.

Conclusion and outlook

The goals and strategies as well as the perceptions of oppositional groups in Hong Kong during the 1970s, and the reaction of the government, contributed to an empowering of pressure group politics. Oppositional groups were largely divided, and had diverse members and strong leaders. They were able to form only weak, issue-oriented alliances. The incentives for joining oppositional groups were largely social, but in some cases groups were able to improve the lives of their members. Thus, membership sometimes did have material benefits. These groups were very active in using multiple forms of communication to achieve their goals. This is one of the most important aspects distinguishing the Hong Kong movement from Singapore's.

Most members of the opposition considered stability and prosperity their most important goal. The fact that they had very little influence, furthermore, created a widespread sense of powerlessness. However, the government's failure to fulfill its promises often resulted in discontent that led to a foray of activism targeted at the government. It also spurred the development of oppositional groups. The goals of Hong Kong's oppositional groups were very moderate and interested merely in reforms. The lack of institutionalization of opposition, however, forced most of the activists to pursue non-institutionalized tactics such as sit-ins, boycotts, or public protests.

The focus of this chapter was on Hong Kong's opposition during the 1970s, because it directly relates to the opposition in Singapore detailed in the next chapter. The development of political groups in Hong Kong between 1984 and the present, as well as the future of these groups, will be discussed in Chapter 9. However, first we need to understand why Singapore's opposition has rarely dared to protest against an equally centralized government. While both movements share a sense of powerlessness, Singapore's oppositional groups have largely been willing to submit their interests to those of the country and, by extension, of the ruling elite. While in Hong Kong, challengers considered it their duty to oppose the government, Singaporean members of the opposition have frequently asserted that they are "not opposing for the sake of opposing."

8 Oppositional groups in Singapore
Contention denied

In this chapter, we turn our attention to oppositional groups in Singapore, which share with Hong Kong's opposition the desire for stability and prosperity but which, in contrast, have largely been unable and sometimes even unwilling to directly challenge the regime. Moreover, due to a lack of confrontation and contentious politics, there has not been any significant pressure for further democratization of the political system.

Singapore is not known for its lively politics; on the contrary, a single-party ruling elite has dominated much of modern Singaporean history. As Chapter 6 demonstrates, the government has successfully depoliticized Singapore's society. However, since the 1980s, with the first election of an opposition politician, Singaporean politics has experienced the return of a small and disunited, yet sometimes assertive, oppositional movement. Contrary to Huff's (1999) opinion, there has been significant political change in Singapore, even if the city-state has not developed toward greater democratization.

This chapter will explore the organization of the opposition, how its perceptions of the government and the society in which it lives shape its behavior, and what goals and tactics the opposition has used to influence the political system. This will show that the government has been successful in defining the dominant discourse in which the opposition has to act. The prevailing fear of the government and the emphasis on stability have significantly weakened the opposition. Furthermore, without a truly revolutionary goal, the opposition has been limited to propagating idealistic values such as democracy and freedom. Finally, divergent tactics have led to serious disagreements between oppositional groups, which has resulted in a very fragmented democracy movement.

Oppositional groups in Singapore

Oppositional groups in Singapore are opposition parties, some of which participate in elections and some of which have a small number of elected representatives in parliament, and *independent* civil society groups, which in their present form have existed only since the early 1990s. There are more than twenty opposition parties registered, but only very few of them participate in elections (Table 8.1). It is even more difficult to establish an authoritative list of civil society groups, because in the Singaporean context it is almost impossible to assess the degree of independence of self-described civil society groups. In this book their ability and willingness to challenge the government will be considered a key criterion of their independence. Table 8.2 lists a selected number of civil society groups, of which only the first four have played some role in recent Singapore politics.

There are even some unregistered oppositional groups in Singapore. It should be noted that the government controls the registration of civil society groups through the Societies Act, which states that all groups need to be registered with the Registrar of Societies and the government can reject the registration of any group. In the case of the homosexual advocacy group People Like Us, the government made use of this power when it rejected its application as a society in 1997, and again in 2004. While in 1997 the government even failed to provide the reasons for the rejection, in 2004 it

Table 8.1 Important Opposition Parties in Singapore (as of 2006)

Party	Founded	Members in parliament
Workers' Party of Singapore (WP)	1957	Low Thia Khiang (elected) Sylvia Lim (nominated)
Singapore Democratic Party (SDP)	1980	-
National Solidarity Party (NSP)	1987	-
Singapore Democratic Alliance (SDA)	2001	Chiam See Tong (elected, member of Singapore People's Party)
Singapore People's Party (SPP)	1994	
Pertubuhan Kebangsaan Melayu Singapura (Singapore Malay National Organisation)	1965	
Singapore Justice Party (SJP)	1972	

Table 8.2 Selected civil society groups in Singapore

Group	Founded	Goal	Members
Nature Society of Singapore (NSS)	1992	Environmental issues	1,500
Association of Women for Action & Research (AWARE)	1984	Gender issues	400
Think Centre	1999	Political	20 (~8 active)
Association of Muslim Professionals (AMP)	1991	Ethnic (Malay)	unknown
Singapore National Front	1991	Ethnic (Malay)	unknown
Eurasian Association Singapore	1919	Ethnic (Eurasian)	2,952

asserted that the application was rejected because of the conservative moral values of the majority of Singaporeans (People Like Us 2005).

Organizational strength

The strength of the opposition in Singapore is hard to assess. It receives little support from major business groups and therefore has limited financial resources. However, its members and leaders have shown a determination that is remarkable. The following discussion will shed light on who the members and leaders of oppositional groups are, what reasons there are for joining the opposition, and how communication works within these groups and with the population at large.

Members

The members of Singapore's opposition are on average much younger than those of the ruling party. Moreover, most of them belong to the new middle class. As a whole, only a very few opposition members reveal themselves publicly in this role. In Singapore's sensitive environment, it is difficult to assess the support opposition parties have within the public at large. As Chua (1995: 660) has argued "being in the opposition can be a perilous activity in this small city-state where the state is pervasive in every sphere of social life." Thousands of people may attend opposition rallies during election periods,[1] because they can remain anonymous, but most people do not become involved in oppositional politics. This suggests that apathy cannot be the only reason for the lack of participation in formalized opposition.

There is a difference between groups who are trying to challenge the government on a specific issue, such as the Nature Society of Singapore, and those that have a much broader agenda as opposition parties or political pressure groups, such as the Think Centre. The latter tend to keep their formal membership numbers secret or very vague. The Workers' Party states on its website that the party has "a few hundred active members and the WP Youth Wing has about 100 members." One reason for the secrecy is probably the idea that the membership numbers would indicate strength or weakness. Since becoming a formal member of an opposition party in Singapore is perceived to be a personal risk, few are willing to join these parties (Lim 2007). It should be noted that this fear does not necessarily apply to those who do join. An informal survey of members of the Workers' Party, a moderate opposition party, shows that there is little fear for their personal careers among the party's activists.

Because membership in opposition parties can be risky, and in civil society groups is largely useless, Singaporeans have become apathetic. The lack of influence in politics has translated into a desire to focus solely on one's private life, which has led to the criticism that Singapore society is very materialistic. The lack of participation in politics is to the chagrin of the few politically active, as Melvin Tan (2002) of the Workers' Party makes clear:

Building a strong opposition or rather, stronger political parties, in Singapore, cannot be left to a few Singaporeans in the current alternative groups. If Singaporeans do not want to join or assist them, they should at least vote some of them into one or two GRCs.

(Tan 2002)

Because the author thinks Singaporeans want opposition parties but fail to support them, he blames the people for the opposition's lack of success. He attributes to Singaporeans a "not-in-my-backyard" attitude when they are too afraid to vote for the opposition in light of the threats from the ruling party. The article thus paints an essentially pessimistic vision for the future of opposition parties unless there is fundamental change in the attitudes of Singaporeans.

Leaders

The leaders of Singapore's oppositional groups are highly educated professionals of the rising middle class. The candidates of the Workers' Party for the 2006 election, for example, were mainly lawyers, teachers, and business people. Furthermore, on average opposition leaders are younger than those of the ruling party. The youngest candidate of the 2006 election, Abdul Salim bin Harun, a Malay, was just 25 years old when he contested the Ang Mo Kio GRC. The chairman of the Workers' Party, Sylvia Lim, born in 1965, is nearly 20 years younger than the chairman of the People's Action Party, Lim Boon Heng, who was born in 1946.

The leaders of the oppositional groups are well aware of their limited ability to influence the government. For example, the president of the Association of Women for Action and Research (AWARE), Tan Joo Hymn, said in 2006:

We have sent well-researched position papers to various ministers or MPs over the years, but there has not been much interest on their part to dialogue with us about our findings. There is a lack of an established tradition—unlike, for example, in the United States or even Britain—of politicians having dialogues with established non-governmental organisations. Changing the minds of Parliamentarians here is incredibly difficult.
(quoted in *ST* 28 Oct 2006)

The frustration is understandable because the organization has accomplished very little since its founding in 1985, despite adhering to the government's demand for well researched claims.

The disappointment of oppositional group members at not being able to influence the political system is partially the reason for the development of very different leadership choices among the active opposition parties. While the majority of opposition leaders favor moderate tactics, a few prominent figures in the movement have propagated a more aggressive approach in order to challenge the ruling elite's domination in parliament and in society. The differences between the leaders of the Workers' Party (WP) and the Singapore Democratic Party (SDP) provide an illustration of this variation.

At the time of the return of the opposition, the Workers' Party under the leadership of the late J.B. Jeyaretnam[2] was aggressively pushing for political change. In response, Chiam See Tong founded the SDP in 1980, with the goal of being only a "constructive" opposition in a democratic system. The major ideological claim of the SDP at the time was that the political system needed an opposition (Hussin 2004: 168–69). In 1993, Chiam's moderate leadership style proved to be problematic when a new member of the party, Dr Chee Soon Juan, was ousted from his university position for allegedly mishandling university funds and went on a hunger strike. Chiam was very displeased with Chee's tactics. However, he was challenged from within his own party and eventually had to concede the leadership to Chee. Chiam left the SDP and founded a new party, the Singapore People's Party (SPP).

The Workers' Party became more moderate over the years and J.B. Jeyaretnam was increasingly isolated within his own party, which was influenced by numerous lawsuits from the government. He resigned in 2001 because he was unable to maintain his NCMP when he could not pay the fines resulting from defamation lawsuits and was declared bankrupt. The relatively moderate Low Thia Khiang, who holds one of two elected seats in parliament, took over the position of Secretary-General.

The divergent leadership styles, however, are also the result of the ruling party's selective attacks on members of the opposition. Dr Chee Soon Juan is a case in point: when he joined the opposition he could not have expected to lose everything. Being a neurologist with ambitions in the scientific field, he most likely intended to remain part of the academic community. When he was sacked from his university post almost immediately after becoming a member of the Singapore Democratic Party for allegedly using money from his research fund to send his wife's PhD thesis to an American university, he blamed the government because the head of his department was a member of the ruling party (Hussin 2004). This case can be seen as reflective of a tactic that singles out individual members of the opposition and attempts to discredit them. Other prominent examples are Tang Liang Hong and James Gomez from the Workers' Party, who were singled out for a misstep that the ruling party could exploit. Comments from the past sufficed to brand Tang as a racist, and Gomez fell victim of an error he made while submitting his registration forms for the 2006 election, which was then trumped up on national television. For the government, this strategy has been very successful, because it has left the opposition in disarray.

Incentives: why do members join?

Unlike in Hong Kong, oppositional groups in Singapore have far fewer tangible incentives for members to participate. While Hong Kong's oppositional groups provided extensive social services, which were supported by the government, Singaporean groups, in contrast, are not able to provide similar incentives.[3] On the contrary, there are many disincentives, as joining the opposition means risking one's livelihood, which is closely tied to the state, and being monitored by the government (Chua 1995). Who would want to risk his or her material well-being by becoming part of the opposition?

Opposition parties provide members with an idealized vision of a perfect future, and the faithful members of these groups hope to achieve a perfect society. For most members of the registered opposition parties, the reasons for joining are mostly idealistic. They tend to emphasize the need to increase democracy and improve society. For example, Arthero Lim of the Singapore Democratic Alliance mentions his reason for joining an opposition party: "My political beliefs have always been 'serving for the larger good and social justice'" (Interview with Arthero Lim 2006).

Even though the influence of opposition parties is minimal, most of those who become members do so because they feel that the opposition is important and can have an impact on the policy-making process. For many of these young activists, the PAP has become too paternalistic and arrogant. One of the most important issues that motivate these members is the need for a tolerant and open decision-making process that does not exclude alternative opinions. They reject the ruling elite's belief that it is the only actor that is capable of finding the best solution. For example, Goh Meng Seng, a 37-year-old businessman and member of the Workers' Party, told *The Void Deck*:

> It was in 2001, on the run up to polling day, one PAP veteran in one heated argument over internet forums (soc.culture.singapore) has questioned me why I want to support the opposition parties that have no working faculties at all? This made me think hard and I come to the conclusion that I either shut up, pack up and emigrate or I join one credible alternative political party, contribute, make a difference and make it work.
>
> (Goh 2005)

The lack of power of these opposition parties apparently does not discourage young, idealistic members from joining. Goh asserts that while many of the younger generation, and especially those that are interested in public affairs, tend to emigrate, for the young idealistic writer this is not an option because he believes that he can "make a difference."

Communication network

Oppositional groups in Singapore are faced with a great number of restrictions on their ability to communicate with the masses, and even with their own members. This affects both pressure groups and political parties alike, even though groups with a specifically political goal have faced the greatest difficulty. When members of political parties want to hold a rally or give a speech, the government often refuses to grant a permit. An example of this occurred in 1999, when moderate opposition member Chiam See Tong wanted to give a political speech at a party anniversary dinner but was not permitted to do so (Gomez 2006).

Unlike in Hong Kong, Singapore's ruling elite has made it nearly impossible for oppositional groups to make strategic use of mass media to communicate their goals or mobilize for their activities. This contradicts Chan Heng Chee's 1975 argument that the newspapers in an "administrative state" allow the articulation of alternative viewpoints because opposition in the press is not organized. Since Chan's article, this has changed in Singapore, as the media has become virtually absorbed into the state in the form of government-linked corporations. At the same time, the development of the Singapore media has been one of centralization and monopolization. Furthermore, the government's tactics prompt self-censorship. An example for this is the out-of-bounds (OB) markers, which are used as warnings against those who overstep the line between permissible and impermissible criticism. This measure was first used against a critical letter-to-the-editor from the novelist Catherine Lim in 1994, in which she alleged that there was an affective divide between the government and the people. The arbitrary nature of this tool makes it difficult to know what constitutes illegal oppositional activity (Ho 2003). As a result, self-censorship is widespread and reporting in the press is overwhelmingly pro-government. In addition, the Singapore government has also used the threat of defamation lawsuits against the foreign press. It has made it clear that non-Singaporean media may not become involved in politics, and if they do they are fined or even banned. A recent case is the banning of the *Far Eastern Economic Review* after it published an interview with the opposition politician Dr Chee Soon Juan.[4] In 2008, the Singapore High Court found the journal guilty of defamation (*Reuters* 24 Sept. 2008).

Restrictions on the ability of opposition parties to communicate with the public even extend to their own publications. The Workers' Party, for example, has complained that it is always a challenge to get its party newspaper, *The Hammer*, published because it needs to pass the censors (Interview with Sylvia Lim 2005). A paper, however, is one of the best methods to reach a large number of Singaporeans and also the most important means by which the opposition parties can raise money. The Workers' Party paper, for example, costs S$2 (approximately US$1.30). With this paper, the party tries to reach out to all literate members of the society, as it is multi-lingual, with English on the front cover and Simplified Chinese on the back. The other two official languages, Malay and Tamil, are also used for articles, but their proportion of the overall newspaper is much smaller than English or Chinese. This corresponds to the ethnic proportion of the city-state. The articles in the various languages, moreover, are not translations but are targeted specifically at the four different official ethnic groups.

More recently, the communication network among members of the Singaporean opposition, and also among people who are sympathetic toward the opposition, has grown substantially, due to the introduction of the internet. Early attempts by the government to control online content have failed to stem the rising tide of criticism on the internet (Rodan 1998; Lee and Kan 2008). The major opposition parties have quite extensive websites with which they try to reach one of the most connected societies in the world (Rahim 2006a). The Singapore Democratic Party, for instance, publishes updates on party activities and criticism of the government nearly every day. The party has recently also introduced a policy discussion board on which it posts well-researched proposals which are open for public discussion.

In contrast, the Workers' Party's party website is updated less often and does not contain so much criticism. Instead, the Workers' Party mostly publishes the parliamentary speeches of its members, along with news and information about the party and its manifesto, in addition to its newspaper. The headings of the various articles do not summarize the main criticisms of the speeches and articles, which are mostly moderate and very technical. Even though the party has recently started to use Twitter, this has been used mostly to highlight party activities and not to criticize the government. Furthermore, unlike the SDP, the Workers' Party does not allow general users to leave comments on its website. The other political parties that have significant websites are comparable in content and design to that of the Workers' Party. The National Solidarity Party and the Singapore People's Party also publish speeches and news on their main pages, but their headlines are more concise. They also do not allow users to post comments on their site. This demonstrates that, except for the SDP, the opposition has not yet made full use of the potential of the internet, which has developed from information sharing to interactive communication. The careful approach of these opposition parties can in part be attributed to the unwillingness of the opposition to antagonize the ruling party.

The "imperial image" in Singapore: inability to imagine change

The socially constructed emotions and behavioral patterns that are associated with a stable "imperial image" can be seen in Table 8.3. First of all, there is a desire for stability, which, as in Hong Kong, guides members of the opposition. This is also coupled with a sense of powerlessness.

Second, many members of the fledgling opposition have spoken of a culture of fear, which is prevalent in the city-state. The government's repeated use of repression against the opposition, and the threat of future actions, have discouraged some people from participating in politics. This shows that the use

Table 8.3 Cognitive image of oppositional groups in Singapore

	Group strength	Emotions and policy disposition	Goals and tactic
Strong Imperial Image	split, weak	desire for stability, fear, avoid conflict, submission	reform goals and institutionalized tactics dominate

of selective repression can be very effective. Third, it will be shown that perceptions of inferiority have led to a tendency to conflict avoidance. When the government has been able to perform very well, oppositional groups in Singapore have largely accepted their inferior position in the political system. Most Singaporeans have, furthermore, largely avoided participating in politics. Finally, this has led to the submission of oppositional goals to those of the ruling elite. They have repeatedly abandoned their interests in favor of the so-called "national interest," which has been successfully defined by the government. This has therefore largely served to debilitate these groups.

The desire for stability

Similarly to Hong Kong, Singaporean citizens as well as members of Singapore's oppositional groups place great emphasis on the stability[5] and prosperity of the city-state. It is not easy for oppositional groups to not recognize the contributions of the ruling party and disagree with the PAP's motivations when they are economic growth, social harmony, and political stability. Dr Chee Soon Juan, arguably the most vocal dissident, has, like most in the Singaporean opposition, been an admirer of the modernization of Singapore. In 1994 he declared that "under the rule of the PAP, Singapore developed quickly. Its economy grew from strength to strength and became the envy of countries near and far" (Chee 1994: 3). And in 2001, he also noted: "There are many compliments that could be paid to Singapore, that it has an ultra-modern airport, pristinely kept gardens and parks, and even a competent civil service" (Chee 2001: 72). These two statements show that even a strong opponent of the Singaporean regime has to acknowledge the government's achievements in regard to the city-state's progress.

Economic growth has often played a crucial role in the writings of the opposition. The Workers' Party, for example, considers the goal of economic development to be the most important objective: "We recognise the absolute importance of maintaining and increasing Singapore's economic prosperity" (Workers' Party of Singapore 1988, 1994). At the same time, the Workers' Party agrees with many of the ruling party's priorities. For instance, it agrees with the PAP that Singapore's economy should be open. At the same time, the WP tries to distinguish itself from the ruling party by arguing that only a democratic system can truly guarantee this stability. The SDP agrees with this argumentation in its 2006 manifesto, when it states that "Democracy remains the surest way forward for nations yearning for progress and stability. Singapore is not exempted. To achieve this, major political reform cannot be avoided" (Singapore Democratic Party 2006b). The Singapore Democratic Party has, therefore, linked the government's strict controls and lack of transparency to the possibility that Singapore's stability is only a mirage (Singapore Democratic Party 2006c). The party thus tries to convince the Singaporean electorate that the present stability could easily disappear during an economic crisis. The lack of democracy in Singapore has not yet, however, led to instability or major conflicts. An average Singaporean might therefore conclude that there is no need for democracy or for opposition parties.

A major problem for the opposition is that in Singapore the ruling PAP is often associated with *economic growth* and *stability*, which makes it very difficult to articulate an alternative vision. This becomes evident in this quote from the news section of the Workers' Party website, which reports on party leader Sylvia Lim's dialogue with youths at the National University of Singapore's Political Association Forum on 30 March 2005:

> One participant asked where Workers' Party stood, since the ruling PAP stood for "economic growth and stability". Ms Lim observed that the GDP growth figures should be looked at more closely due to comparisons with years of low growth and due to concerns about the uneven distribution of growth among Singaporeans. One of Workers' Party's concern is that while it can see the rationale for being pro-business, this was carried very far, even at the expense of workers, as seen by the recent amendments to the Employment Act to remove certain rights of low wage-earners to being paid for extra work.
>
> (Workers' Party of Singapore 2005)

This shows that Sylvia Lim was not really able to provide an effective answer to the participants' question. It is not easy for the Workers' Party leader to make the case that her party is a better guarantor of stability than is the ruling party. Instead, she argues that not all Singaporeans have profited equally from economic growth—which may be factual, but which is a complicated argument many of her listeners may not have understood.

The sense of powerlessness

Singapore's opposition parties also have a strong sense of powerlessness. This naturally comes from the realistic assessment of the chances of the opposition. In an interview after the 2006 election, the Chairman of the Workers' Party, Sylvia Lim, expressed this sense of powerlessness:

Q: Did you feel that you were given justified media coverage during the elections?

A: I think this round, generally, the English and Chinese papers did not represent the Workers' Party in a bad light. And because of this, it affected voters' perception of us as well. So people started to think, "Hey, Workers' Party is not crazy." But then, we could have had more coverage vis-à-vis PAP, but that's the way things are.

Q: "The way things are." Is that a resigned statement or ... ?

A: It's born out of a sense of realism and also from having worked with people who have been in opposition politics longer.

(S. Lim 2006)

This exchange demonstrates that the opposition leader grudgingly accepts the inferior position of her party. Instead of being a visionary, she has chosen to be a realist and pragmatist. For this reason, the WP leader supports the idea of gradual change even though she also acknowledges that the "people are too resigned to the fact that the status quo will remain, that there's no inclination for change, and that's wrong" (ibid.). This sentiment is echoed by Dr Chee Soon Juan who writes that "the first step of liberating ourselves from PAP oppression is to recognise that we are not powerless" (Chee 2005: 8). Still, he argues that the sense of powerlessness prevalent in present-day Singapore is "crippling" any attempts to achieve democracy in Singapore.

This desire for stability cannot be regarded in isolation from the culture of fear. On the contrary, the apprehension of a common national threat has been the rallying tool of the ruling elite for the last 50 years. For this reason, we need to analyze how fear impacts on oppositional groups.

The "fear factor"

A number of members of the opposition have asserted that the fear[6] of becoming involved in politics is permeating activities of oppositional groups. Most Singaporeans, they charge, do not dare to get involved in politics because they are afraid that participation will lead to government retributions. For instance, J.B. Jeyaretnam told the parliament in an emotional speech: "I have found in this country a fear that grips our people" (Jeyaretnam 2000: 4). Another fervent opposition politician, Dr Chee Soon Juan, has also pointed to the fear that is part of Singaporean society. In 2001, he wrote: "Fear remains a firm feature of the national psyche" (Chee 2001: 34).

This fear is created through the threat of arrest without a warrant, the use of defamation suits to bankrupt members of the opposition, the attempt to link personal benefits (like upgrading of apartment blocks) to votes for candidates of the ruling party, and other tactics that aim to stifle the opposition. For Dr Chee, the most important reason for this fear is the government's ability to arbitrarily arrest anyone without a warrant.

> Even if there had been no ISA arrests (since 1987), such terror tactics need not be applied on a frequent basis. A single episode can have enough impact to re-instill the dread that a citizen may be hauled away at the whim of the government and find no recourse in the justice system.
>
> (Chee 2001: 36)

The government's use of "extreme tactics," such as suing the opposition or threatening an individual's job prospects, has also raised the level of fear, Dr Chee argues. He uses himself as an example to prove his case: after he had become a member of the Singapore Democratic Party he was sacked from his university position as a neuropsychologist for allegedly misusing a little over S$200. He was sued, and lost the case, in which the judge awarded the plaintiffs S$450,000. Dr Chee had to sell his house and other possessions. The fear of not finding a job discourages many from entering politics. It is therefore not surprising that many are afraid to become opposition candidates.

A survey conducted in 2000 revealed that 93 percent of Singaporeans are afraid to speak up in public against government policies that they oppose. At the same time, 62 percent prefer to complain to their friends and family about political issues (Leong 2000). Professor Eddie Kuo, Dean of the School of Communications Studies of Nanyang Technological University blames the government:

> Many are still afraid to disagree with the Government in public, due partly to the different signals the Government has sent in the past on how far they would tolerate them. This is not a desirable situation and the Government also knows that. More channels for people to air their views are expected to come.
>
> (quoted in Leong 2000)

At the same time, this fear appears to be less important in relation to elections, which are secret (even though all ballots are numbered). Despite threats against inhabitants of opposition wards during the 2006 general election, Singaporeans still voted for the opposition in those wards that were already represented by opposition members. This shows that fear alone cannot explain the PAP's continuing success in the polls.

Recently, some people in the opposition see a shift in the role of fear in the behavior of oppositional groups. One of them is Dr Geh Min of the Nature Society (Singapore), who said in 2004, at the time when she became a nominated member of parliament:

> A couple of decades ago, fear prevented people from speaking up. Then later, it was apathy. But we are in a very interesting time now, because PM Lee seems to want to be even more open and consultative in his style of government.
>
> (quoted in *ST* 3 Dec. 2004)

The environmental activist considers it a positive sign than an increasing number of people have shown a willingness to become nominated members of parliament. Singaporeans now consider it worthwhile to participate in politics. Goh Meng Seng of the Workers' Party sees a different shift that explains the unwillingness of Singaporeans to become more active in politics:

> It is not "fear" alone that prevented a mass support of Chee's protest moves. If Fear is that pervasive, there would not be tens of thousands of Singaporeans attending WP's political rallies in the last elections. The culture of "Fear" is definitely wading off but the fundamental desire of stability is still very much intact.
>
> (E-mail from Goh Meng Seng 2006)

The increase in members of the Workers' Party who actively participate in politics shows that fear does not play the same role as it did in the past. This is corroborated with a survey of members of the Workers' Party which showed that fear did not play a role in their decision to join the party.

However, at the same time it is important to note that these opposition members are careful about what they support and say. As long as the government uses repressive tactics against some of its critics, it is safe to assume that "the Singapore polity resonates with a climate of fear, which gives rise to the prevalent practice of self-censorship, to the extent that many avoid or even vilify participation in activities that are held in the public sphere" (Lee 2002: 103). In this context, the novelist Catherine Lim has even suggested that "the new model of governance is the systematic use of fear to silence existing dissident voices and discourage potential ones" (Lim 2007). Fear, furthermore, is still reflected in the behavior of the opposition, as Chia Ti Lik, former member of the PAP and the Workers' Party, argues in his profile. Furthermore, he states that "Fear is the last thing an opposition party should have. Fear is what paralyses a people when they face an arrogant and high-handed government" (Chia 2009). Despite this wish, however, the opposition continues to avoid conflict and submit its interests to those of the ruling elite. These two aspects of the "imperial image" are the focus of the following discussion.

An opposition that avoids conflict

This fear or apprehension of becoming involved in politics, coupled with a strong sense of powerlessness, is closely linked to a preference for avoiding conflict. Oppositional groups tend to go out of their way to refrain from antagonizing the ruling elite. This, of course, is the result of the government's use of lawsuits, bankruptcy, or just verbal insults against the opposition. Even apparently small signs of opposition are met with a disproportionate response. The Singaporean government's attitude to protests can be illustrated by its reaction to a minor public demonstration of discontent about an unopened MRT station, in the form of white paper-cut elephants. Even though a government minister saw nothing wrong in this kind of display, the police started a full-fledged investigation (Zakir 2006). The message was clear: Singaporeans do not protest, under any circumstances. It is therefore not surprising that many are trying to do everything to avoid potentially confrontational behavior toward the government.

The opposition parties, which not only draw their constituency from the population, but are also deeply rooted in Singaporean society, have also adopted a nonconflictual stance. Since the election of J.B. Jeyaretnam, most opposition parties have repeatedly stated that they intend to be a constructive opposition and, except during the last election, they have never contested more than half of the seats. This strategy was meant to send the signal that the opposition was not threatening the ruling elite's power.

Political discourse in Singapore has many examples of this kind of behavior. The opposition and the population have often accepted certain government rhetoric that is meant to weaken the opposition. One such attempt has been the government's claim that the opposition is only "opposing for the sake of opposing," which is repeated very frequently. For instance, Minister Lim Swee Say used this argument in his rebuttal of opposition MP Low Thia Khiang's criticism of the decision to allow the construction of casinos in Singapore:

> Sir, Mr. Low wants the WP to be a major party offering alternative visions for Singapore and strategies to Singaporeans. Yet on this important issue with long term implications, Mr. Low has no constructive ideas to offer. After a long silence, he now decides *to oppose for the sake of opposing*—not on principle or in the best interests of Singaporeans, but out of political interest of the WP; not as opinion leader, but as opinion follower.
>
> (Interview with S. Lim 2005; emphasis added)

This comment is interesting because it suggests that there is something like objective truth. The ruling party, it is suggested, does not act in terms of special interests but for the good of the people. In contrast, Lim accuses the Workers' Party of being partisans who are only interested in their own party's interest.

The opposition has by and large accepted the idea that partisanship is detrimental to the survival of Singapore. For instance, the Workers' Party has stated: "We did not set up the Workers' Party because we want to 'oppose' the government or oppose for the sake of opposing" (*The Hammer* 2002). This notion not only rejects partisanship but also entails the widespread belief that politicians must fulfill certain qualifications. Only a party that has highly educated members can be a credible opposition (*The Hammer* 2001). The opposition continuously strives to attract more qualified, i.e. more university-educated professionals, to join the party and become candidates. In turn, the government tries to discredit members of the opposition on the basis of their qualifications, even if they are highly educated. An example of this is the criticism of Workers' Party candidate James Gomez, a PhD student, for failing to fill out a form.

Furthermore, some self-confessed members of the opposition even reject the notion that the opposition's primary function is to act as a check on the government. Steve Chia, Secretary General of the National Solidarity Party (NSP) and Non-Constituency Member of Parliament at the time, told the parliament in 2002:

> Sir, by definition, I am from the Opposition. However, what am I opposing? We do not oppose for the sake of opposing. What is there to oppose if a policy is for the good of the people? If it is not good for

the people or the country, I believe many Government party members will join me in opposing such a policy. Are they then considered the Opposition as well?

(Chia 2002)

Chia even rejects the idea of "opposition" when he considers himself as someone who will not oppose policy that is for the "good of the people." While Chia avoids confrontation by conceding to the government with regard to the definition of what is good for the people, he even rejects the distinction between oppositional and ruling elite groups.

Aside of the SDP, a number of opposition members in other parties, however, are also in favor of a more confrontational politics. For instance, an argument in favor of a checks-and-balance system for Singapore was made in the Workers' Party paper, *The Hammer*:

We cannot sit in our comfort zone and hope for more able and qualified people to stand for election. We need to realise that for a candidate to win an election, it is not only his manifesto, ability and qualifications that count; the electorate would also want to see a strong team and grass-root support as well.

(Xin 2003)

This article stands in contrast to the majority of texts written by the Workers' Party. However, the use of a pseudonym (Xin Ren, presumably Chinese for "New Man") indicates the unwillingness of the author to identify herself. Perhaps the article constitutes an attempt to test the attitude of Singaporeans to this new approach. However, since no prominent politician has aggressively promoted this idea, there is not yet widespread support for it within moderate opposition parties. Instead of revealing a change in attitude, the use of a pseudonym again reflects the prevailing tendency to avoid conflict.

Finally, the avoidance of conflict can also mean voluntary exile. A number of opposition politicians have chosen to leave the country, often fearing for their own future or even life in Singapore. Tan Wah Piow, a student leader in the 1970s, for example, decided to move to Great Britain in 1976 after he was released from prison. Fearing for his life because he had been drafted into the artillery despite his physique, he chose to move to London, where he currently works as a very successful attorney (Tan 1987). Another prominent dissident who has emigrated is Francis Seow, solicitor-general from 1967 to 1971 and president of the Law Society from 1986 to 1988. When, under Seow's leadership, the Society criticized proposed amendments to the Newspaper and Printing Press Act, he was arrested in 1988 on the allegation that he had illegally received funds in support of the opposition. He was released after 72 days in prison. When he was invited to a meeting of Human Rights Watch in the United States he decided to become an exile (Seow 1998: 254).

Submitting to the "national interest"

An aspect of the opposition's nonconflictual attitude is its willingness to submit the groups' interests to that of the "national interest," even in the absence of a national crisis. The Workers' Party 2006 manifesto, for example, provides a very good example of this stance:

> WP is Pro-Singapore and believes national interest should precede party interest.
>   As such we would be prepared to support government policies if they are for the common good of the nation. However we will also not hesitate to take a confrontational stand against the ruling party when there is a need to do so.
>
> (Workers' Party of Singapore 2006)

The WP does not question what and who defines the national interest. Instead of proclaiming that the WP's interests are congruent with the nation, the statement suggests that there may be goals that are against the national interest. Since these are not mentioned, goals such as political rights or civil liberties could possibly be included. Furthermore, the party allows the government to define the national interest, which indicates the party's readiness to accept subjugation to the ruling elite. Even though the party makes the case for confrontation, this possibility is heavily circumscribed by the previous assertions. From this statement, it remains unclear how the party could legitimately oppose a certain policy if the government asserted that it was in the national interest.

Another aspect of the opposition's submission to the ruling elite is the acceptance of the notion that there are neutral, scientific, and objective solutions to problems facing the country. For this reason, the opposition has recognized the need to have highly trained individuals in politics. In the media, as well as in the writings of the opposition, there is still a tendency to compare the opposition unfavorably with the PAP in terms of talent. As a consequence, opposition parties have focused greatly on attracting highly educated individuals, and at the same time have neglected to mobilize the less-educated masses. While this reflects the notion that Singapore is a "meritocracy",[7] it also raises problems of legitimizing the existence of opposition parties. If the purpose of opposition is only to ensure the perfect functioning of the state, it minimizes the role of the opposition and seriously restricts its ability to challenge the government.

Goals

Reform goals

Similarly to Hong Kong, the goals of Singapore's oppositional groups also tend to be very moderate and overwhelmingly reform-oriented. The

Singaporean opposition rarely questions the political order. On the contrary, most oppositional groups have merely demanded reforms to the political system. It is therefore not surprising that opposition parties in Singapore can almost all be characterized as moderate, left-wing catch-all parties that have accepted most of the ruling elites' basic tenets and only demand improvement in the performance of the government. For instance, while the opposition recognizes the need for economic growth and stability, it tries to distinguish itself from the government by demanding a more equitable distribution of the country's wealth. However, even though almost all of the opposition parties demand that economic growth in Singapore should not be the sole domain of the wealthy few, they also do not demand radical changes in economic policy.

The 2006 Workers' Party manifesto exemplifies the kind of reforms that the opposition demands. It is structured under fourteen headings, covering a wide array of issues that face Singapore, from civil liberties to labor policy and the Central Provident Fund (CPF). The first point on the list concerns the role of government in relation to civil liberties, which is of central concern to opposition parties, which are almost completely excluded from the political system. The WP rightly points out:

> the PAP has consistently tinkered with the structure and processes of government to ensure minimal accountability to the public. Parliamentary elections have been organized such as to foster minimal participation from voters and minimal contest from alternative parties. Citizen activism is encouraged only if the PAP government "leads."
>
> (Workers' Party of Singapore 2006)

According to the WP, the problem in Singapore is not the political system per se but the way in which the PAP rules the country. The ruling party should not restrict citizens' ability to participate in politics. While the introduction of greater democracy could be regarded as revolutionary (see next section), the Workers' Party actually proposes that the ruling party should not abuse Singapore's political system in its favor. The party thus accuses the PAP of partisanship, which it also regards as detrimental to Singapore.

The focus on reforms also entails that the opposition's goals are often similar to those of the ruling party. For example, the WP demands that the bureaucracy should abide by the rules of professionalism and neutrality, which are an inherent aspect of the administrative state and reflect the government's own understanding. Furthermore, the party also considers multiracialism and meritocracy, which have been major concerns of the PAP government since the founding of Singapore, to be of great importance. It propagates a policy approach that is very similar to the rhetoric of the ruling party. Finally, the Workers' Party agrees with the ruling party on the importance of the military. It calls for improvement in the operations of the military not only by placing an emphasis on the acquisition of military equipment, but also in regard to the concerns of military personnel.

While the opposition agrees with the ruling elite in many respects, it also needs to explain what difference the opposition would make. For example, the moderate Workers' Party has stated:

> While it is true that WP and PAP may be fighting on the same platform for the country seeking the betterment of life of Singaporeans, the mindset, focus and considerations would be different in policy formulation.
>
> (Workers' Party of Singapore 2007)

The Workers' Party does not see any fundamental difference between its goals and those of the ruling party. Instead, the WP would bring important reforms to the political system that would enhance Singapore's success. In essence, the party argues that it would perform even better than the ruling party.

The emphasis on reforms has influenced the role of opposition parties in Singapore. While the WP is not in power and does not consider it realistic that it could gain power, it aims to function as a pressure group targeting political reforms. To this end, the party uses phrases such as "We urge the government … " to press for certain policy changes. The party's manifesto, furthermore, starts with a list of past policy proposals which the PAP has implemented:

> To begin with, WP is pleased to note that some of the ideas from our 1994 Manifesto have been implemented by the government. For instance, in the area of education, the government has implemented compulsory primary education and 10 years of formal education to equip our citizens with basic knowledge and academic skills. WP also proposed reducing the class size to 20 and is pleased that MOE is reducing the class size to 30 today.
>
> (Workers' Party of Singapore 2006)

With this opening, the WP emphasizes that it has been successful in convincing the government to adopt its suggestions. This type of statement not only gives the party a purpose, it also clarifies the role of the opposition in Singapore. While the party is not in power and unable to get into power, it can still act as a pressure group. This is especially important in Singapore, where pressure groups such as those in Hong Kong do not exist.

Revolutionary goals

There are very few voices that call for revolutionary change, and even those demands cannot be seen as a complete rejection of the present order. At most, opposition parties target the hegemony of the ruling party, the PAP, and those restrictions on political freedoms that are perceived to be an obstacle to a truly advanced society. The reason for this is mostly an idealistic optimism that a democratic society would be better capable of dealing with all of the country's problems. Democracy is rarely regarded as a process that enables the negotiation of divergent societal interests.

Because the government has successfully created the impression that it is able to solve all of the country's problems, the opposition has faced great difficulty in promoting the idea of democracy. To a certain degree, this impression has been strengthened by a media which is biased in favor of the government. The government has thus far been able to avoid any serious economic or political crisis. Most oppositional groups have therefore attempted to emphasize that democracy does not risk the prosperity of the city-state. The Workers' Party manifesto (1988, 1994), for example, stated: "Political authoritarianism does not just harm our standard of living. It also harms our quality of life. We need democracy and freedom of expression for our full cultural, social and personal development." In Singapore, oppositional groups such as the WP perceive democracy as the final fulfillment of the developmental state, which had to rely on authoritarianism for economic development. It is argued that once the country is developed, the strong state will slowly withdraw and allow the development of independent groups. To the chagrin of many in the opposition, the Singaporean rulers have decided to greatly limit the liberalization process, in order to maintain as much power as possible.

The most "revolutionary" party in Singapore is the Singapore Democratic Party (SDP), which aggressively advocates the introduction of liberal democracy and rejects ruling elite claims that Singapore needs a special Asian version of democracy. Furthermore, the party believes that democracy would be beneficial to economic growth because it enables entrepreneurs to be more creative, and consequently to create more jobs:

> Not only does democracy not hinder economic growth, it actually facilitates growth. We all know that creative thinking is what makes entrepreneurs successful, and it is through these entrepreneurs that jobs are created.
>
> (Singapore Democratic Party 2006d)

The SDP's rhetoric is targeted at the government's claim that democracy has a negative impact on growth and consequently leads to instability.

In recent years, Dr Chee has pushed more aggressively for liberal democracy, in order to amend the deficiencies in Singapore's developmental model. In 2001, he asserted that the government had not been instrumental in the development of the city-state after all. Instead, he attributed economic growth to the efforts of the people of Singapore:

> I have a confession to make. Like many Singaporeans, I have always been under the impression—until recently, that is—that the People's Action Party (PAP) is the reason that Singapore is the success story that it is today, and that without the party's leadership, the island would just be another impoverished economy trying to work its way out of a political malaise.
>
> (Chee 2001: 1)

While Singapore's success is undeniable, Dr Chee instead points to the increasing disparity between rich and poor as a serious shortcoming of the

PAP's developmental plan. The ruling elite, he asserts, is getting richer while the poor, who have no say in politics, are falling behind. Dr Chee's solution for problems like this is democracy. He compares authoritarianism with a building that lacks a fire exit. The fire exit, he says, may not be the most attractive part of a building, but it is essential. Democracy is needed in times of crisis because it provides this fire exit. He asserts: "Singaporeans, unfortunately, have been so busy focusing on accumulating material wealth that they have utterly and perilously neglected to construct the fire escape of democracy" (Chee 2001: 8). Dr Chee thus makes it clear that, in times of crisis, Singapore needs to have democracy in order to remain stable and prosperous. However, this functional understanding of democracy seems to be inaccessible to most Singaporeans, because Chee's claims have not yet been able to convince a significant number of people.

Tactics

Non-institutionalized tactics

In Singapore, the use of non-institutionalized tactics is exceptionally rare. From the mid-1970s there was not a single public protest, perhaps because they were closely linked to the possibility of a riot. The first public protest in a long time occurred in 2005, when four demonstrators stood in front of the Central Provident Fund (CPF) building to protest against the lack of transparency and democracy in Singapore. The protesters, who were closely aligned to the Singapore Democratic Party, were careful about obeying the law. They chose to send only four demonstrators, because this was the maximum allowed for an unregistered protest. Nevertheless, a police unit in riot gear was sent to the scene to disperse the peaceful demonstration. This was justified in terms of the interest of public safety. The protest was technically *not* non-institutionalized, because the activists attempted to stay within the framework of the law. The first non-institutionalized protest occurred in 2006, during the World Bank and International Monetary Fund (IMF) meeting, and was in clear violation of the law. The protesters had repeatedly asked for a permit for the protest, but had been rebuffed on each occasion.

Only recently, Dr Chee Soon Juan has argued in favor of breaking laws that obstruct the ability of the opposition to influence the political system and that therefore are not for the common good of society. He lists a number of laws in the Singapore context that he deems to be unjust: the Films Act, the Public Donations Act, Singapore Broadcasting Act, the Trades Union Act, the Parliamentary Elections Act, and the Internal Security Act (see Chapter 4 for an overview of these laws). In order to challenge the government, Dr Chee champions the methods of non-violence, as practiced by Mahatma Gandhi or Martin Luther King, to "pressure the PAP to give us back our rights of free speech and assembly" (Chee 2005: 64). The main tactic for achieving this goal, in the author's opinion, is the use of illegal assemblies, because mass demonstrations could show the discontent of Singaporeans and pressure the regime to change.

This change of tactic, mainly supported by Dr Chee Soon Juan and the Singapore Democratic Party, however, is still a very new and isolated phenomenon and cannot be seen as characteristic of the opposition. Many Singaporeans even frown on what appears to them to be extreme and unproductive behavior. The comment of Daniel Ong, a student at Nanyang University, can be seen as representative of the perception that many Singaporeans have of the outspoken dissident:

> He talked about the lack of freedom of speech and the widening income gap, especially between working Singaporeans and the ministers. His stirring speech made sense at times, at least for someone who heard him for the first time. However, what I failed to hear was anything concrete to remedy the problem or plans to improve the situation.
>
> ...
>
> It was no surprise that he found himself with so little support, at least from me. I simply cannot attach any credibility to a bankrupt opposition politician, much less want him running the constituency I live in. I want someone with credibility and action, not someone who gets into the headlines for all the wrong reasons.
>
> (Ong 2006)

Even though Dr Chee apparently delivered a "stirring" speech, the student's preconceptions are unchanged. He accepts the widespread notion that the activist should deliver an alternative, because only then would he be credible. His attitude is even condescending when he asserts that Dr Chee's speech only "made sense at times." The author is certainly unaware of the books that Dr Chee wrote in the 1990s. Furthermore, he credits the lack of wider participation in the activities of the democracy activist to a lack of credibility because he is "bankrupt." This, however, neglects the fact that the activist has been bankrupted because he was willing to challenge the government verbally. However, the text reveals the sentiments of many Singaporeans, who believe that protests are not a legitimate tactic when confronting the ruling elite.

So far, non-institutionalized tactics are very rare and are even seen as an aberration and dangerously radical by most members of the opposition. There was no one in the opposition, for example, who publicly voiced support for Dr Chee's unregistered demonstration. The rejection of non-institutionalized tactics seems to have weakened the oppositional movement, because its willingness to participate in government-sanctioned channels legitimizes the present system in which the opposition has virtually no influence on the policy-making process and in which opposition is seen as destructive to the survival of the nation. The various institutionalized forms of tactic for the opposition will be discussed in the following section.

Institutionalized tactics

While non-institutionalized tactics are a very new phenomenon and are also restricted to a handful of supporters around Dr Chee Soon Juan, the mainstream of the opposition favors the use of institutionalized tactics to achieve its goals. It is interesting that even Dr Chee and the SDP have not entirely rejected institutionalized tactics, as the party still contests elections. Its website explains this two-pronged approach:

> Boycotting elections is a worthy gambit if all opposition parties would cooperate and take a united stand. Given present circumstances, however, this is unlikely to happen. ... In the meantime the Singapore Democrats will take part in elections because election rallies are an important opportunity to reach out and educate the people of the strengths of democracy. We will not stop there, however. The SDP will also urge the proactive use of non-violent action to work towards reforming the election system.
>
> (Singapore Democratic Party 2006a)

The strategy of boycotting elections is rejected for two reasons. First of all, the SDP cannot find allies for this tactic and, being a very small party, its boycott would not make any impact. Second, elections provide the party with an important opportunity to reach out to the population. This shows that the party is worried that without institutional guarantees it will not be able to pursue its goals. At the same time, the party also advocates non-institutionalized tactics to press for institutional reform and not, as might be expected, for regime change.

Except for the 2006 illegal protest, the opposition has remained willing to adhere to the rules set by the system and the ruling PAP. The use of institutionalized means is often seen as the only legitimate way of challenging the ruling party's monopoly. Moreover, most members of the opposition reject tactics that include any action that bends or even breaks existing laws. The perception is that these laws cannot be broken, because their validity is generally accepted. For example, WP chairman Sylvia Lim recently said: "I'm idealistic, but I'm also a very practical person. So I would make sacrifices for my ideals, but still try not to break the law in doing that" (quoted in S. Lim 2006).

Perhaps the most common use of institutionalized tactics is the willingness of opposition members to become part of government institutions. Members of Singapore's oppositional groups have not only been elected to parliament but also been nominated by the government as Non-Constituency Members of Parliament (NCMPs) (opposition parties) and as nominated members (civil society groups) to serve in parliament (Table 8.4). Similarly to Hong Kong, this is an attempt to co-opt moderate members of the opposition into government institutions. Unlike in Hong Kong, the opposition at first rejected the possibility of nomination, because its main goal was to be elected to

Table 8.4 List of Non-Constituency Members of Parliament

Opposition member	Party affiliation	Duration
Dr. Lee Siew Choh	Workers' Party	1988–1991
J.B. Jeyaretnam	Workers' Party	1997–2001
Steve Chia	National Solidarity Party	2001–2006
Sylvia Lim	Workers' Party	2006–

parliament. While in 1984 the Workers' Party refused to select anyone to serve as an NCMP because it was a "second-class seat," the first opposition member to accept the offer was Dr Lee Siew Choh in 1988. After he was selected, he lost the backing of the Workers' Party and his overall influence waned. According to Hussin Mutalib, however, he performed well in parliament, where he was able to question many government bills (Hussin 2004: 328). In 1991 no one was selected as an NCMP because the opposition was able to get four members elected. The opinion of the opposition toward the scheme changed over time, so that in 1997 even the outspoken J.B. Jeyaretnam accepted the seat, reversing his earlier decision to reject the offer. In parliament he was not treated as an ordinary MP, because he did not receive any replies to his questions. The government's reason for this was that he was not representing a constituency (Hussin 2004: 329).

In 1989 the government introduced a similar scheme, the Nominated Members of Parliament, which became law in 1990, with the difference that NMPs are required to be free of party affiliation. The continuing success of the opposition at the polls was a major reason for the introduction of the scheme. Deputy Prime Minister Goh Chok Tong made it clear during the second reading of the bill that the scheme was meant to "evolve a more consensual style of government where alternative views are heard and constructive dissent accommodated" (quoted in *ST* 30 Nov. 1989: 18). The word "consultative" is especially important because it suggests that elected members of parliament are too contentious. The nominated members of parliament are supposed to be interested only in "constructive dissent" and not to challenge the government. Goh therefore makes it clear that the scheme is intended to create an opposition that is supportive of the regime.

The nominated members are selected by a PAP-dominated committee, which means that the NMPs have to fulfill qualifications set by the PAP. Since NMPs are only nominated for two years, after which they may be renominated, they tend to avoid being overly critical. Hussin Mutalib illustrates this with a comparison of two NMPs, namely Chia Shi Teck and Associate Professor Walter Woon. While the former voiced his criticism in parliament and dared to challenge the ruling party, the latter became a supporter of the regime. His "comments in parliamentary debates made him to be perceived by the general public (perhaps incorrectly) as someone who had converted to the cause of the Establishment" (Hussin 2004: 332). Chia Shi Teck was not renominated when his two years were up, while Walter Woon later became ambassador to Germany and Belgium.

While the NMP scheme excludes members of the opposition parties, members of Singapore's newly emerging civil society have been selected for this position. In 1992, the one-time president and founding member of AWARE, Dr Kanwaljit Soin, was chosen as NMP. In December 2004, the president of the Nature Society (Singapore), Dr Geh Min, was also selected. She commented on her reasoning for accepting this position despite the fact that there is a widespread perception that NMPs lack power:

> I am aware of that criticism, and I must say I partially agree which is why I didn't come in earlier. But past NMPs have shown that the nominated position is not a purely nominal one.
>
> I keep reminding myself that I am not representing my own personal views or pushing narrow interests, that I must represent as large a section of people as possible.
>
> (quoted in: *ST* 3 Dec. 2004)

While the ability of NMPs to affect the policy-making process is very limited, the civil society activist argues, it is still better to become part of parliament, because she can potentially influence some legislation. Furthermore, the environmentalist sees her role in parliament not as a representative on environmental issues but rather as someone who will serve society at large. Environmental issues or her own views are described as "narrow interests," and are therefore rejected.

Even though Dr Geh Min has rejected the notion of pressure group politics, she has focused on environmental and women's issues while in parliament. Speaking about a bill to limit the import and export of endangered species, which she considered an issue of "national security," she remarked: "I would like to clarify that I am not talking about protecting animals against people. ... I am going to concentrate on protecting people from wildlife" (*Singapore Hansard* 17 Jan. 2006). Despite its being a purely environmental issue, the environmental activist attempted to frame it as an issue for society at large. In this debate, Dr Geh was able to claim success.

In another debate, however, she was not successful. She had argued for a central coordinating body to protect marine life and bio-diversity in the southern islands, but the government rejected her proposal for financial reasons. In response, Minister for Trade and Industry Heng Chee How argued that the primary considerations of the Singapore government were economic. Environmental studies would be done on a case-by-case basis when the need arose (ibid.). These kinds of studies, however, have the disadvantage that they are conducted at the discretion of the government and that the influence of outside actors is restricted. A central coordinating institution could have provided environmental groups with greater influence in issues concerning the protection of the ocean.

Civil society groups thus far have been very careful in their approach to the government. They differ greatly from the pressure groups that influenced Hong Kong politics in the 1970s. The Nature Society's former president, Associate Professor Wee Yeow Chin, for example, has rejected the term "pressure group" because his group's objective is merely that of sharing information with the government. He argues, "(w)e are level-headed and look at things rationally," suggesting that pressure groups are not rational (quoted in *ST* 2 Oct. 1993). The pro-government *Straits Times* explained the Singaporean type of civil society groups:

> It is an approach that differs markedly from how the rich and powerful lobby groups operate in the United States. There, they fund political parties and even set the agenda. The Singapore way, on the other hand, is quiet advocacy and public consultation, say political watchers.
>
> (Ibid.)

Even though civil society groups have had very little influence on government policy, there has been an increase in group activity which targets policy changes. The almost exclusive use of institutionalized tactics, however, has not significantly increased the influence of oppositional groups.

Conclusion and outlook

The ruling elite groups in Singapore have been exceptionally successful in containing contention. The opposition has accepted that economic growth and stability are the most important goals of a government. At the same time, the inability to influence the policy-making process has engendered a strong sense of powerlessness. Furthermore, the government has also created fear within the opposition, which has created insecurity regarding the limits of opposition. Potential members of the challenger groups have been deterred from joining opposition parties for fear of a harsh government response. Many oppositional groups, furthermore, have been careful in avoiding direct confrontation with the government. This has even led some to subordinate their interests to those of the ruling elite groups.

We can see from the choice of goals and tactics that the opposition has been unable to increase its strength vis-à-vis the government. Moderate, reform-oriented objectives dominate much of the opposition's rhetoric. The opposition recognizes the successes of the government and sees democracy only as the final step toward the status of a fully developed nation.

In terms of tactics, Singapore's opposition is deeply divided. Even though some propagate more aggressive, non-institutionalized tactics, this kind of approach is rejected by most oppositional groups. They attempt to exert pressure on the government through participation in elections, through nomination to parliament, or through their publications. The fear of a strong social-control response makes these groups very careful in their interactions with the ruling elite groups. However, the lack of a direct challenge to the government has seriously weakened these groups. The isolation of the few individuals who propagate faster and more revolutionary change has resulted in deep division into small, separate oppositional groups.

The next and final chapter looks at the goals and tactics of the political groups in the two city-states from a comparative perspective. While the opposition in Hong Kong did not shy away from non-institutionalized tactics, oppositional groups in Singapore have almost always stayed within the institutional framework. I will argue that this can in part be attributed to the varying success of the two government's strategies of co-option and coercion. Furthermore, the effective implementation of government programs has also had an impact on the oppositions' choices of tactic. The book will conclude by looking at possible future scenarios for the two city-states.

9 Comparing ruling elite strategies in Hong Kong and Singapore

Implications for the future

While Hong Kong experienced a rising opposition movement in the 1970s and 1980s, Singapore's leaders have successfully contained nearly all contentious politics in the city-state. This occurred in a climate in which ruling elite and oppositional groups both share similar goals. While the oppositional groups usually stress reform goals over revolutionary demands, Singapore and Hong Kong's rulers prioritize economic growth and government efficiency (Table 9.1). The main difference between these two states can be found in the tactics of the oppositional and ruling elite groups. While Hong Kong's leaders opted most often for co-option and the opposition relied mostly on non-institutionalized tactics, such as protests, sit-ins, or strikes, Singapore's rulers have been much more willing to resort to repression when necessary and opposition has been largely resigned to remaining within the institutional framework. These strategies have had an impact on the differences in the organizational structure of the two opposition movements. While Hong Kong's challengers had enough funding to finance social activities, Singapore's opposition has difficulties even in financing election deposits and campaigns.

While the differences in the tactics of the ruling elites partially explain why the opposition opts for certain tactics, another reason needs to be taken into account, namely the ability of the government to achieve its goals. The two cases demonstrate that it is much more difficult for Singapore's opposition to argue or even protest for greater democratization than it was the case in Hong Kong. This can be attributed to government efficiency and effectiveness in fulfilling the demands of the population, which demonstrates why performance legitimacy plays such an important role for these authoritarian regimes

Table 9.1 Comparison of goals and tactics of oppositional and ruling elite groups

	goals	tactics
Hong Kong ruling elite	progressive	moderate
Singapore ruling elite	progressive	balanced
Hong Kong opposition	reform	non-institutionalized
Singapore opposition	reform	institutionalized

with democratic features, which Stubbs (2001) has called "soft-authoritarian" regimes. It should be noted that government performance can also be influenced through persuasive propaganda, which requires control over the media, as the case of Singapore shows. In reverse, this also means that conspicuous government deficiencies can be instrumentalized to challenge the ruling elite.

These conclusions allow us to propose different scenarios for the future development of contentious politics in the two city-states. On the one hand, Hong Kong's democracy movement reached its zenith when it was able to mobilize about 500,000 people on 1 July 2003 (*SCMP* 2 July 2003). Since then, support for the movement has ebbed somewhat (Chan 2008) and the future of the opposition largely depends on the government's willingness to proceed with the introduction of popular elections to the Chief Executive by 2017 (delayed from the original date of 2007) and also on the government's ability to provide efficient and effective government. In contrast, recent increases in contentious politics in Singapore, coupled with repeated government missteps, could be indicative of greater contention and perhaps democratization in the future.

Balancing co-option and coercion

Modernization increases the demand for greater participation among the more educated members of the middle class. This can lead to contention, which poses a potential challenge for authoritarian regimes that aim to monopolize the national agenda. Consequently, the ruling elite groups must devise methods that are designed to weaken organized political opposition. The two cases demonstrate that the governments have had differing success in weakening oppositional groups. Both governments have attempted, on the one hand, to co-opt members of the opposition into the government and, on the other, to use force against selected members of the opposition. The comparison reveals that these two tactics have to be carefully balanced in order to have the desired result. The case of Singapore clearly demonstrates that, in order to be successful, co-option has to be applied whenever possible, coercion when absolutely necessary. In contrast, the Hong Kong government was forced to rely mainly on co-option because its self-proclaimed liberal attitude restricted the use of coercion.

Since the leaders in Singapore and Hong Kong believe that persuasion provides the best remedy against political competition, they have most often opted to co-opt dissenting voices into the institutional framework. To this end, both city-states have first of all tried to entice members of the opposition to participate in government institutions. In Hong Kong, there were nominated Unofficials in the Legislative and Executive Councils, and in Singapore, the government introduced nominated members of parliament (NMP) and non-constituency members of parliament (NCMP). Furthermore, co-option is also achieved through active participation in elections. In Singapore, all opposition parties take part in elections even though these are skewed heavily in favor of the ruling party. In Hong Kong, elections to the Urban Council, an institution that had little influence, also provided an institutional outlet for opposition members. Furthermore, in both cases the governments institutionalized a number of feedback channels, which were to foster consultation between the government and the people and thus intended to replace the need for representative government. In Singapore, the government established, among others, the Feedback Unit, Consultative Committees, and Meet-the-MP sessions. In Hong Kong in the 1970s, examples of feedback institutions were the City District Officers (CDOs) Scheme, Advisory Boards and Councils, and the UMELCO office.

The demand for more activists to be nominated to government positions, which would supposedly increase the representation of the population, even often originated from members in the opposition. The opposition was convinced that greater representation in these positions would increase its influence over the policy-making process. It is thus not surprising that it was often willing to accept or even actively seek these positions. In Hong Kong, elected members of the Urban Council and pressure group activists regarded nomination to the Legislative Council as an important step in the direction of a more representative government (Chapter 7). In Singapore, members of the opposition have similarly accepted nomination as non-voting members to parliament. Even the most vocal opposition member of the early movement, J.B. Jeyaretnam, has accepted the position of NCMP, even though he rejected it at first (see Chapter 8).

However, the rising political contention could not entirely be absorbed into the present institutions and therefore the ruling elite groups in both city-states felt forced to apply coercion against members of the opposition. In Singapore, repression of the opposition enabled the People's Action Party to take control of almost all aspects of the state. This started with the arrest of opposition members during Operation Cold Store in 1963 (Haas 1999), continued with the incorporation of the labor movement into a close tripartite union with the government during the mid-1960s (Rosa 1990), and was completed with the repression of student protests in 1974 (Tan 1987) and the termination of an independently owned press in 1977 (Mauzy and Milne 2002). While particularly in the first half of 1970s, the Hong Kong government was more reluctant to apply outright repression against oppositional groups, the government increasingly used repressive tactics in the latter half of the 1970s (Chapter 5).

The two governments have employed the tactic of co-option and coercion with differing levels of success. The reason for this can be found in the way coercion was framed. In Hong Kong, the use of coercion was regarded as an illegitimate act on the part of the government because it attempted to radicalize what was normal, such as peaceful protests and pressure groups. The frequent assertion that the government was acting against "troublemakers" did not succeed in legitimizing coercion. The overwhelmingly negative reaction to the institution of the Standing Committee on Pressure Groups (SCOPG) is a good example for this (Chapter 5). In contrast, the Singaporean government has largely succeeded in framing coercion as a necessary tool against radical opposition, even though these "extremists" are rather moderate in their demands and tactics. This has contributed to a split within the opposition, as it pits moderates against more outspoken members. The Singaporean government constantly fine-tunes its approach and, as Garry Rodan (2006a: 5) observes, "beginning from around the early–mid 1980s, more technocratic, administrative and legalistic techniques and ideologies of state political repression and co-option emerge." As a result, while the government tends to attack all members of the opposition, it makes things easier for less contentious members. Repression is reserved to those who are regarded as threatening to the political regime. In this context, non-institutionalized tactics, such as public protests or strikes, are completely delegitimized. Furthermore, the limits of opposition are kept very vague. There are, for example, the so-called "OB markers" (out-of-bound markers) for deviating opinions, which were first issued against Catherine Lim, a Singaporean novelist, for suggesting that there was an "effective divide" between the PAP and the people (Lim 1994). Prime Minister Goh Chok Tong told Lim that if she wanted to state her political views in public she should join a political party (*ST* 17 Dec. 1994). The uncertainty created by measures such as these is supposed to discourage individuals from publicly voicing alternative viewpoints that the government disagrees with.

The reason for the differences in the ability of the ruling elite groups to balance co-option and coercion lies in the historical roots of the two city-states. Since Singapore is an independent country, the first generation of the ruling elite was also the founding generation and so the ruling party could rely on its nationalist origins. In contrast, Hong Kong's colonial regime could not localize as much as would have been necessary to control the society in a similar way. It was, therefore, a combination of fortuitous events and a deliberate strategy on the part of the Singaporean ruling elite that allowed it to monopolize power. However, maintaining this control and continuing to contain political contention also means a strong reliance on performance legitimacy, as the following section will show.

Successful regime performance

Even though the ability to carefully balance co-option and coercion is an effective strategy for reducing political contention, regime performance is also crucial for the strength of modernizing and industrializing "soft-authoritarian" regimes such as Singapore and Hong Kong, because they depend on performance legitimacy (Stubbs 2001). In Singapore, Chan Heng Chee argued in 1971 that "The survival of the political system will depend on the ability of the leadership to handle both the economic and political problems so that the established political order will be accepted as effective and legitimate and a change of system will be unnecessary." (Chan 1971: 11). Most of the people of the two city-states during the 1970s and early 1980s approved of their government because it was able to guarantee prosperity and stability. Furthermore, rapid economic growth led to significant improvements in the living conditions of most of the people.

The ruling elite's emphasis on performance has the consequence of fostering congruence between its goals and those of the opposition. Both aim for improvement of society and the economy for the benefit of all people. This is reflected in the fact that almost all oppositional groups in Singapore and Hong Kong reject partisanship, pursue mostly reform-oriented goals, and do not want fundamental changes. In Hong Kong during the 1970s and 1980s, the demand for greater democratization was not a call for a fully elected Legislative Council. Democracy activists in the 1970s instead demanded a greater share of elected members on various councils and a widening of the franchise. In Singapore, most members of the opposition have until recently claimed that they want to be a constructive opposition and are not intent on replacing the ruling party (Vasil 2000). This changed in the 2006 election, when the opposition contested more than half of the seats.

During times of relatively good government performance, there is a lack of broad support for oppositional groups. Because the democratic opposition regards democracy as the panacea for all of society's problems, it needs to convince the public that the tactics (soft-authoritarian methods) and not the goals (good government) of the ruling groups need to be changed. However, in the meantime, the opposition does not fundamentally question the legitimacy of the political regime and therefore contributes to its strength.

The two city-states demonstrate that the level of regime performance has an influence on the development of opportunities that allow oppositional groups to increase their influence. Modernization processes, such as an increasingly complex political system and a rising middle class, lead to challenges for the ruling elite groups. The question of whether these challenges will translate into opportunities for the opposition depends on the ability of the ruling elite to deal successfully with these challenges. Inefficiencies in government policies slowly undermine the legitimacy of the government, which, in turn, results in opportunities for challengers. For instance, shortcomings in government policies provided opportunities for Hong Kong's opposition during the 1970s, when it increasingly considered it to be its task and even duty to challenge the government for the benefit of the society. In contrast, in Singapore, the successful implementation of government policies did not create the same number of opportunities. However, there were instances, such as after the proposal to introduce the Graduate Mothers Programme, when the opposition was empowered to challenge the regime, which resulted in electoral gains.

Regime performance should not, however, be regarded merely as an objective criterion. On the contrary, the perception of regime performance is just as crucial. The representation of the government in the media, for instance, has a great effect on the interpretation of its performance. While a free press in Hong Kong often reported on government shortcomings, Singapore's press is overwhelmingly pro-government, as its role is to help in the nation-building process and not to critically examine government policies. Furthermore, attempts to blame individuals or circumstances beyond the control of the government for failures increase its capacity to demonstrate effectiveness. In Hong Kong, the threat from Communist China enhanced the government's prestige in the eyes of Hong Kongers, many of whom were refugees from China. The Singaporean government often blames shortcomings on individual scapegoats. For example, when Mas Selamat Kastari, a terrorist suspect who planned to crash a hijacked plane into Changi Airport, escaped from his detention center in Singapore on 27 February 2008 (*ST* 27 Feb. 2008), many bloggers considered this a failure on the part of the government (*Agence France-Presse* 3 March 2008). A massive manhunt failed to recapture the suspect. After two months, the government tried to blame individuals at the prison for the failure. On 27 May 2008, nine officers and guards were penalized for the security lapse. Furthermore, the superintendent of the facility was relieved of his post (*ST* 27 May 2008).

The ability of the ruling elite groups to deal with the challenges of modernization, industrialization, and the growing complexity of the political system partially explain the differences in the level of contentious politics. When viewed comparatively, the Singaporean government has been far more successful in achieving its goals than was its Hong Kong counterpart. This can be exemplified with reference to the strategies of the two governments in regard to the serious housing problems that were widespread during the onset of modernization. For the Singapore and Hong Kong governments housing was a top priority. When we compare their two programs and their effect on the legitimacy of the government, it becomes evident that shortcomings provided opportunities for oppositional groups. In Singapore, the government's Housing Development Board (HDB) built too many units in the 1980s, which partially explains the 1985–86 economic crisis. This crisis also provided the opposition with an opportunity (Castells et al. 1990). However, from the point of view of political mobilization, building an excessive number of houses was not seen to be as problematic as building too few, as was the case in Hong Kong. In the British colony, the issue of housing played an important role in a number of disputes during the 1970s and 1980s, many of which dealt with the shortage of public housing estates. Because Singapore's public housing program was much more successful than Hong Kong's, the government was able to secure the support of a majority of Singaporeans (Yeung and Drakakis-Smith 1982).

The reason for this difference can be found in the state capacity of the two city-states. While Hong Kong's government in the 1970s promoted "positive non-interventionism" (which justified the increasing involvement of the state in society when it was necessary to maintain social stability), it could not match the Singapore government's developmental state, which was closely linked to society (Cheung 2008). As is the case in the ability of the ruling elite groups to balance co-option and coercion, historical origins also influenced this outcome. Due to the colonial nature of the Hong Kong government, it was not able to act with the same decisiveness and conviction as did Singapore's government. The Hong Kong rulers of the 1970s and 1980s were largely expatriates, who needed the support of the Chinese business elite. In contrast, the Singaporean government, which conducts periodic elections, is able to claim a mandate and act in the "interest of the nation." The ruling elite groups in Singapore were thus also marked by greater cohesiveness than their counterparts in Hong Kong. This enabled the former to concentrate on developmental goals while the latter's still dominating laissez-faire attitude severely limited the government's capacities.

Future scenarios

It is always risky to venture predictions about the future, especially in cases of political development, which to a large degree depend on the political decisions of individuals, as this book has shown. Based on the developments in Hong Kong in the 1970s and early 1980s, it is possible to make some suggestions as to the future political development of Hong Kong and Singapore. The question will be whether the relationship between the oppositional and the ruling elite groups will drastically change in the future. First we will consider the possibility of renewed authoritarianism in Hong Kong and a weakened democracy movement. Despite recent setbacks for the activists and a declining interest in the issue of democracy within the population, some scholars remain optimistic about the future of the movement (Sing 2009). Then we will turn to Singapore, where recent increases in political activity could be interpreted as a precursor of the development of a strengthened democracy movement. This would follow the predictions of some authors such as Chua Beng Huat, who considers political contention an "unavoidable political effect ... of capitalist development" (Chua 1994: 667). Furthermore, Inglehart and Welzel predict that Singapore will democratize by 2015, because "it is producing a social infrastructure that should give rise to growing demands for democracy" (Inglehart and Welzel 2005: 160–61).

Declining interest in democracy in Hong Kong after 2003

Even though this study has compared Singapore with Hong Kong during the 1970s and 1980s, developments during this time also enable us to evaluate Hong Kong's present situation and suggest future developments. After Hong Kong's reversion to the mainland, the already growing active democratization movement gained worldwide attention when it was able to draw around 500,000 people onto the streets in 2003. However, since its zenith in 2003, amid poor performance by then Chief Executive Tung Chee Hwa, its importance has again declined. When the Hong Kong government postponed the introduction of universal suffrage for the election of the chief executive from 2007 to 2017, activists could not mobilize as many people as before. For many, the issue of democracy became less important. This section first returns to 1984 and traces the rise of the democracy movement and then attempts to answer the question why interest in democracy seems to fade after 2003 and what this means for the future of the democracy movement in Hong Kong.

The era after the 1984 Joint Declaration to return Hong Kong to the Chinese government by 1997 was a time of great change. First and foremost, the decision to hand over power created a "lame duck" administration for 13 years. This can be regarded as a legitimacy crisis for the government, and had a significant impact on the relationship between ruling elite and oppositional groups (Scott 1989). Middle-class intellectuals became disenchanted with the government because they had not been consulted on the negotiations between the PRC and Great Britain over the future of the colony. These intellectuals had developed a strong affinity to the city-state, which found expression in the so-called "Hong Kong Man" (Lo 1997: 105) and the Hong Kong identity (Tsang 2004). This group felt that the British government should not have made the concessions that it did in the Sino-British Agreement. At the same time, this period has to be seen as the conclusion of the transition from colonial rule to self-government—without, however, resulting in independence.

These political developments had a great influence on the behavior of oppositional groups in Hong Kong. Legislative Councilor Rita Fan said in 1985: "Hongkong is entering a new era. We Hongkong people will take up the responsibility of administration while other people only play a secondary role" (quoted in Leung 1985). It was thus a moment that was seen by the people of Hong Kong as an opportunity to become more involved in the way in which the city-state would be governed. The rise of public protests (Table 9.2) and the increase of social conflict (Table 9.3) after 1984 clearly show this shift in the mindset of the people. The newly found opportunities provided a welcome basis for oppositional behavior.

This had the result that some pronounced apathy a "myth of the past" (Choi 1985), but the 1985 elections still only motivated half a million, or 37.5

Table 9.2 Public protests in Hong Kong between 1984 and 1989

	1984	1985	1986	1987	1988	1989
No. of applications	69	191	251	264	375	497
Disallowed	7.2%	1.6%	2%	1.9%	2.1%	1%

Source: Adapted from Wong 1990.

Table 9.3 Number of social conflicts in Hong Kong 1984–1989

Year	1984	1985	1986	1987	1988	1989	1990	1991	1992	1993	1994	1995
#	70	80	136	300	322	525	509	358	462	410	404	362

Sources: Adapted from Cheung and Louie 1991:10; Lau and Wan 1997: 7

percent of the population, to cast their vote—even less than in the 1982 District Board election (Staff reporters 1985). The result can be blamed in part on confusion over the true influence of the District Boards in policy making. There were still few guidelines on how the process of consultation was to be institutionalized. Another reason for the low turnout was the fact that elected members remained in the minority. Despite these shortcomings, the government considered the voter turnout a victory: "It has often been said in the past that Hongkong could not introduce democracy because its people were not ready: obviously this axiom is no longer true" (Yang 1985). That year was also the first time that members of the Legislative Council were elected from functional constituencies and members of the urban and regional councils. In other words, only a few hundred people were eligible to cast their votes.

Another event that proved significant for the behavior of oppositional groups was the 1989 Tiananmen massacre. According to the *New York Times*, tens of thousands of people protested in Hong Kong against the Beijing government's violent crackdown on student protesters (Bernstein 1989). The event also altered British policy toward Hong Kong (Lo 1997: 109). In the years between 1989 and 1997, the colonial government pushed more aggressively for greater democratization. Immediately after 1989, many in Hong Kong supported the British colonial government in its belated push for greater democratization. The people favored the drafting of a Bill of Rights for Hong Kong and demanded to be allowed to emigrate to Britain if they so chose. For instance, the "Hong Kong People Saving Hong Kong Campaign" united a great number of prominent politicians immediately after the incident (Ching 1994). Consequently, the Hong Kong government introduced a number of institutional changes after 1989. For example, the first direct elections of the Legislative Council took place in 1991.

However, demands for stability and prosperity continued to play a central role in the political discourse. They were seen as key factors for the vitality of the territory. They formed the fundamental principles of the Basic Law, which became the new de facto constitution of the future Special Administrative Region (SAR). Democratization was seen as a guarantor of this stability. Greater democracy could guarantee continuing autonomy, which, in light of the potential dangers of Communism, was considered crucial in maintaining prosperity.

After 1997, support for Chief Executive Tung Chee-hwa, handpicked by the Beijing government and then elected by an electoral college of 400, quickly evaporated as it became clear that he lacked the legitimacy to introduce policies that would enhance his ability to strengthen his performance legitimacy (Scott 2007). Only six years into his administration, the issue of passing security legislation, as stipulated by Article 23 of the Basic Law, met with strong resistance from democracy activists and the population. The opposition was successful in framing the issue as a grave threat to the stability of the territory, and on 1 July 2003 around 500,000 people took to the streets to mobilize against the law. The protesters were successful when the government backed down from passing the law after James Tien of the pro-Beijing Liberal Party resigned because he had wanted the controversial legislation delayed (*SCMP* 8 July 2003). Eventually, discontent with Tung's performance led to his resignation in March 2005.

Since the resignation of Tung Chee-hwa and the election of Donald Tsang, support for the Chief Executive has significantly improved. For instance, support for the Chief Executive in February of 2009 was at 54.9 percent, even though this was a significant decline on the previous year, and was down from 71.4 percent only four years earlier (U.S. Department of State 2006). In terms of co-optation, the government has greatly enhanced its support among the business community, which, since the weakening of the Liberal Party, has become more closely aligned with the pro-China faction (Sing 2009). However, the government's connection to society continues to be weak and lacking in political trust (Cheung 2008). So far, the post-colonial government has successfully curtailed the introduction of greater democratization in Hong Kong. At the same time, Hong Kongers are still easily mobilized for political campaigns when there are salient issues. However, there is potential for a renewed depoliticization of society, should the government appear to be successful in the management of society and the economy, and increasingly use co-optation or repression against its critics.

In the 2008 election for the Legislative Council, the pro-democratic camp of political parties was able to hold on to its majority of seats even though its overall number of seats declined from 25 to 23. Furthermore, the election results fell short of the massive support needed for pressuring the Chinese government to accede to the demands of full democracy. Sing Ming (2009), however, argues that these election results should not be regarded as a defeat for the democracy movement and that activists are still able to promote the cause of democracy. There are a number of signficant challenges to the democrats, such as possible voter intimidation, deliberate use of scandals, the greater financial resources of pro-Beijing parties, deepening links between local businesses and the mainland, and the bias toward pro-China parties in functional constituencies. Furthermore, there is a slow erosion of free speech, as became evident with the resignation of three radio show hosts in 2004 after they had received threats from the Chinese government and organized crime. In addition, most of the media in the Special Administrative Region lean toward the pro-Beijing front (Cheng 2005).

The future development of Hong Kong must take the "China factor" into account. Any demand for greater participation must also secure the approval of Beijing, which needs to recognize Hong Kong's potential as a model for the People's Republic. Furthermore, the PRC must also be convinced that a democratic Hong Kong is nothing to fear. Under present conditions, this is not so much a molehill as a steep mountain to climb. If Hong Kong's democrats can make it plausible that economic growth and the stability of the Special Administrative Territory depend on the implementation of greater democracy, then it is possible that China will accede to some of their demands. Lack of government performance will significantly enhance the chances of the democrats in promoting their cause.

Rising contention in Singapore

In recent years, some members of Singapore's opposition movement have gradually been willing to employ more non-institutionalized or only partially institutionalized tactics. Chapter 8 has detailed some of the more recent efforts by Dr Chee Soon Juan to promote civil disobedience in Singapore. However, the majority of the population remain largely alienated from the liberal activist, who has been the victim of a massive propaganda campaign against his character. At the same time, other acts of contentious politics have either been mostly spontaneous (for instance the protest of approximately thirty people against the dismissal of "mrbrown" from his *Straits Times* column)[1] or confined to the internet. Nonetheless, the government has recognized this pressure and tries to channel the rising discontent, for instance, by making concessions as to what is permissible on the internet and by relaxing rules on public speeches at Speakers' Corner, while at the same time trying to find new ways to limit the influence of challengers. This reflects a similar pattern to that in Hong Kong during the 1970s, and we may well ask ourselves whether this may only be the beginning of a more active and lively political environment.

In Singapore, independent websites and the "blogosphere" are becoming an alternative source of information. In Hong Kong during the 1970s this alternative source had been the free and largely independent press. The government has so far decided to tolerate these online discussions and, unlike the People's Republic of China, has not blocked many websites, none of which arc political.[2] In contrast to the traditional media, the information provided by these websites is largely critical of the government. While much of the content is emotional dissatisfaction, some online journalists, such as Au Waipang, known for his website Yawning Bread, have done a remarkable job in investigative journalism. Even though the internet is more heterogeneous and still not as widespread as traditional media, its significance is continually growing in one of the world's most connected countries.

How declining performance can strengthen the opposition can be demonstrated by the 2005 National Kidney Foundation (NKF) scandal, which spurred a number of internet commentaries. One of them is an article from Yawning Bread, which attempts to draw parallels between the scandal involving the chairman of the charity and the political system, something that the ruling elite has strongly rejected. The chairman, T.T. Durai, had lost a defamation lawsuit against the *Straits Times*, which had printed a critical report that had alleged wastefulness and extravagance at the NKF. Yawning Bread alleged that this was similar to the government's tactic of using defamation lawsuits against members of the opposition (see Chapter 6). Furthermore, the article highlighted problems with government oversight. While the NKF had lost its status as an institution entitled to collect tax-exempt donations in December 2001, its status was renewed when a different government institution, the Health Ministry, became responsible for these entitlements.

The impact of articles such as this is hard to estimate, since it is impossible to know how many people read these websites and, since anybody can publish articles online, it is also uncertain how much credibility websites such as Yawning Bread have. However, as a consequence of the scandal, opposition members conducted one of their first protests in years. It was in response to this scandal that four people protested silently on 11 August 2005 in front of the CPF building to call for greater transparency. Even though the government dispersed the protesters and no report about it was published in the mainstream media, news of the event quickly spread across the city. The internet carried photos and a video of the demonstration that allowed Singaporeans to evaluate the protest for themselves. The action of the government again motivated protesters to increase pressure on the government, which led to another protest during the World Bank/IMF meeting of 16–19 September 2006. On 1 September 2008, the Singapore government dropped the requirement for Singapore residents to register for a permit to protest at Speakers' Corner, which has already led to a number of protests. While Table 9.4 suggests a rise in political activity, it should be mentioned that much of it

Table 9.4 Major political activity in Singapore since 2006

Date	Number of participants	Description
16 Sep. 2006	6	"Empower Singaporeans Rally and March": unlicensed demonstration for human rights
7 July 2006	30	Silent protest in support of the blogger mrbrown
10 Dec. 2006	20	Freedom walk in commemoration for Human Rights Day
11 Aug. 2007	39	Social event for gays and lesbians (Pink Run)
15 Mar. 2008	20	Protest against rising living costs with "Tak Boleh Tahan"–T-shirts
27 April 2008	100s–2,500	Democracy activists from Myanmar (Burma) demonstrate against their country's constitution
7 Sep. 2008	1,600	Petition against opening a dorm for foreign workers in Serangoon Gardens
5 Oct. 2008	60	Nanyang students protest against censorship of campus paper at Speakers' Corner
11 Oct. 2008	600	Investors protest against losses from structured notes issued by Lehmann Brothers
16 Feb. 2009	50	Bangladeshi migrant workers protest in front of Ministry of Manpower building for work and overdue pay
27 Feb. 2009	100	Another protest by Bangladeshi migrant workers

Sources: SDP 2007; Reuters 2006, 2008, 2009; BurmaNet News 2008
Note: The numbers for the 27 April 2008 protest vary between "hundreds of protesters" (*Reuters*) and (BurmaNet News).

continues to be within the still very limited legal space in Singapore. Only a very few daring members of the opposition and foreigners such as Burmese activists have dared to flout these regulations.

Looking into the future, it is possible to imagine that discontent will even grow. For this it is necessary to mention some of the current issues in Singapore. One issue that increased the level of discontent was the rise in the goods and services tax (GST) in 2007, which was largely condemned by a wide spectrum of internet authors. Furthermore, the news that in 2006 more foreigners than locals found jobs in Singapore was hotly debated. Closely linked to this is the government proposal to increase the population from 4.5 million to 6.5 million over the next 50 years through an influx of foreign "talents," which has raised serious concern (Koh 2007). The escape of a terrorist leader, rising living costs, serious problematic investments by Temasek, the government's investment corporation, and as yet unknown problems as a result of the world financial crisis have raised serious questions about governance which could eventually undermine the performance-based legitimacy of the government.

Perhaps the greatest impact on the government's ability to control the opposition would be an unmanaged governance crisis, which would lead to an erosion of government legitimacy. Discontent would lead to contentious politics, which would increase pressure for democratization. While the government will probably try to minimize calls for greater liberalization, increasing societal pressure may eventually force the government to choose between repression and allowing other groups greater participation. The government's focus on pragmatism suggests that it would consider the costs of repression too high and opt for allowing the opposition more influence. As a result, the government might relax the rules that greatly restrict oppositional behavior and a slow democratization process would be the result.

However, small political changes such as these in Singapore should not be overestimated, because the government's strategy of dividing the opposition and presenting efficient rule by externalizing newly arising challenges—such as the issue of the escape of a terrorist subject discussed earlier—has been very effective. As long as the government is able to maintain the status quo there is very little hope for the weak oppositional movement. Civil society groups will continue to lack the legitimacy to become involved in political cases. Opposition parties are unlikely to find common ground on which they can agree. Differences of opinion on the right choice of tactic will continue to weaken their ability to create larger coalitions.

Finally, even though the internet plays an increasingly important role in politics, the government has also adapted its forms of control to meet these online challenges. For instance, before the 2006 election, the government warned that "the streaming of explicit political content by individuals during the election period is prohibited under the Election Advertising Regulations" (*Singapore Hansard* 3 April 2006). When, despite these regulations, the Singapore Democratic Party posted a political podcast, the government threatened to take action against the party. The SDP complied immediately with the order and took down its podcast. The government has, furthermore, been very vague about what is permissible content. For example, Prime Minister Lee Hsien Loong said in his 2006 National Day Message:

> Singaporeans should express themselves freely but responsibly. We need to help solve problems and build our nation, not chip away at the pillars of our society. We will not always agree with one another, but we must stay cohesive and united in our common vision for Singapore.
>
> (Lee 2006b)

From the viewpoint of the ruling elite groups, the internet poses a serious risk to their monopoly on power. The government is therefore closely monitoring the internet (Rahim 2006a). Furthermore, the *Straits Times* reported on 7 February 2007 that the PAP had created a "new media capabilities group," which consists of PAP members who anonymously rebut online criticism (Li 2007).

More traditional attempts to control internet content have also been tested. The threat of a defamation lawsuit was used in 2005 against US-based Singaporean blogger Chen Jiahao (known as AcidFlask), who in response voluntarily restricted access to his blog and later publicly apologized for his comments, which had been critical of government scholarships. Two years later, three people were prosecuted under the Sedition Act for writing insensitive comments about religion on their blogs (Lee and Kan 2008). In 2008, a Singaporean court sentenced Gopalan Nair, a US citizen, to three months in jail for writing in his blog that a judge had "prostituted herself" (*Reuters* 18 Sep. 2008). In February of 2009, the government even gave an explicit warning to bloggers when Community Development, Youth and Sports Minister Vivian Balakrishnan said: "if need be, we can identify you, and if we have to, we will be prepared to prosecute you" (quoted in Cheney 2009). As a result, bloggers practice self-censorship to avoid government retribution (Lee and Kan 2008). This shows that even though the internet has increased the space for oppositional groups, the government's balanced strategy of co-option and coercion continues to weaken potential challengers.

From contention to democratization

This book has demonstrated that two aspects are most important in the mobilization of the opposition. If, on the one hand, there are popular perceptions of government inefficiencies and, on the other, there is a relatively low level of co-option and coercion, then oppositional groups can increase their strength. The continuing lack of democracy in Hong Kong, however, demonstrates amply that contentious politics does not necessarily lead to democratization. Public protest alone cannot force authoritarian leaders to relinquish power. It therefore remains a mystery when greater contention leads to democratization and not to riots and other violent activity. It is therefore important to understand under what conditions oppositional groups are successful in increasing their power to pressure the government for greater democratization. Future research should focus on an analysis of the goals and tactics of the two groups during the democratization phase. If we accept that splits in the ruling elite coalition increase the likelihood of democratization, we need to know what could cause this alliance to fall apart.

However, when there is a lack of significant societal pressure, such as in Singapore, it is highly unlikely that a country will democratize in the near future. In effect, this book has demonstrated that the level of contention is also a reflection of the unity within the ruling elite. Singapore's strong state lacks significant fissures or factions that could impede the decision making of its leaders, who are still able to skillfully implement their long-term strategies. Nevertheless, the present global financial crisis will increase pressure on the government. While it seems likely that it will increase the opportunities for oppositional groups, it is not certain that the opposition will decide to change its tactics, nor that a change would increase pressure for democratization.

Notes

1 Introduction and methodology

1 While Sing (2004b) argues that Hong Kong before 1984 was an exception to modernization theory, I argue that the rise in contentious politics during this time is an early indicator of the changing relationship between different groups in society. The contrast to Singapore, which for most of the last 50 years has lacked contention, is especially pertinent.

2 George W. Bush said this about Prime Minister Lee Hsien Loong at the University Cultural Centre Theatre of the National University of Singapore in November 2006: "I also had a very fine meeting with Prime Minister Lee earlier. I've come to know him as a wise man. I appreciate his good counsel. He's a friend and a partner, and he's a strong voice for peace and prosperity in Asia" (White House 2006).

3 The most comprehensive overview of opposition parties comes from Hussin (2000 and 2004). Gomez (2006) describes the impact of lack of freedom of speech on the opposition. Barr (2003) studies one of Singapore's most famous opposition politicians, J.B. Jeyaretnam.

4 For example there is the important collection of articles in Gillian Koh and Ooi Giok Ling's *State-Society Relations in Singapore* (2000). Other studies include Lee 2002 and 2005; and Chong 2005.

5 Important works about the role of the state in Singapore's authoritarian regime are by Quah (1980), Chan (1975) and Hamilton-Hart (2000). Rodan (2004) discusses the relationship between bureaucratic authoritarianism and transparency reforms.

6 One of the earliest studies of Singapore's institutions is Quah's (1975) comparison of the Singapore Improvement Trust and the Housing and Development Board. Schein (1996) details the inner workings of the Economic Development Board. Francis T. Seow (2006) has provided a very important analysis of Singapore's judiciary. Furthermore, there are important works that provide an overview of Singapore's institutions (such as Yeo 2002; Mauzy and Milne 2002).

7 The Singapore elite has been the focus of a large body of research. The most important early work comes from Chen (1978), who referred to the "power elite". More recent prominent works are by Vennewald (1994a, 1994b), who speaks of a dominance of technocrats within the elite and Worthington (2003). Furthermore, the ruling People's Action Party has been the focus of a number of important studies (e.g., Chan 1976; Mauzy and Milne 2002).

8 In the context of this book, the most helpful studies on the government and the elite are Harris 1978; Miners 1981; and Scott 1989. Society is covered in Lau 1982 and Lam 2004, of which the latter tries to challenge some of the basic assumptions in the former.

2 Modernization and the political process model

1 Political stability in this context can be defined as "the regularity of the flow of political exchanges" (Ake 1975: 273). The opposite of political stability is, therefore, contentious politics. A major problem in Hong Kong and Singapore is, however, that stability is not clearly defined and is often used to advance the political agenda of the various actors. For instance, in Hong Kong oppositional groups legitimized their use of contentious politics with reference to the need for stability (see Chapter 7).

2 For a detailed description of these incentives, see Clark and Wilson 1961.

3 Table 2.1 does not consider the enemy image, the barbarian image, the degenerate image, the rogue image, and the ally image because these are largely irrelevant in the context of this book.

4 Cottam and Cottam (2001) identify three possibilities for when people accept their inferiority: first of all, people usually share the general belief that the world is just, and therefore inferiority is seen as the fault of the subordinate group. Second, disadvantaged groups may accept their position when they do not regard the other group as comparable. Third, the relationship is rarely an all-or-nothing relationship in which only one group profits. In extreme cases groups in a society may be blamed for the problems, and the poor treatment of this group is based on this assumption.

5 It could be argued that Singapore's present political system is that of a continuation of the political control of a "colonial–imperial relationship", yet with the difference that Singapore's leaders are home-grown and therefore do not have the same legitimacy deficit as a colonial regime.

3 Depoliticization and the rise of social protest in Hong Kong during the 1970s

1 This classification is taken from Sing Ming's (2004b) analysis of Hong Kong's democratization. It should be noted, however, that in 2004 Hong Kong was considered "semi-competitive, partially pluralist." The competitive elements in Hong Kong in the 1970s were still too rudimentary to justify the present classification.

2 Freedom House constantly gave Hong Kong a rating of 2 (on a scale of 1 = best to 7 = worst) in terms of civil liberties during the 1970s, and a 3 in terms of political rights in the first half of the 1970s and a 4 in the latter half of the 1970s and in the 1980s. This latter aspect is confusing, considering the improvements in terms of political rights at the beginning of the 1980s. Also strange is the fact that Hong Kong's status changed between free and partly free, despite little change in terms of the ratings. It should be noted that these ratings are not available on the internet and need to be requested directly from the organization.

3 Those found guilty were an Italian parish priest, four students, five social workers, and a doctor. They were all placed on a bond of good behavior of HK$300 for 18 months.

4 These were the editors of the main left-wing newspapers *Afternoon News, Hong Kong Evening News, Tin Fung Daily News*. They received a suspension for six months, sentences of three years' imprisonment and fines of up to US$2,000 (see Chang 1982: 84)

5 The Letters Patent states that "the Governor shall in no case, except where the offence has been of a political nature unaccompanied by any grave crime, make it a condition of any pardon or remission of sentence that the offender shall be banished from or shall absent himself or be removed from the colony" (Letters Patent XV).

6 Chinese is meant as a term covering all the Chinese languages; in Hong Kong it mostly refers to Cantonese.

7 Population statistics are from www.demographia.com/db-hkhist.htm, while estimates of the eligible votes are from the *SCMP* (1970) and the *Hong Kong Standard* (1981).

8 Urban Councilors originally did not receive a salary for their duties and elections therefore often provided a platform for a few motivated people, who often had very few resources.

4 Expanding political opportunities and limiting institutional structures in Singapore

1 After World War II, the British dissolved the Straits Settlement and on 1 April 1946 Singapore became an independent Crown Colony.
2 Originally termed "civic society," because the government wanted to enhance the civic life in Singapore. According to Lee (2002), the term "civic" was used because the intention was not only to increase participation but also to develop a unitary national identity.
3 Other reasons that Koh (1997) mentions are progress, changes in the international business environment, and the need to retain talent according to market practices.
4 In contrast to single-member constituencies, group representation constituencies (GRCs) are constituencies of three to six candidates with at least one minority candidate, who are elected as a group with a plurality of the vote. Officially, this measure is intended to ensure minority representation in parliament.
5 A candidate for the presidency needs to have been a member of the government for at least three years, a chairman or chief executive officer of a statutory board, a chairman of a company with a paid-up capital of at least S$100 million, or to have been in a comparable position. Furthermore, he should not be a member of a political party or engage in commercial business. Perhaps most importantly, the candidate needs to satisfy the Presidential Elections Committee's idea of personal characteristics, which means that the committee can control the selection of candidates (Singapore Constitution, Article 19).

5 Ruling elite groups in Hong Kong during the 1970s

1 The first Clean Hong Kong campaign was introduced for just one year in 1948 (Director of Audit 2005).
2 The municipal council was, unlike the Urban Council, supposed to deal with most civic affairs.

6 Ruling elite groups in Singapore

1 This includes the military, the police force, and any other part of the government.
2 A comparison of the salaries of selected heads of state can be found on the website of the Singapore Democratic Party: www.singaporedemocrat.org/ministers'%20pay. html (based on data from *Asian Wall Street Journal* 10 July 2000)
3 Grassroots leaders receive some benefits, such as priority placements in housing and education (Koh 1998).
4 These were the Singapore 21 Committee in 1997, which produced its report in 1999, and the Remaking Singapore Committee, established in 2002, which published its report in 2003.
5 To minimize opposition from conservatives, the government decided to introduce measures that would require Singapore citizens, among other things, to pay an entrance fee of S$100 for every entry or S$2000 a year (*ST* 19 April 2005).
6 For an overview of the housing program in Singapore, see Phang 2007.

7 Oppositional groups in Hong Kong

1 The group leaders, however, rejected this assertion: "The Conservancy Association is in no way tied to the commercial firms (including the oil companies) which

support it, nor does it feel obliged to look after the interests of the wealthy members of the population (from which most of its members come) to the detriment of the rest" (Ding and Webster 1973).

2 Brook Bernacchi denied any connection to the scandal and the club launched an investigation into the allegations. Apparently some members had used a branch office and an apartment for the purposes of illegal gambling (Wai, 1988).

3 For a definition of political stability, see Chapter 2, note 1.

4 The functional constituencies represent professional and special interest groups and make up half of the 60 seat Legislative Council as of 2009.

5 In 1972, the Yaumati boat people had been given the choice either to move into public housing or to continue to be boat people permanently. Of these, 355 families accepted the offer, while 413 rejected it, in part because they did not want to move far away from the coast.

8 Oppositional groups in Singapore

1 In recent elections, opposition rallies have attracted large crowds. During the 2006 election, even Lee Hsien Loong's teenage son was present at one of them (*Reuters* 6 May 2006). Videos and speeches from past election rallies can be viewed at the Singapore Elections Rally Archive: http://sgrally.blogspot.com.

2 Sadly, J.B. Jeyaretnam died on 30 September 2008, only months after forming a new political party, the Reform Party.

3 It should be noted that, for instance, the Workers' Party does conduct welfare activities and social events such as cycling trips, bowling sessions, or casual meetings. I do not consider this an important incentive because, in my opinion, it only marginally enhances the ability of the party to attract members.

4 The article "Singapore's 'Martyr,' Chee Soon Juan," written by Hugo Restall and published in July 2006 drew parallels between the National Kidney Foundation scandal and the Singapore government. For more on the scandal, see Chapter 9.

5 For a definition of political stability, see Chapter 2, note 1.

6 This is not the fear we associate with imminent dangers, it more closely resembles a sense of anxiety about what the consequences might be for those who get too involved in politics and directly challenge the government.

7 For the myth of meritocracy, see Barr 2006 and Rodan 2006a.

9 Comparing ruling elite strategies in Hong Kong and Singapore

1 The protest was organized via SMS messages, which urged people on 9 July 2006 to appear in brown shirts at City Hall MRT. The police later dropped all charges, claiming that there had been no breach in public order (*ST* 22 July 2006).

2 The Censorship Survey 2003 conducted by the Ministry for Information, Communication, and the Arts stated that there were 100 banned websites in Singapore, mostly with sexual content (MICA 2003).

Bibliography

"AP and Irrawaddy: Overseas Burmese protest Constitution," in: *BurmaNet News*, 28 April 2008, www.burmanet.org/news/2008/04/28/ap-and-irrawaddy-overseas-burmese-protest-constitution/ (Online Access: 23/02/09).

"Competitiveness Scoreboard 2006," in: *World Competitiveness Yearbook (WCY)*, www.imd.ch/research/publications/wcy/competitiveness_scoreboard_2006.cfm?bhcp =1 (Online Access: 02/25/07).

"Singapore gov't butt of jokes after prison escape," in: *Agence France-Presse*, 3 March 2008.

"The political parallels to the NKF scandal," in: *Yawning Bread*, December 2005, www.yawningbread.org/arch_2005/yax-527.htm (Online Access: 02/23/09).

A Concerned Resident. 1975. "A bigger say in the government of Hongkong," in: *Hong Kong Standard*, 28 January.

Acemoglu, Daron and James A. Robinson. 2001. "A Theory of Democratic Transitions," in: *The American Economic Review*, 91:4, pp. 938–63.

Ake, Claude. 1975. " A Definition of Political Stability," in: *Comparative Politics*, 7:2, pp. 271–83.

Alagappa, Muthiah. 1995. "Introduction," in: Muthiah Alagappa (ed.), *Political Legitimacy in Southeast Asia: The Quest for Moral Authority*. Stanford, CA: Stanford University Press.

Alagappa, Muthiah. 2004. "Civil Society and Political Change: An Analytical Framework," in: Muthiah Alagappa (ed.), *Civil Society and Political Change in Asia*. Stanford, CA: Stanford University Press.

Amnesty International. 2008. "Singapore," in: *Amnesty International Report 2008*. http://thereport.amnesty.org/eng/Regions/Asia-Pacific/Singapore (Online Access: 02/ 24/09).

Anonymous. 1980. "Recent Developments in the Hong Kong Government," in: *Hong Kong Journal of Public Administration*, 2:2, pp. 86–89.

Arat, Zehra F. 1988. "Democracy and Economic Development: Modernization Theory Revisited," in: *Comparative Politics*, 21:1, pp. 21–36.

Arato, Andrew. 2000. *Civil Society, Constitution, and Legitimacy*. Lanham, MD: Rowman and Littlefield.

Baird, David. 1970a. "Hongkong: The Rubber Stamps Silently," in: *Far Eastern Economic Review*, 67:6, p. 8.

Baird, David. 1970b. "Reform Club 'knocking some chips off the government wall'" in: *South China Morning Post*, 21 January, p. 1.

Balji, P.N. 2006. "The Gomez affair: Is there something we don't know?" in: *Channel NewsAsia* website, www.channelnewsasia.com/stories/analysis/view/205946/1/.html (Online Access: 05/05/06).

Barmer, Naazneen, Ely Ratner and Regine Spector. 2008. "Open Authoritarianism: How Some Illiberal States Thrive in the Liberal International Order," paper presented at the 2008 Annual Meeting of the American Political Science Association, 18–31 August.

Barr, Michael D. 1998. "Lee Kuan Yew's 'Socialism' Reconsidered," in: *Access: History*, 2:1, pp. 33–54.

Barr, Michael D. 2000. "Trade Unions in an Elitist Society: The Singapore Story," in: *Australian Journal of Politics & History*, 46:4, pp. 480–96.

Barr, Michael D. 2003. "J.B. Jeyeratnam: Three Decades as Lee Kuan Yew's *bête noir*," in: *Journal of Contemporary Asia*, 33:3, pp. 299–317.

Barr, Michael D. 2006. "The Charade Of Meritocracy," in: *Far Eastern Economic Review*, October, www.feer.com/articles1/2006/0610/free/p018.html (Online Access: 11/01/06).

Barrett, Vickie. 1979. "In full—the speech that was not delivered," in: *Hong Kong Standard*, 17 October.

Beatty, Bob. 2003. *Democracy, Asian Values, and Hong Kong.* Westport, CT, and London: Praeger.

Bellows, Thomas. 1985. "Bureaucracy and Development in Singapore," in: *The Asian Journal of Public Administration*, 7:1, pp. 55–69.

Bendix, Reinhard. 1978. *Kings or People: Power and the Mandate to Rule.* Berkeley and Los Angeles, CA: University of California Press.

Berlins, Marcel. 1974. "The last pearl of the Empire loses its luster," in: *London Times*, 9 January.

Bermeo, Nancy. 1990. "Rethinking Regime Change," in: *Comparative Politics*, 22, pp. 359–77.

Bernstein, Richard. 1989. "Vast Hong Kong Crowd Protests Beijing's Action," in: *The New York Times*, 5 June, www.nytimes.com/specials/hongkong/archive/89065vast-hong-kong.html (Online Access: 01/29/07).

Bhavani, K. 2006. "Distorting the truth, mr brown?" in: *Today*, 3 July.

Bloodworth, Dennis. 1986. *The Tiger and the Trojan Horse.* Singapore: Times Books International.

Boix, Charles. 2003. *Democracy and Redistribution.* Cambridge: Cambridge University Press.

Bollen, Kenneth A. 1979. "Political Democracy and the Timing of Development," in: *American Sociological Review*, 44, pp. 572–87.

Bordens, Kenneth S. and Irwin A. Horowitz. 2002. *Social Psychology.* Mahwah, NJ: Lawrence Erlbaum.

Boudreau, Vince. 2004. *Resisting Dictatorship: Repression and Protest in Southeast Asia.* Cambrige: Cambridge University Press.

Bradley, C. Paul. 1965. "Leftist Fissures in Singapore Politics," in: *The Western Political Quarterly*, 18:2, pp. 292–308.

Bremridge, J.H. 1975. "A little more tilting by Government seems overdue," in: *South China Morning Post*, 13 July.

Brooker, Paul. 2000. *Non-Democratic Regimes: Theory, Government and Politics.* New York: Palgrave Publishers.

Brown, David. 1993. "The Corporatist Management of Ethnicity in Contemporary Singapore," in: Garry Rodan (ed.), *Singapore Changes Guard: Social, Political, Economic Directions in the 1990s.* Melbourne: Longman.

Brown, David and David Jones. 1995. "Singapore and the Myth of the Liberalising Middle Class," in: *Pacific Review*, 7:1, pp. 79–87.

Burton, John. 2005. "Public anger over charity chief's salary," in: *Financial Times*, 14 July, www.ft.com/cms/s/67657c0e-f3f7–11d9-af32–00000e2511c8.html (Online Access: 02/10/07).

Burton, John. 2006. "Straits under strain: why inequality is centre stage in Singapore's election," in: *Financial Times*, 4 May, p. 11.

Butenhoff, Linda. 1999. *Social Movements and Political Reform in Hong Kong.* Westport and London: Praeger.

Campbell, Duncan. 1980. "Colonialism: A Secret Plan for Dictatorship" in: *New Statesman*, 12 December.

Carothers, Thomas. 2002. "The end of the transition paradigm," in: *Journal of Democracy*, 13:1, pp. 5–21.

Case, William F. 1996. "Can the 'Halfway House' Stand? Semidemocracy and Elite Theory in Three Southeast Asian Countries," in: *Comparative Politics*, 28:4, pp. 437–68.

Case, William F. 2002. *Politics in Asia: Democracy or Less.* Richmond: Curzon.

Case, William. 2005. "Southeast Asia's Hybrid Regimes: When Do Voters Change Them?" in: *Journal of East Asian Studies*, 5, pp. 220–27.

Castells, Manuel et. al. 1990. *The Shek Kip Mei Syndrome: Economic Development and Public Housing in Hong Kong and Singapore.* London: Pion.

Central Intelligence Agency. 2009. *The 2008 World Factbook.* https://www.cia.gov/library/publications/the-world-factbook/index.html (Online Access: 02/24/09).

Chalmers, Ian. 1992. "Loosening State Control in Singapore: The Emergence of Local Capital as a Political Force," in: *Southeast Asian Journal of Social Science*, 20:2, pp. 57–83.

Chan Hean Boon. 1996. "Opposition for the sake of opposition wastes time," in: *The Straits Times*, 25 October 2001, p. H6.

Chan Heng Chee. 1971. *Singapore: The Politics of Survival.* Singapore: Oxford University Press.

Chan Heng Chee. 1975. "Politics in an Administrative State: Where has the Politics Gone?" in: Seah Chee Meow (ed.), *Trends in Singapore: Proceedings and Background Paper.* Singapore: Singapore University Press.

Chan Heng Chee. 1976. *The Dynamics of One Party Dominance: The PAP at the Grass-roots.* Singapore: Singapore University Press.

Chan Heng Chee. 1989. "The PAP and the Structuring of the Political System," in: Kernial Singh Sandhu and Paul Wheatley (eds), *Management of Success: The Moulding of Modern Singapore.* Singapore: Institute of Southeast Asian Studies.

Chan Heng Chee. 2000. "The Role of Intellectuals in Singapore Politics: An Essay," in: Verinder Grover (ed.), *Singapore: Government and Politics.* New Delhi: Deep and Deep Publications.

Chan Sek Keong. 2006. "Welcome Reference for the Chief Justice: Response by the Honorable the Chief Justice Chan Sek Keong," 22 April, http://app.supremecourt.gov.sg/default.aspx?pgid=1001&printFriendly = true (Online Access: 01/16/06).

Chan, Garmen. 1981. "Nine candidates set for Urbco poll race," in: *Hong Kong Standard*, 7 February.

Chan, Ho Mun. 2004. "The Ethics of Care and Political Practices in Hong Kong," in: Chua Beng Huat (ed.), *Communitarian Politics in Asia*. London and New York: RoutledgeCurzon.

Chan, John. 2008. "Beijing delays direct elections in Hong Kong for another decade," in: *World Socialist Web Site*, www.wsws.org/articles/2008/jan2008/hkon-j14.shtml (Online Access: 02/20/09).

Chang Kuo-sin. 1982. "Hong Kong," in: John Lent (ed.), *Newspapers in Asia: Contemporary Trends and Problems*. Hong Kong: Heinemann Asia.

ChannelNews Asia. Various dates. Online: www.channelnewsasia.com.

Chao Hick Tin. 2007. "Speech by the Attorney General at the Opening of the Legal Year," Supreme Court Auditorium, 6 January, http://app.supremecourt.gov.sg/default.aspx?pgid=1621&printFriendly = true (Online Access: 01/16/06).

Chee Soon Juan. 1994. *Dare to Change: An Alternative Vision for Singapore*. Singapore: Singapore Democratic Party.

Chee Soon Juan. 1995. *Singapore, My Home Too*. Singapore: Melodies Press.

Chee Soon Juan. 2001. *Your Future, My Faith, Our Freedom: A Democratic Blueprint for Singapore*. Singapore Open Centre, 2001.

Chee Soon Juan. 2005. *The Power of Courage: Effecting Political Change in Singapore through Nonviolence*. Singapore: Melodies Press.

Chee Soon Juan. 2007. "CSJ refutes AG on the 'rule of law' in Singapore," Open Letter to Chao Hick Tin, Attorney-General, in: *Singapore Democratic Party* website, http://singaporedemocrat.org/articleChees_AG1.html (Online Access: 01/16/06).

Chen, Peter S.J. 1978. "The Power Elite in Singapore," in: Ong Jin Hui, Tong Chee Kiong and Tan Ern Ser (eds), *Understanding Singapore Society*. Singapore: Times Academic Press.

Cheney, Satish. 2009. "Govt says policies on new media will evolve as new challenges crop up," in: *Channel NewsAsia*, 21 February, www.channelnewsasia.com/stories/singaporelocalnews/view/410619/1/.html (Online Access: 02/27/09).

Cheng Tong Yung. 1982. *The Economy of Hong Kong*. Hong Kong: Far East Publications.

Cheng, Joseph S.Y. 1999. "Political Participation in Hong Kong: Theoretic Issues and Historical Issues," in: Joseph Y.S. Cheng. (ed.), *Political Participation in Hong Kong: Theoretical Issues and Historical Legacy*. Hong Kong: City University of Hong Kong Press.

Cheng, Joseph S.Y. 2005. "Hong Kong's Democrats Stumble," in: *Journal of Democracy*, 16:1, pp. 138–52.

Cheung, Anthony B.L. 1997. "Reform in Search of Politics: The Case of Hong Kong's Aborted Attempt Corporatise Public Broadcasting," in: *Asian Journal of Public Administration*, 19:2, pp. 276–302.

Cheung, Anthony B.L. 2008. "The story of two administrative states: state capacity in Hong Kong and Singapore," in: *The Pacific Review*, 21:2, pp. 121–45.

Cheung, Anthony Bing-leung and Kin-sheun Louie. 1991. *Social Conflicts in Hong Kong, 1975–1986: Trends and Implications*. Hong Kong: Hong Kong Institute of Asia-Pacific Studies.

Chia Ti Lik. 2009. "About Me," in: *Chia Ti Lik's Blog*, http://chiatilik.wordpress.com/about/ (Online Access: 03/27/09).

Chia, Steve. 2002. "Motion of Thanks: PRESIDENT'S ADDRESS at Opening of 10th Session of Singapore's Parliament," in: *National Solidarity Party* website, www.nsp.sg/speech_transcript.php?more=8 (Online Access: 01/16/2006).

Chin, James. 2007. "The General Election in Singapore, May 2006," in: *Electoral Studies*, 26:3, pp. 703–7.

Ching, Frank. 1994. "Toward Colonial Sunset: The Wilson Regime, 1987–86," in: Ming K. Chan (ed.), *Precarious Balance: Hong Kong Between China and Britain, 1842–1992*. Armonk: M.E. Sharpe, pp. 173–98.

Chiu, Stephen, Khong-chong Ho and Tai-lok Lui. 1995. "A Tale of Two Cities Rekindled: Hong Kong and Singapore's Divergent Paths to Industrialism," in: *Journal of Developing Societies*, 11, pp. 98–128.

Choi, Frank. 1985. "Poll results show 'a new awareness,'" in: *South China Morning Post*, 11 March.

Chong, Terence. 2005. "Civil Society in Singapore: Popular Discourses and Concepts," in: *SOJOURN*, 20:2, pp. 273–301.

Chow Soo Shee. 2006. "Wrong to take progress and peace for granted," in: *Straits Times*, 18 April.

Chua Beng-Huat. 1994. "Arrested development: democratisation in Singapore," in: *Third World Quarterly*, 15:4, pp. 655–68.

Chua Beng-Huat. 1995. *Communitarian ideology and democracy in Singapore*. London and New York: Routledge.

Chua Beng-Huat. 1997. *Political Legitimacy and Housing——Stakeholding in Singapore*. London and New York: Routledge.

Chua Beng-Huat. 2000. "The Relative Autonomies of State and Civil Society in Singapore," in: Gillian Koh and Ooi Giok Ling (eds), *State-Society Relations in Singapore*. Singapore: Oxford University Press.

Clark, Peter B., and James Q. Wilson. 1961. "Incentive Systems: A Theory of Organizations," in: *Administrative Science Quarterly*, 6:2, pp. 129–66.

Cooper, John. 1970. *The Colony in Conflict: The Hong Kong Disturbances May 1967–January 1968*. Hong Kong: Swindon.

Cottam, Martha L. and Richard W. Cottam. 2001. *Nationalism and Politics: The Political Behavior of Nation States*. Boulder and London: Lynne Rienner.

Crandall, Christian S. and Ryan K. Beasley. 2001. "A Perceptual Theory of Legitimacy: Politics, Prejudice, Social Institutions and Moral Value," in: John T. Jost and Brenda Major (eds), *The Psychology of Legitimacy. Emerging Perspectives on Ideology, Justice, and Intergroup Relations*. Cambridge: Cambridge University Press.

Crouch, Harold and James W. Morley. 1999. "The Dynamics of Political Change," in: James W. Morley (ed.), *Driven by Growth: Political Change in the Asia-Pacific Region*. Revised edition. Armonk, N.Y.: M.E. Sharpe.

Dahl, Robert A. 1971. *Polyarchy: Participation and Opposition*. New Haven and London: Yale University Press.

Davies, S.N.G. 1983. "Bureaucracy and People in Hong Kong ... Like a Horse and Carriage? (Review Article)" in: *The Asian Journal of Public Administration*, 5:1, pp. 103–14.

Deutsch, Karl W. 1961. "Social Mobilization and Political Development" in: *The American Political Science Review*, 55:3, pp. 493–514.

Diamond, Larry. 2002. "Elections Without Democracy: Thinking about Hybrid Regimes," in: *Journal of Democracy*, 13:2, pp. 21–35.

Diamond, Larry, Juan Linz, and Seymour Martin Lipset (eds). 1989. *Democracy in Developing Countries*. Boulder: Lynne Rienner.

Ding, Dr. L.K. and Michael Webster. 1973. "Where conservation must give way to economics. ... ," in: *South China Morning Post*, 14 September.

Director of Audit. 2005. "The Government's Efforts in Developing Sustainable Systems to Keep Hong Kong Clean," in: *Report No. 45 of the Director of Audit*, Chapter 8, www.aud.gov.hk/pdf_e/e45ch08_summary.pdf (Online Access: 01/22/07).

Dix, Robert H. 1982. "The Breakdown of Authoritarian Regimes," in: *The Western Political Quarterly*, 35:4, pp. 554–73.

do Rosario, Louise. 1981. "Szeto Wah, doyen of HK pressure groups," in: *Hong Kong Standard*, 23 March.

Downey, Bernard. 1975. "New machinery for the judiciary," in: *South China Morning Post*, 16 October.

Economist Intelligence Unit. 2008. *The Economist Intelligence Unit's Index of Democracy 2008*. http://a330.g.akamai.net/7/330/25828/20081021185552/graphics. eiu.com/PDF/Democracy%20Index%202008.pdf (Online Access: 02/24/09).

Elias, Penelope. 1973. "Plea to extend Urbco franchise," in: *South China Morning Post*, 10 March.

Elliot, Elsie. 1977. "Why the Urban Council is ineffective," in: *South China Morning Post*, 18 April.

Elliot, Elsie. 1981. "White Paper kills democracy," in: *South China Morning Post*, 16 January.

Elliot, Elsie, Dr Denny Huang and Tsin Sai-nin. 1978. "A Demand for Political Reform," Open Letter to the British Foreign Secretary, Dr David Owen, in: *The Star*, 20 November.

Emmerson, Donald K. 1995. "Singapore and the 'Asian Values' Debate," in: *Journal of Democracy*, 6:4, pp. 295–319.

Endacott, George B. 1973. *A History of Hong Kong*. Hong Kong: Oxford University Press.

Epstein, David L. et al. 2006. "Democratic Transitions," in: *American Journal of Political Science*, 50:3, pp. 551–69.

Ertman, Thomas. 1998. "Democracy and dictatorship in interwar western Europe revisited" in: *World Politics*, 50:3, pp. 475–505.

Faure, David. 2003. *Colonialism and the Hong Kong Mentality*. Hong Kong: Centre of Asian Studies, The University of Hong Kong.

Forss, Pearl. 2007. "Middle class wage stagnation could lead to social instability," in: *Channel NewsAsia* website, 11 January, www.channelnewsasia.com/stories/singaporelocalnews/view/251939/1/.html (Online Access: 01/20/07).

Freedom House. 2006. *Freedom in the World ratings: Hong Kong*.

Fukuyama, Francis. 1995. "The Primacy of Culture," in: *Journal of Democracy*, 6:1, pp. 7–14.

Gamson, William A. 1975. *The Strategy of Social Protest*. Homewood, IL: Dorsey Press.

Gan Kim Yong. 2006. "Message from the PPC chairman," in: *Petir*, January / February, www.pap.org.sg/petir_view.php?id=25 (Online Access: 03/04/07).

Geddes, Barbara and John Zaller. 1989. "Sources of Popular Support for Authoritarian Regimes," in: *American Journal of Political Science*, 33:2, pp. 319–27.

Geiger, Theodore and Frances M. Geiger. 1973. *Tales of Two City-states: The Development Progress of Hong Kong and Singapore*. Washington, DC: National Planning Association.

Gellner, Ernest. 1964. *Thought and Change*. London: Weidenfeld and Nicholson.

Gellner, Ernest. 1983. *Nations and Nationalism*. Ithaca, NY: Cornell University Press.

George, Cherian. 2007. "Consolidating authoritarian rule: calibrated coercion in Singapore," in: *The Pacific Review*, 20:2, pp. 127–45.

Gill, Graeme J. 2000. *The Dynamics of Democratization: Elites, Civil Society and the Transition Process.* New York: St. Martin's Press.

Goh Chok Tong. 1994. "Social Values, Singapore Style," in: *Current History*, 93:587, pp. 417–22.

Goh Meng Seng. 2005. "The Void Deck Interview," in: *Singapore Alternatives*, 6 April, http://singaporealternatives.blogspot.com/2005/04/void-deck-interview.html (Online Access: 06/06/07).

Goldstone, Jack A. 2003. "Introduction: Bridging Institutionalized and Non-institutionalized Politics," in: Jack A. Goldstone (ed.), *States, Parties, and Social Movements.* Cambridge: Cambridge University Press.

Gomez, James. 2000. *Self-Censorship: Singapore's Shame.* Singapore: Think Centre.

Gomez, James. 2001. "The Singapore Media: What Needs to Be Done?" in: *Solidarity*, 11:2, www.hrsolidarity.net/mainfile.php/2001vol11no2/22/ (Online Access: 03/04/07).

Gomez, James. 2006. "Restricting Free Speech: The Impact on Opposition Parties in Singapore," in: *The Copenhagen Journal of Asian Studies*, 23, pp. 105–31.

Goodstadt, L.F. 1970. "The Fixers," in: *Far Eastern Economic Review*, 30 July, pp. 21–23.

Goodstadt, Leo F. 2005. *Uneasy Partners: The Conflict between Public Interest and Private Profit in Hong Kong.* Hong Kong: Hong Kong University Press.

Goodstadt, Leo F. 2006. "Government without Statistics: Policy-making in Hong Kong 1925–85, with special reference to Economic and Financial Management," in: *HKIMR Working Paper*, No.6, www.hkimr.org/cms/upload/publication_app/pub_full_0_2_128_wp200606_text.pdf (Online Access: 01/17/07).

Goodstadt, Leo. 1971. "Hongkong: They Must Be Joking," in: *Far Eastern Economic Review*, 20 February.

Goodwin, Jeff and James M. Jasper. 1999. "Caught in a Winding, Snarling Vine: the Structural Bias of the Political Process Model," in: *Sociological Forum*, 14:1, pp. 27–54.

Goodwin, Jeff, James M. Jasper, and Francesca Polletta. 2001. "Introduction: Why Emotions Matter," in: Jeff Goodwin, James M. Jasper, and Francesca Polletta (eds), *Passionate Politics: Emotions and Social Movements.* Chicago, IL: University of Chicago Press, pp. 1–24.

Graham, Natalie. 1976. "Conservancy Association makes a big impact," in: *The Star*, 17 August.

Greenless, Donald. 2006. "Courts in Singapore come under scrutiny: Canadian case questions their fairness as foreign investors watch with interest," in: *International Harald Tribune*, 9 May 2006.

Haas, Michael. 1999. "A Political History," in: Michael Haas (ed.), *The Singapore Puzzle.* Greenwood, CT: Praeger.

Hack, Karl and Kevin Blackburn. 2004. *Did Singapore Have to Fall? Churchill and the Impregnable Fortress.* London and New York: Routledge.

Haggard, Stephan and Robert R. Kaufman. 1995. *The Political Economy of Democratic Transitions.* Princeton, NJ: Princeton University Press.

Hamilton-Hart, Natasha. 2000. "The Singapore State Revisited," in: *The Pacific Review*, 13:2, pp. 195–216.

Han Fook Kwang, Warren Fernandez and Sumiko Tan. 1998. *Lee Kuan Yew: The Man and His Ideas.* Singapore: Singapore Press Holdings.

Han, Minzhu (ed.). 1990. *Cries For Democracy: Writings and Speeches from the 1989 Chinese Democracy Movement.* Princeton, NJ: Princeton University Press.

Harris, Peter. 1978. *Hong Kong: A Study in Bureaucratic Politics.* Hong Kong: Heinemann Asia.

Harris, Peter. 1982. "British Political Institutions in a Chinese Setting: The Case of the Crown Colony of Hong Kong," in: *Parliamentary Affairs*, 35:2, pp. 181–92.

Hawkins, Darren. 2001. "Democratization Theory and Nontransitions: Insights from Cuba," in: *Comparative Politics*, 33:4, pp. 441–61.

Hicks, Douglas A. 2003. *Religion and the Workplace: Pluralism, Spirituality, Leadership.* Cambridge: Cambridge University Press.

Hill, Michael and Lian Kwen Fee. 1995. *The Politics of Nation Building and Citizenship in Singapore.* London and New York: Routledge.

Ho Khai Leong. 2003. *Shared Responsibilities, Unshared Power: The Politics of Policy-Making in Singapore.* Singapore: Eastern Universities Press.

Ho Shuet Ying. 1986. "Public Housing," in: Joseph Y.S. Cheng (ed.), *Hong Kong in Transition.* Hong Kong: Oxford University Press, pp. 331–53.

Hoadley, J. Stephen. 1973. "Political Participation of Hong Kong Chinese: Patterns and Trends," in: *Asian Survey*, 13:6, p. 604–16.

Hong Kong Government. 1971. *White Paper: The Urban Council.* Hong Kong: Government Printer.

Hong Kong Government. 1973. *Hong Kong 1973: A Review of 1972.* Hong Kong: Hong Kong Government Printer.

Hong Kong Government. 1974. *Hong Kong 1974: Report for the Year 1973.* Hong Kong: Hong Kong Government Printer.

Hong Kong Hansard. Hong Kong: Government Printer.

Hong Kong Journal. 2005. "Timeline," in: *Hong Kong Journal* website, www.hkjournal.org/timeline/timeline1900s.html (Online Access: 07/08/08).

Hong Kong Observers. 1976. "Proposals for tax systems in HK," in: *South China Morning Post*, July 27.

Hong Kong Observers. 1983. *Pressure Points: A Social Critique by the Hong Kong Observers.* 2nd edn. Hong Kong: Summerson.

Hong Kong Standard. Various issues, 1970–92.

Hong Professional Teachers' Union (HKPTU) pamphlets from 1983, 1984.

Honi Soit. 1979. "Demand for reforms is seen as a threat to stability," in: *Hong Kong Standard*, 7 March.

Housing and Development Board. 2008. *HDB Annual Report 2007/2008.* Singapore: Government Printer.

Huang, Denny. 1976. "Govt has failed to support 'Clean Hongkong Campaign,'" in: *The Star*, 31 March.

Huang, Esther. 2006. "Speakers' Corner or SNEAKERS' CORNER?" in: *The Electric New Paper,* 18 April, http://newpaper.asia1.com.sg/printfriendly/0,4139,105175,00.html (Online Access: 01/16/07).

Huckshorn, Robert. 1984. *Political Parties in America.* Monterey, CA: Brooks/Cole.

Huff, W.G. 1994. *The Economic Growth of Singapore: Trade and Development in the Twentieth Century.* Cambridge: Cambridge University Press.

Huff, W.G. 1999. "Turning the Corner in Singapore's Developmental State?" in: *Asian Survey*, 39:2, pp. 214–42.

Huidobro, Maria del Mar Francesch. 2005. "A 'disciplined governance' approach to government-NGOs relations: the structures and dynamics of environmental politics and management in Singapore." Unpublished thesis, University of Hong Kong.

Huntington, Samuel P. 1968. *Political Order in Changing Societies.* New Haven and London: Yale University Press.

Huntington, Samuel P. 1970. "Social and Institutional Dynamics of One-Party Systems," in: Samuel Huntington and Clement H. Moore (eds), *Authoritarian Politics in Modern Society: The Dynamics of Established One-Party Systems.* New York and London: Basic Books.

Huntington, Samuel P. 1984. "Will More Countries Become Democratic?" in: *Political Science Quarterly,* 99, pp. 193–218.

Huntington, Samuel P. 1991. *The Third Wave: Democratization in the Late Twentieth Century.* Norman, OK: University of Oklahoma Press.

Huntington, Samuel P. 1996. "Democracy for the Long Haul," in: *Journal of Democracy,* 7:2, pp. 3–13.

Huque, Ahmed Shafiqul, Grace O. M. Lee and Anthony B.L. Cheung (eds). 1998. *The Civil Service in Hong Kong: Continuity and Change.* Hong Kong: Hong Kong University Press.

Hussin Mutalib. 1997. "Singapore's First Elected Presidency: The Political Motivations," in: Kevin Y.L. Tan and Lam Peng Er (eds), *Managing Political Change in Singapore: The Elected Presidency.* London: Routledge.

Hussin Mutalib. 2000. "Illiberal democracy and the future of opposition in Singapore," in: *Third World Quality,* 21:2, pp 313–42.

Hussin Mutalib. 2004. *Parties and Politics: A Study of Opposition Parties and the PAP in Singapore.* 2nd edn. Singapore: Marshall Cavendish Academic.

Huxley, Tim. 2000. *Defending the Lion City: The Armed Forces of Singapore.* St. Leonards, Australia: Allen & Unwin.

Inglehart, Ronald. 1997. *Modernization and Postmodernization: Cultural, Economic, and Political Change in 43 Societies.* Princeton: Princeton University Press.

Inglehart, Ronald and Wayne E. Baker. 2000. "Modernization, cultural change, and the persistence of traditional values," in: *American Sociological Review,* 65: 1, pp. 19–51.

Inglehart, Ronald and Christian Welzel. 2005. *Modernization, Cultural Change, and Democracy: The Human Development Sequence.* New York: Cambridge University Press.

International Coalition for Religious Freedom. 2004. "Singapore," in: *Religious Freedom World Report,* www.religiousfreedom.com/wrpt/asiapac/singapore.htm (Online Access: 04/01/07).

Jao, Y.C. 1997. "Hong Kong as a Financial Centre for Greater China," in: Joseph C. H. Chai, Y. Y. Kueh and Clement Allan Tisdell. *China and the Asia Pacific Economy.* New York: Nova Science Publishers.

Jayasuriya, Kanishka. 1996. "The rule of law and capitalism in East Asia," in: *The Pacific Review,* 9:3, pp. 367–88.

Jeyaretnam, J.B. 2000. *Make it Right for Singapore: Speeches in Parliament 1997–1999.* Singapore: JEYA Publishers.

Jeyaretnam, J.B. 2005. "Introduction," in: Chee Soon Juan. *The Power of Courage: Effecting Political Change in Singapore through Nonviolence.* Singapore: Melodies Press.

Jones, Catherine. 1990. *Promoting Prosperity: The Hong Kong Way of Social Policy.* Hong Kong: The Chinese University Press.

Jones, David Martin. 1997. "Asian Values and the Constitutional Order of Contemporary Singapore," in: *Constitutional Political Economy,* 8, pp. 283–300.

Jose, Jim and Christine Doran. 1997. "Marriage and Marginalisation In Singaporean Politics," in: *Journal of Contemporary Asia,* 27:4, pp. 475–88.

Kan, Yuet-keung. 1973. "Come invest in Hongkong," in: *South China Morning Post*, June 17.

Kane, Tim, Kim R. Holmes, and Mary Anastasia O'Grady (eds). 2007. *2007 Index of Economic Freedom*. Washington, DC: The Heritage Foundation and the Wall Street Journal.

Keong, Victor. 2004. "Speakers' Corner now requires only simple registration," in: *Straits Times*, 20 September.

Kim, Sunhyuk. 2000. *The Politics of Democratization in Korea: The Role of Civil Society*. Pittsburgh, PA: University of Pittsburgh Press.

Kim, Yung-Myung. 1997. "'Asian-Style Democracy': A Critique from East Asia," in: *Asian Survey*, 37:12, pp. 1119–34

King, Ambrose Yeo-chi. 1975. "Administrative Absorption of Politics in Hong Kong: Emphasis on the Grass Roots Level," in: *Asian Survey*, 15:5, pp. 422–39.

Koh Buck Song. 1998. "The PAP cadre system," in: *The Straits Times*, 4 April, www.singapore-window.org/80404st1.htm (Online Access: 02/11/07).

Koh Gui Qing. 2007. "Singapore woos immigrants to boost population," in: *Reuters*, 25 March, www.boston.com/news/world/asia/articles/2007/03/26/singapore_woos_immigrants_to_boost_population/ (Online Access: 04/14/07).

Koh, Gillian. 1997. "Bureaucratic Rationality in an Evolving Developmentalist State: Challenges to Governance in Singapore," in: *Asian Journal of Political Science*, 5:2, pp. 114–41.

Koh, Gillian and Giok Ling Ooi (eds). 2000. *State-Society Relations in Singapore*. Singapore: Oxford University Press.

Kolesnikov-Jessop, Sonia. 2007. "Singapore Sling," in: *Newsweek*, 29 January, www.msnbc.msn.com/id/16725528/site/newsweek/ (Online Access: 07/14/2007).

Kuan Hsin-chi. 1979. "Political Stability and Change in Hong Kong," in: Tzong-biau Lin, Rance P.L. Lee and Udo-Ernst Simonis (eds), *Hong Kong: Economic, Social and Political Studies in Development*. White Plains: M.E. Sharpe.

Kuan Hsin-chi and Lau Siu-kai. 2002. "Traditional Orientations and Political Participation in Three Chinese Societies," in: *Journal of Contemporary China*, 11, pp. 297–318.

La Porta, Rafael, Florencio Lopez-de-Silanes, Andrei Shleifer, and Robert Vishny. 2000. "Investor protection and corporate governance," in: *Journal of Financial Economics*, 58, pp. 3–27.

Lam Peng Er. 1999. "Singapore: Rich State, Illiberal Regime," in: James W. Morley (ed.), *Driven by Growth: Political Change in the Asia-Pacific Region*. Armonk, NY: M.E. Sharpe, pp. 255–74.

Lam Wai-man. 2004. *Understanding the Political Culture of Hong Kong*. Armonk, NY, and London: M.E. Sharpe.

Lau Siu-kai. 1981. "Utilitarianistic Familism: The Basis of Political Stability," in: Ambrose Y.C. King, Rance P.L. Lee (eds), *Social Life and Development in Hong Kong*. Hong Kong: The Chinese University Press.

Lau Siu-kai. 1982. *Society and Politics in Hong Kong*. Hong Kong: The Chinese University Press.

Lau Siu-kai and Kuan Hsin-chi. 1988. *The Ethos of the Hong Kong Chinese*. Hong Kong: Chinese University Press.

Lau Siu-kai and Kuan Hsin-chi. 2000. "Partial Democratization, 'Foundation Moment' and Political Parties in Hong Kong," *China Quarterly*, 163, pp. 705–20.

Lau Siu-kai and Wan Po-san. 1997. *Social Conflicts in Hong Kong 1987–1995*. Hong Kong: Hong Kong Institute of Asia-Pacific Studies.

Lau, Emily. 1986. "The News Media," in: Joseph Y.S. Cheng (ed.), *Hong Kong in Transition*. Hong Kong: Oxford University Press.

Lau, Emily. 1988. "Club reforms its aims for the future battles," in: *Hong Kong Standard*, 27 November.

Lee Hsien Loong. 2006a. English text of National Day Rally 2006 Speech in Mandarin, Sunday 20 August 2006, at the University Cultural Centre, NUS, http://app. sprinter.gov.sg/data/pr/2006082008.htm (Online Access: 02/11/07).

Lee Hsien Loong. 2006b. "National Day Message," in: *MFA Press Release*, http://app. mfa.gov.sg/pr/read_content.asp?View,5015, (Online Access: 07/21/07).

Lee Kuan Yew. 1992. "Democracy, human rights, and the realities," speech to The Create 21 Asahi Forum, Tokyo, 10 November, published in: *Speeches*,16:6, Singapore: Ministry of Information and the Arts, p. 20.

Lee Kuan Yew. 2000. *From Third World to First. The Singapore Story: 1965–2000*. New York: Harper Collins.

Lee, J.M. 1967. *Colonial Development and Good Government*. Oxford: Clarendon Press.

Lee, Mary. 1979. "Keeping the public in Order," in: *Far Eastern Economic Review*, 9 March.

Lee, Terence. 2002. "The Politics of Civil Society in Singapore," in: *Asian Studies Review*, 26:1, pp. 97–117.

Lee, Terence. 2005. "Gestural Politics: Civil Society in 'New' Singapore,' in: *SOJOURN*, 20:2, pp. 132–54.

Lee, Terence and Cornelius Kan. 2008. "Blogosphereic Pressures in Singapore: Internet Discourses and the 2006 General Election," in: *Working Paper*, 150, Murdoch University, http://wwwarc.murdoch.edu.au/wp/wp150.pdf (Online Access: 02/25/09).

Lent, John (ed.). 1982. *Newspapers in Asia: Contemporary Trends and Problems*. Hong Kong: Heinemann Asia.

Leong Weng Kam. 2000. "The Silent Majority," in: *The Straits Times*, 15 August, p. 35.

LePoer, Barbara Leitch (ed.). 1989. *Singapore: A Country Study*. Washington, DC: Library of Congress, http://lcweb2.loc.gov/frd/cs/sgtoc.html#sg0062 (Online Access: 12/30/06).

Lethbridge, H.J. 1978. *Hong Kong: Stability and Change. A Collection of Essays*. Hong Kong: Oxford University Press.

Leung, Benjamin K.P. 1996. *Perspectives on Hong Kong Society*. Oxford and New York: Oxford University Press.

Leung, Benjamin K.P. 2000. "The Student Movement in Hong Kong: Transition to a Democratizing Society," in: Stephen Wing Kai Chiu and Tai Lok Lui (eds), *The Dynamics of Social Movement in Hong Kong*. Hong Kong: Hong Kong University Press, pp. 209–26.

Leung, Benjamin and Stephen Chiu. 1991. *A Social History of Industrial Strikes and the Labour Movement in Hong Kong, 1946–1989*. Hong Kong: Social Sciences Research Centre Occasional Paper, 3.

Leung, Stanley. 1985. "Students' role in 'era of changes,'" in: *South China Morning Post*, 3 February.

Levin, David and Y.C. Jao. 1988. "Introduction," in: Y.C. Jao et al. (eds), *Labour Movement in a Changing Society: The Experience of Hong Kong*. Hong Kong: Centre of Asian Studies, University of Hong Kong.

Levitsky, Steven and Lucan A. Way. 2002. "The Rise of Competitive Authoritarianism," in: *Journal of Democracy*, 13:2, pp. 51–65.

Li Xueying. 2007. "PAP moves to counter criticism of party, Govt in cyberspace," in: *The Straits Times*, 3 February.

Li, Nancy. 1978. "Angry parents, students hold sit-in today," in: *Hong Kong Standard*, 14 July.

Lijphart, Arend. 1975. "The Comparable-Cases Strategy in Comparative Research," in: *Comparative Political Studies*, 8: 2, pp. 158–75.

Lim Swee Say. 2005. *Speech by Lim Swee Say on Proposal to Develop Irson on 20 April 2005*, http://app.sprinter.gov.sg/data/pr/2005042001.htm (Online Access: 05/10/06).

Lim, Catherine. 1994. "The PAP and the people-A Great Affective Divide," in: *The Straits Times*, 3 September.

Lim, Catherine. 2007. "An Open Letter to the Prime Minister," in: *catherinelim.sg*, http://catherinelim.sg/2007/11/04/an-open-letter-to-the-prime-minister/ (Online Access: 10/12/08).

Lim, Linda Y.C. 1983. "Singapore's Success: The Myth of the Free Market Economy," in: *Asian Survey*, 23:6, pp. 752–64.

Lim, Linda, Pang Eng Fong and Ronald Findlay. 1993. "Singapore," in: Ronald Findlay and Stanislaw Wellisz (eds), *Five Small Economies*. Oxford: Oxford University Press, pp. 93–139.

Lim, Sharon. 2006. "Interview: Sylvia Lim," in: *I-S Magazine*, www.littlespeck.com/content/politics/CTrendsPolitics-060627.htm (Online Access: 10/12/06).

Lingle, Christopher. 1994. "Smoke over parts of Asia obscures some profound concerns," in: *International Herald Tribune*, 7 October.

Linz, Juan and Alfred Stepan. 1996. *Problems of Democratic Transition and Consolidation: Southern Europe, South America, and Post-Communist Europe*. Baltimore, MD: John Hopkins University Press.

Linz, Juan. 1978. *The Breakdown of Democratic Regimes: Crisis, Breakdown and Reequilibration*. Baltimore, MD: Johns Hopkins University.

Lipset, Seymour Martin. 1959. "Some Social Requisites of Democracy: Economic Development and Legitimacy," in: *The American Political Science Review*, 53:1, pp. 69–105.

Lloyd, Trevor. 2001. *Empire: A History of the British Empire*. London: Hambledon Continuum.

Lo Shiu-hing. 1988. "Decolonization and Political Development in Hong Kong: Citizen Participation," in: *Asian Survey*, 28:6, pp. 613–29.

Lo Shiu-hing. 1997. *The Politics of Democratization in Hong Kong*. Houndmills: Macmillan Press.

Lo Shiu-hing. 2001. *Governing Hong Kong: Legitimacy, Communication and Political Decay*. New York: Nova Science Publishers.

Lowe, C.J.G. 1980. "How the Government in Hong Kong Makes Policy," in: *Hong Kong Journal of Public Administration*, 2:2, December, pp. 63–70.

Lui, Tai-lok. 1999. "Pressure Group Politics in Hong Kong," in: Joseph Y.S. Cheng. (ed.), *Political Participation in Hong Kong: Theoretical Issues and Historical Legacy*. Hong Kong: City University of Hong Kong Press, pp. 149–73.

Lui, Tai-lok and Stephen W.K. Chiu. 1997. "The Structuring of Social Movements in Contemporary Hong Kong," in: *China Information*, 12:1–2, pp. 97–113.

Lui, Tai-lok and Stephen W.K. Chiu. 1999. "Social Movements and Public Discourse on Politics," in: Tak-Wing Ngo (ed.), *Hong Kong's History: State and Society under Colonial Rule*. London and New York: Routledge.

Lui, Tai-lok and Stephen W.K. Chiu. 2000. "Introduction——Changing Political Opportunities and the Shaping of Collective Action: Social Movements in Hong Kong," in: Chiu, Stephen Wing Kai and Tai Lok Lui (eds), *The Dynamics of Social Movement in Hong Kong*. Hong Kong: Hong Kong University Press, pp. 1–20.

Lui, Terry. 1988. "Changing Civil Servants' Values," in: Ian Scott and John P. Burns (eds), *The Hong Kong Civil Service and its Future*. Hong Kong: Oxford University Press

Ma Fook-Tong, Stephen. 1986. "Urban Neighbourhood Mobilization in the Changing Political Scenes of Hong Kong." Unpublished dissertation, Master of Social Sciences in Urban Studies, University of Hong Kong, Hong Kong.

Ma Ngok. 2007. *Political Development in Hong Kong: State, Political Society, and Civil Society*. Hong Kong: Hong Kong University Press.

Ma Ngok and Choy Chi-keung. 2003. *Xuanju Zhidu de Zhengzhi Xiaoguo: Gangshi Bili Daibiaozhi de Jingyan (Political Consequences of Electoral Systems: The Hong Kong Proportional Representation System)*. Hong Kong: City University of Hong Kong Press.

Mainwaring, Scott. 1992. "Transitions to Democracy and Democratic Consolidation: Theoretical and Comparative Issues," in: Scott Mainwaring, Guillermo O'Donnell, and J. Samuel Valenzuela (eds), *Issues in Democratic Consolidation*. Notre Dame, IL: University of Notre Dame, pp. 294–341.

Mangold, Tom. 1975. "Tigers and Flies——Tom Mangold on police corruption in Hong Kong," in: *The Listener*, 16 January, pp. 66–68.

Mauzy, Diane K. 2006. "The Challenge to Democracy: Singapore's and Malaysia's Resilient Hybrid Regimes," in: *Taiwan Journal of Democracy*, 2:2, pp. 47–68

Mauzy, Diane K. and R.S. Milne. 2002. *Singapore Politics Under the People's Action Party*. London and New York: Routledge.

Maxwell, Bruce. 1973. "Lobbying in the Lamma Island refinery stakes," in: *South China Morning Post*, 12 September.

McAdam, Doug. 1982. *Political Process and the Development of Black Insurgency, 1930–1970*. Chicago, IL: University Press of Chicago.

McAdam, Doug. 1996. "Conceptional origins, current problems, future directions," in: Doug McAdam, John D. McCarthy, and Mayer N. Zald (eds), *Comparative Perspectives on Social Movements: Political Opportunities, mobilizing structures, and cultural framings*. Cambridge: Cambridge University Press.

McAdam, Doug, Sidney Tarrow, and Charles Tilly. 2001. *Dynamics of Contention*. Cambridge: Cambridge University Press.

Means, Gordon Paul. 1996. "Soft Authoritarianism in Malaysia and Singapore," in: *Journal of Democracy*, 7:4, pp. 103–17.

Meyer, David R. 2000. *Hong Kong as a Global Metropolis*. Cambridge: Cambridge University Press.

Miners, Norman. 1981. *The Government and Politics of Hong Kong*. Hong Kong: Oxford University Press.

Miners, Norman. 1994. "The Transformation of the Hong Kong Legislative Council 1970–94: From Consensus to Confrontation," in: *Asian Journal of Public Administration*, 16:2, pp. 224–48.

Miners, Norman. 1996. "Consultation with Business Interests: The Case of Hong Kong," in: *Asian Journal of Public Administration*, 18:2, pp. 245–56.

Ministry of Information, Communications and the Arts. 2003. Report of the Censorship Review Committee 2003. www.mda.gov.sg/wms.file/mobj/mobj.316.Censorship_Review_2003.pdf (Online access: 03/04/09).

Ministry of Manpower. 2007. "Trade Unions: Statistics—Strikes," in: *Ministry of Manpower* website, www.mom.gov.sg/publish/momportal/en/communities/workplace_standards/trade_unions/Statistics/strikes.html (Online Access: 07/02/07).

Moore, Barrington Jr. 1966. *Social Origins of Dictatorship and Democracy: Lord and Peasant in the Making of the Modern World.* Boston, MA: Beacon Press.

Muhula, Raymond. 2006. "Contentious politics and democratization in Africa: The social movement dimension of regime change and transition in Kenya, 1988–2002." Dissertation, ProQuest.

Nathan, Andrew J. 2003. "Authoritarian Resilience," in: *Journal of Democracy*, 14:1, pp. 6–17.

NationMaster.com. 2009. www.nationmaster.com (Online Access: 02/24/09).

Neher, Clark D. 1999. "The Case for Singapore," in: Michael Haas (ed.), *The Singapore Puzzle*. Greenwood: Praeger.

NEXUS. 2008. *Introduction to TD Badge Programme.* www.totaldefence.sg/imindef/mindef_websites/topics/totaldefence/resources/td_badge_programme.-imindefPars./td_intro_09.pdf (Online Access: 02/01/2009).

Ng Wei Joo. 1997. "Jeya: Why the Workers' Party lost in Cheng San," in: *The Straits Times*, 28 January, p. 27.

Ng, Julia. 2006. "PAP's new candidates, MP-elects chide opposition for lack of vision," in: *Channel NewsAsia* website, May 3, www.channelnewsasia.com/stories/singaporelocalnews/view/206295/1/.html (Online Access: 01/21/07).

Ngiam Kee Jin. 2000. "Coping with the Asian Financial Crisis: The Singapore Experience," in: *Visiting Researchers Series*, No. 8, www.iseas.edu.sg/vr82000.pdf (Online Access: 02/25/07).

Ngo Tak-wing. 1993. "Civil Society and Political Liberalization in Taiwan," in: *Bulletin of Concerned Asian Scholars*, 25:1, pp. 3–15.

Ngo, Tak-wing. 1999. "Industrial History and the Artifice of Laissez-faire," in: Tak-Wing Ngo (ed.), *Hong Kong's History: State and Society under Colonial Rule*. London and New York: Routledge.

O'Donnell, Guillermo. 1973. *Modernization and Bureaucratic Authoritarianism: Studies in South American Politics.* Berkeley, CA: Insitute of International Studies.

O'Donnell, Guillermo and Philippe C. Schmitter. 1986. *Transitions from Authoritarian Rule: Tentative Conclusions about Uncertain Democracies.* Baltimore, MD, and London: Johns Hopkins University Press.

Olson, Mancur. 1965. *The Logic of Collective Action. Public Goods and the Theory of Groups.* Cambridge, MA: Harvard University Press.

Ong, Daniel. 2006. "Protest or Performance Art?" in: *The Nanyang Chronicle*, 13:4, p. 26.

Ortmann, Stephan. 2009. *Legitimacy and the National Threat in Singapore.* Saarbrücken: VDM Verlag Dr. Müller.

Ott, Dana. 2000. *Small Is Democratic: An Examination of State Size and Democratic Development.* New York: Garland Publishing.

Ottaway, Marina. 2003. *Democracy Challenged: The Rise of Semi-Authoritarianism.* Washington, DC: Carnegie Endowment for International Peace.

Owen, Nicholas. 1971. "Economic Policy," in: Keith Hopkins (ed.), *Hong Kong: The Industrial Colony: A Political, Social and Economic Survey.* Hong Kong: Oxford University Press.

Owen, Nicholas. 1999. "Critics of Empire in Britain," in: Judith M. Brown and W.M. Roger Louis (eds), *The Oxford History of the British Empire: The Twentieth Century.* Oxford: Oxford University Press.

Pang Gek Choo. 1998. "Upgrading link swung vote in GE," in: *Straits Times*, 12 January.

Peebles, Gavin and Peter Wilson. 2002. *Economic Growth and Development in Singapore: Past and Future*. Cheltenham and Northampton: Edward Elgar.

Peh Shing Huei. 2006. "What a load of rubbish, Singapore," in: *Straits Times*, 1 September.

People Like Us. 2005. "History in brief," in: *People Like Us* website, www.plu.sg/main/index2.htm (Online Access 11/31/06).

People's Action Party. 2006. "Beyond Feedback," in: *Petir Magazine*, November/December, www.pap.org.sg/articleview.php?folder=PT&id = 1366 (Online Access: 01/16/2007).

People's Action Party. 2009. "About PAP," in: *People's Action Party* website, www.pap.org.sg/about.shtml (Online Access: 02/25/09).

Phang, Sock-Yong. 2007. "The Singapore Model of Housing and the Welfare State," in: Richard Groves, Alan Murie and C.J. Watson (eds), *Housing and the New Welfare State. Perspectives from East Asia and Europe*. Aldershot: Ashgate, pp. 15–44.

Porio, Emma. 2002. "Civil Society and Democratization in Asia: Prospects and Challenges in the New Millennium," in: Yue-man Yeung (ed.), *New Challenges for Development and Modernization: Hong Kong and the Asia-Pacific Region in the New Millennium*. Hong Kong: The Chinese University Press.

Przeworski, Adam. 1986. "Some Problems in the Study of the Transition to Democracy," in: Guillermo O'Donnell, Philippe C. Schmitter and Laurence Whitehead (eds), *Transitions from Authoritarian Rule: Comparative Perspectives*. Volume III. Baltimore, MD, and London: Johns Hopkins University Press.

Przeworski, Adam. 1991. *Democracy and the Market: Political and Economic Reforms in Eastern Europe and Latin America*. Cambridge: Cambridge University Press.

Przeworski, Adam and Fernando Limongi. 1997. "Modernization: Theories and Facts," in: *World Politics*, 49, pp. 155–83.

Przeworski, Adam and Henry Teune. 1970. *The Logic of Comparative Social Inquiry*. Malabar, FL: Krieger Publishing.

Public Opinion Programme. 2009. *HK Pop Site*, http://hkupop.hku.hk/ (Online Access: 02/23/09).

Quah, Jon S.T. 1975. "Administrative Reform and Development Administration in Singapore: A Comparative Study of the Singapore Improvement Trust and the Housing and Development Board." Unpublished PhD. thesis, Florida State University.

Quah, Jon S.T. 1980. "The Public Bureaucracy and Social Change in Singapore," in: *The Asian Journal of Public Administration*, 2:2, pp. 16–37.

Quah, Jon S.T. 1990. "Government Policies and Nation-Building," in: Jon S.T. Quah (ed.), *In Search of Singapore's National Values*. Singapore: Times Academic Press.

Quah, Jon S.T. and Stella R. Quah. 1989. "The Limits of Government Intervention," in: Kernial Singh Sandhu and Paul Wheatley (eds), *Management of Success: The Moulding of Modern Singapore*. Singapore: Institute of Southeast Asian Studies.

Rahim, Farah Abdul. 2006a. "Blogging activity up during Singapore election campaigning," in: *Channel NewsAsia* website, 12 May, www.channelnewsasia.com/stories/singaporelocalnews/view/207967/1/.html (Online Access: 07/21/07)

Rahim, Farah Abdul. 2006b. "SM Goh concerned Potong Pasir, Hougang residents will lose out on upgrading," in: *Channel NewsAsia* website, 26 March, www.channelnewsasia.com/stories/singaporelocalnews/view/199982/1/.html (Online Access: 07/20/07).

Rajaratnam, S. 1975. "Non-Communist Subversion in Singapore," in: Seah Chee Meow (ed.), *Trends in Singapore: Proceedings and Background Papers*. Singapore: Singapore University Press.

Rajaratnam, S. 1966. "The National Pledge," in: *Infomap*, www.sg/explore/symbols_pl edge.htm (Online Access: 02/25/09).

Ramesh, S. 2006. "Singapore economy grew 9.4% in H1, full-year forecast raised: PM Lee," in: *Channel NewsAsia* website, 8 August, www.channelnewsasia.com/stories/ singaporelocalnews/view/223791/1/.html (Online Access: 03/16/07).

Rear, John. 1971. "One Brand of Politics," in: Keith Hopkins (ed.), *Hong Kong: The Industrial Colony. A Political, Social and Economic Survey*. Hong Kong: Oxford University Press. pp. 55–139.

Reform Club. 1975. *Election Chronicle*.

Reform Club. 1977. *A Survey on the Public's Attitudes towards Elected Representation in Legislative Council*. Hong Kong: Survey Research Hong Kong.

Regnier, Philippe. 1987. *Singapore: City-State in South-East Asia*. Translated from the French by Christopher Hurst. Honolulu: University of Hawaii Press.

Remaking Singapore Committee. 2003. *Changing Mindsets, Deepening Relationships*. Singapore: Government Printer.

Restall, Hugo. 2006. "Singapore's 'Martyr'" in: *Far Eastern Economic Review*, July/ August, www.feer.com/articles1/2006/0607/free/p024.html (Online Access: 01/22/07).

Rodan, Garry. 1992. "Singapore: Emerging Tensions in the 'Dictatorship of the Middle Class,'" in: *The Pacific Review*, 5:4, pp. 370–81.

Rodan, Garry. 1996. "Class transformations and political tensions in Singapore's development," in: Richard Robison and David S.G. Goodman, *The New Rich in Asia: Mobile phones, McDonald's and middle class revolution*. London and New York: Routledge, pp. 17–45.

Rodan, Garry. 1998. "The Internet and Political Control in Singapore," in: *Political Science Quarterly*, 113:1, pp. 63–89.

Rodan, Garry. 2004. *Transparency and Authoritarian Rule in Southeast Asia: Singapore and Malaysia*. London and New York: RoutledgeCurzon.

Rodan, Garry. 2006a. "Singapore's Founding Myths vs. Freedom," in: *Far Eastern Economic Review*, October, http://feer.com/articles1/2006/0610/free/p013.html. (Online Access: 03/26/08).

Rodan, Garry. 2006b. "Singapore's 'Exceptionalism'? Authoritarian Rule and State Transformation," in: Working Paper No. 131, Murdoch University, http://wwwarc. murdoch.edu.au/wp/wp131.pdf (Online Access: 03/26/08).

Rodan, Garry. 2006c. "Lion City Baits Mousy Opposition," in: *Far Eastern Economic Review*, 169:4, pp. 11–17.

Rosa, Linda. 1990. "The Singapore State and Trade Union Incorporation," in: *Journal of Contemporary Asia*, 20:4, pp. 487–507.

Roy, Danny. 1994. "Singapore, China, and the 'Soft Authoritarian' Challenge," in: *Asian Survey*, 34:3, pp. 231–42.

Rudbeck, Jens and Jesper Sigurdsson. 1999. "Contentious Politics and Regime Change: New Perspectives on Democratization," in: *Copenhagen Peace Research Institute*, 12 January, www.ciaonet.org/wps/ruj02/ (Online Access: 01/30/07).

Rueschemeyer, Dietrich, John D. Stephens and Evelyne Huber Stephens. 1992. *Capitalist Development and Democracy*. Cambridge: Polity Press.

Rule, James and Charles Tilly. 1975. "Political Process in Revolutionary France, 1830–32," in: John M. Merriman (ed.), *1830 in France*. New York and London: New Viewpoints.

Russell, David A. 1977. "Call to Friends of Heritage Society," in: *South China Morning Post*, 10 June.

Rustow, Dankwart A. 1970. "Transitions to Democracy," in: *Comparative Politics*, 2:3, pp. 337–63.

Sartori, Giovanni. 1994. "Compare Why and How. Comparing, Miscomparing and the Comparative Method," in: Mattei Dogan and Ali Kazancigil (eds), *Comparing Nations: Concepts, Strategies, Substance*. Oxford: Blackwell, pp. 14–34.

Saw Swee-Hock. 1990. *Changes in the Fertility Policy of Singapore*. IPS Occasional Papers No. 2. Singapore: IPS and Times Academic Press.

Saw Swee-Hock. 1999. *The Population of Singapore*. Singapore: Institute of Southeast Asian Studies.

Schaar, John H. 1981. *Legitimacy in the Modern State*. New Brunswick, NJ: Transaction Publishers.

Schein, Edgar H. 1996. *Strategic Pragmatism: The Culture of Singapore's Economic Development Board*. Cambridge, MA: MIT Press.

Schmitter, Philippe. 1993. "Some Propositions about Civil Society and the Consolidation of Democracy," in: *Reihe Politikwissenschaft*, No. 10.

Schubert, Gunter, Rainer Tetzlaff and Werner Vennewald. 1994. *Demokratisierung und politischer Wandel. Theorie und Anwendung des Konzepts der strategischen und konfliktfähigen Gruppen (SKOG)*. LIT Verlag: Münster and Hamburg.

Scott, Ian and Kathleen Cheek-Milby. 1986. "An Overview of Hong Kong's Social Policy-making Process," in: *Asian Journal of Public Administration*, 8:2, pp. 166–76.

Scott, Ian. 1989. *Political Change and the Crisis of Legitimacy in Hong Kong*. London: Hurst & Company.

Scott, Ian. 2007. "Legitimacy, Governance and Public Policy in Post-Handover Hong Kong," in: *The Asia Pacific Journal of Public Administration*, 29:1, pp. 29–49.

Seow, Francis T. 1997. *The Politics of Judicial Institutions in Singapore*. http://unpan1.un.org/intradoc/groups/public/documents/APCITY/UNPAN002727.pdf (Online Access: 08/15/2006).

Seow, Francis T. 2006. *Beyond Suspicion? The Singapore Judiciary*. Monograph 55, Yale Southeast Asia Studies. New Haven: Yale University Press.

Seu, Yeong Sien. 1992. "Clarity or Controversy—The Meaning of Judicial Independence in Singapore and Malaysia," in: *Singapore Law Review*, 85.

Shee Poon-Kim. 1978. "Singapore in 1977: Stability and Growth," in: *Asian Survey*, 18:2, pp. 194–201.

Shin, Doh Chull. 1994. "On the Third Wave of Democratization: A Synthesis and Evaluation of Recent Theory and Research," in: *World Politics*, 47, pp. 135–70.

Sing, Ming. 1999. "A Changing Political Culture and Democratic Transition: The Case of Hong Kong", in: Joseph Y.S. Cheng (ed.), *Political Participation in Hong Kong: Theoretical Issues and Historical Legacy*. Hong Kong: City University Press.

Sing, Ming. 2004a. "Weak Labor Movements and Opposition Parties: Hong Kong and Singapore," in: *Journal of Contemporary Asia*, 34:4, pp. 449–65.

Sing, Ming. 2004b. *Hong Kong's Tortuous Democratization: A Comparative Analysis*. London: RoutledgeCurzon.

Sing, Ming. 2009. "Hong Kong's Democrats Hold their Own," in: *Journal of Democracy*, 20:1, pp. 98–112.

Singapore Democratic Alliance. 2006. "Statement of the SDA released on 26 January 2006," in: *Singapore People's Party* website, 26 January, www.spp.org.sg/P%20&%20M%20260106.html (Online Access: 02/10/07).

Singapore Democratic Party. 2006a. "How we'll succeed," in: *Singapore Democratic Party* website, www.singaporedemocrat.org/howwesucceed.html (Online Access: 10/12/2006).

Singapore Democratic Party. 2006b. "Manifesto: The Political System," in: *Singapore Democratic Party* website, www.singaporedemocrat.org/manifestopolitics.html (Online Access: 03/08/06).

Singapore Democratic Party. 2006c. "Manifesto: Media," in: *Singapore Democratic Party* website, www.singaporedemocrat.org/manifestomedia.html (Online Access: 03/08/06).

Singapore Democratic Party. 2006d. "Manifesto: The Economy," *Singapore Democratic Party* website, www.singaporedemocrat.org/manifestoeconomy.html (Online Access: 03/08/06).

Singapore Democratic Party. 2007. "The power of the powerless: Dissent growing in Singapore," in: *Singapore Democratic Party* website, www.singaporedemocrat.org/articledissents.html (Online Access: 02/23/09).

Singapore Department of Statistics. 2005. *Homeownership and Equity of HDB Households.* Singapore: Government Printer. www.singstat.gov.sg/papers/op/op-s9.pdf (Online Access: 01/15/06).

Singapore Department of Statistics. 2007. *Yearbook of Statistics, 2007.* Singapore: Government Printers.

Singapore Government. 1991. *White Paper on Shared Values.* Singapore: Singapore National Printers.

Singapore Government. 1994. *Competitive Salaries for Competent and Honest Government.* Singapore: Singapore National Printers.

Singapore Government. 2000. "News Release: Reply to Questions in Parliament on Speakers' Corner," in: *News@Home* (Ministry of Home Affairs website), 25 April, http://www2.mha.gov.sg/mha/detailed.jsp?artid=416&type = 4&root = 0&parent = 0&cat = 0&mode = arc

Singapore Government. 2006. "REACH's role," in: *REACH* website, www.reach.gov.sg/AboutUs/REACHsRoles/tabid/43/Default.aspx (Online Access: 01/16/2007).

Singapore Government. 2006. *Budget Highlights Financial Year 2006/2007: Building Our Strengths, Creating Our Best Home.* www.mof.gov.sg/budget_2006/budget_speech/downloads/FY2006_Budget_Highlights.pdf (Online Access: 03/02/09).

Singapore Government. 2009a. *Budget Highlights Financial Year 2008/2009: Keeping Jobs, Building for The Future.* www.singaporebudget.gov.sg/speech_toc/downloads/FY2009_Budget_Highlights.pdf (Online Access: 03/02/09).

Singapore Government. 2009b. "About Total Defence," in: *Total Defence* website, www.mindef.gov.sg/imindef/mindef_websites/topics/totaldefence/about_td.html (Online Access: 03/13/09).

Singapore Hansard. Singapore: Singapore National Printers.

Slater, Dan. 2005. "Ordering Power: Contentious Politics, State-Building, and Authoritarian Durability in Southeast Asia." Unpublished PhD thesis, Department of Political Science.

Slater, Dan. 2006. "The Architecture of Authoritarianism: Southeast Asia and the Regeneration of Democratization Theory" in: *Taiwan Journal of Democracy*, 2:2, pp. 1–22.

So, Alvin Y. 1990. *Social Change and Development: Modernization, Dependency and World-System Theories.* Newbury Park, CA and London: SAGE Publications.

So, Alvin Y. 1999. *Hong Kong's Embattled Democracy: A Societal Analysis.* Baltimore, MD, and London: Johns Hopkins University Press.

South China Morning Post. Various issues 1970–2009.

Staff reporters. 1985. "Half a million show up for historic poll," in: *South China Morning Post*, 8 March.

Star, The. Various Issues 1970–84.

Stepan, Alfred. 1978. *The State and Society: Peru in Comparative Perspective.* Princeton: Princeton University Press.

Stepan, Alfred. 1990. "On the Tasks of a Democratic Opposition," reprinted in: Alfred Stepan. 2001. *Arguing Comparative Politics.* Oxford: Oxford University Press.

Stepan, Alfred. 1997. "Democratic Opposition and Democratization Theory," in: *Government and. Opposition,* 32:4, pp. 657–73.

Straits Times, The. Various Issues 1990–2008.

Stubbs, Richard. 2001. "Performance Legitimacy and Soft Authoritarianism," in: Amitav Acharya, B. Michael Frolic and Richard Stubbs (eds), *Democracy, Human Rights and Civil Society in Southeast Asia.* Toronto: Joint Centre for Asia Pacific Studies, University of Toronto-York University, pp. 37–54.

Sunday Post——Herald. 1974. "UMELCO awash in trivia," 20 October.

Tan Khee Giap. 2007. "Do the right thing, not what's popular," in: *The Straits Times,* 16 January.

Tan Wah Piow. 1987. *Let the People Judge: Confessions of the Most Wanted Person in Singapore.* Kuala Lumpur: INSAN.

Tan Wah Piow. 1989. *Frame-up: A Singapore court on trial.* Kuala Lumpur: INSAN.

Tan, Eugene Kheng-Boon. 2000. "Law and Values in Governance: The Singapore Way," in: *Hong Kong Law Journal,* 30 Part 1, pp. 91–119.

Tan, Ivan Kok Leong. 2002. "Prohibiting bar-top dancing goes against free spirit, creativity," in: *Straits Times,* 18 July.

Tan, Melvin. 2002. "Opinion—Protect Your 'Weapon'," in: *The Hammer Online,* www.wp.sg/news/hammer_online/03_protect_weapon.htm (Online Access: 10/12/06).

Tan, Melvin. 2004. "Opening Up?" in: *The Hammer Online,* No. 7, www.wp.org.sg/news/hammer_online/07_opening_up.htm (Online Access: 03/08/07).

Tang, Kwong-leung. 1998. *Colonial State and Social Policy: Social Welfare Development in Hong Kong 1842–1997.* Lanham, MD: University Press of America.

Tarrow, Sidney. 1996. "States and opportunities: The political structuring of social movements," in: Doug McAdam, John D. McCarthy, and Mayer N. Zald (eds), *Comparative Perspectives on Social Movements: Political opportunities, mobilizing structures, and cultural framings.* Cambridge: Cambridge University Press.

Thio Li-ann. 1999. "Law and the Administrative State," in: Kevin Y.L. Tan, *The Singapore Legal System.* 2nd edn. Singapore: Singapore University Press.

Thomas, Nicholas. 1999. *Democracy Denied: Identity, Civil Society and Illiberal Democracy in Hong Kong.* Aldershot: Ashgate.

Thompson, Mark R. 1997. "Why Democracy Does Not Always Follow Economic Ripeness," in: Yossi Shain and Aharon Klieman. *Democracy: The Challenges Ahead.* Houndmills: Macmillan Press Ltd., pp. 63–84.

Thompson, Mark R. 2001. "Whatever happened to 'Asian Values'?" in: *Journal of Democracy,* 12:4, pp. 154–65.

Thompson, Mark R. 2002. "Totalitarian and Post-Totalitarian Regimes in Transitions and Non-Transitions from Communism," in: *Totalitarian Movements and Political Religions* 3:1, pp. 79–106.

Thompson, Mark R. 2004. "Pacific Asia after 'Asian values': authoritarianism, democracy, and good governance," in: *Third World Quarterly,* 25:6, pp. 1079–95.

Thompson, Mark R. 2004. *Democratic Revolutions: Asia and Eastern Europe.* London and New York: Routledge.

Thompson, Mark R. 2005. "Vanguard in a Vacuum: Students as a Strategic Group in Pacific Asia'," unpublished paper prepared for the Forschungsgruppe Strategische Gruppe Workshop, 17 and 18 June, KWI, Essen.

Tilly, Charles. 2004. *Social movements, 1768–2004*. Boulder, CO: Paradigm Publishers.

Tipps, Dean C. 1973. "Modernization Theory and the Comparative Study of Societies: A Critical Perspective," in: *Comparative Studies in Society and History*, 15:2, pp. 199–226.

Tong, Sharon. 2006. "SM Goh says Gomez issue has raised questions about latter's character," in: *Channel NewsAsia* website, 1 May, www.channelnewsasia.com/stories/singaporelocalnews/view/205953/1/.html (Online Access: 01/21/06).

Tong, Sharon and S. Ramesh. 2006. "PM Lee says countries worldwide respect and admire Singapore's proven system," in: *Channel NewsAsia* website, 3 May, www.channelnewsasia.com/stories/singaporelocalnews/view/206313/1/.html (Online Access: 01/21/06).

Tor Ching Li. 2006. "Please mind the age gap," in: *Today*, 20 April, www.channelnewsasia.com/stories/singaporelocalnews/view/204003/1/.html (Online Access: 01/11/07).

Towner, Eric. 1973. "HK not ashamed of profit motive," in: *South China Morning Post*, 25 July.

Transparency International. 2008. *2008 Corruption Perception Index*. www.transparency.org/news_room/in_focus/2008/cpi2008/cpi_2008_table (Online Access: 02/24/09).

Trocki, Carl A. 2006. *Singapore: Wealth, Power and the Culture of Control*. Oxford and New York: Routledge.

Tsang, Steve Yui-sang. 1988. *Democracy Shelved: Great Britain, China, and Attempts at Constitutional Reform in Hong Kong, 1945–1952*. Hong Kong: Oxford University Press.

Tsang, Steve. 2004. *A Modern History of Hong Kong*. London and New York: I.B. Tauris.

Tu, Elsie. 2003. *Colonial Hong Kong in the Eyes of Elsie Tu*. Hong Kong: Hong Kong University Press.

Turner, H.A., Patricia Fosh, Margaret Gardner, Keith Hart, Richard Morris, Sek-hong Ng, Michael Quinlan and Dianne Yerbury. 1980. *The Last Colony. But Whose?* Cambridge: Cambridge University Press.

U.S. Department of State. 2006. *Singapore: Country Reports on Human Rights Practices*. www.state.gov/g/drl/rls/hrrpt/2005/61626.htm (Online Access: 03/05/09).

United Nations Development Programme. 2008. *Human Development Index: A statistical update 2008—HDI rankings*. http://hdr.undp.org/en/statistics/ (Online Access: 02/10/09).

Uphoff, Elisabeth. 1991. *Intellectual Property and US Relations with Indonesia, Malaysia, Singapore, and Thailand*. Ithaca, NY: Cornell University Southeast Asia Program Publications.

Vanhanen, Tatu. 2003. *Democratization: A Comparative Analysis of 170 Countries*. London and New York: Routledge.

Vasil, Raj. 2000. *Governing Singapore: Democracy and National Development*. Singapore: Allen & Unwin.

Vennewald, Werner. 1994a. "Technocrats in the State Enterprise System of Singapore," in: Working Paper, No. 32. Canberra: National Library of Australia.

Vennewald, Werner. 1994b. *Singapur: Herrschaft der Professionals und Technokraten—Ohnmacht der Demokratie?* Opladen: Leske + Budrich.

Wai, S.Y. 1988. "28 arrested in gambling raid on Reform Club," in: *Hong Kong Standard*, 16 October.

Walden, John. 1983. *Excellency, Your Gap Is Showing*. Hong Kong: Corporate Communications.

Wan Po-san and Timothy Ka-ying Wong. 2005. *Social Conflicts in Hong Kong, 1996–2002*. Hong Kong: Hong Kong Institute of Asia-Pacific Studies.

Wang, Enbao and Regina F. Titunik. 2000. "Democracy in China: The Practice of Minben," in: Suisheng Zhao (ed.), *China and Democracy: Reconsidering the Prospects for a Democratic China*. New York and London: Routledge.

Weber, Max. 1930. *The Protestant Ethic and the Spirit of Capitalism*. London and Boston: Allen & Unwin.

Wee Siew Kim. 2006. "A Lesson Learnt, Says MP and Dad Wee Siew Kim," in: *The Straits Times*, 24 October.

Welsh, Frank. 1997. *A History of Hong Kong*. 2nd edn. London: Harper Collins.

White, Lynn T. 2005. "Introduction—Dimensions of Legitimacy," in: Lynn T. White (ed.), *Legitimacy: Ambiguities of Political Success or Failure in East and Southeast Asia*. New Jersey: World Scientific.

White, Stephen. 1986. "Economic Performance and Communist Legitimacy," in: *World Politics*, 38:3, pp. 462–82.

White House. 2006. *President Bush Visits National University of Singapore*. Office of the Press Secretary, 16 November, www.whitehouse.gov/news/releases/2006/11/20061116–1.html (Online Access: 07/02/08).

Wiarda, Howard J. 1996. *Corporatism and Comparative Politics: The Other Great "Ism."* Armonk and London: M.E. Sharpe.

Wilding, Paul. 1997. "Social Policy and Social Development in Hong Kong," in: *Asian Journal of Public Administration*, 19:2, pp. 244–75.

Wong, Cheuk-yin. 2001. "The Communist-Inspired Riots in Hong Kong, 1967 a Multi-Actors Approach." Unpublished PhD. Thesis, Hong Kong University.

Wong, Fanny. 1990. "Sharp Increase in Street Protests," in: *South China Morning Post*, 14 April.

Wong, Karen. 2005. "Sacked SIA Captain Ryan Goh, who had his PR status revoked, renews flying licence," in: *The New Paper*, 28 January.

Wong, Ting-Hong. 2002. *Hegemonies Compared: State Formation and Chinese School Politics in Postwar Singapore and Hong Kong*. New York and London: Routledge-Falmer.

Workers' Party of Singapore. 1971. *The Workers' Party Manifesto*. www.wp.org.sg/party/manifesto_1971.htm (Online Access: 08/12/2006).

Workers' Party of Singapore. 1976. *Towards a Caring Society: The Programme of the Workers' Party Singapore 1976*. www.wp.org.sg/party/manifesto_1976.htm (Online Access: 08/12/2006).

Workers' Party of Singapore. 1988. *Towards a Caring Society: The Programme of the Workers' Party '88*. www.wp.org.sg/party/manifesto_1988.htm (Online Access 07/06/06).

Workers' Party of Singapore. 1994. *Towards a Caring Society: Programme of the Workers' Party 1994*. www.wp.org.sg/party/manifesto_1994.htm (Online Access 07/06/06).

Workers' Party of Singapore. 2005. "Sylvia Lim's Dialogue with Youths at NUSPA Forum," in: *Workers' Party* website, 25 March, www.wp.org.sg/news/news_articles/20050330_sl_nuspa.htm (Online Access 07/06/06).

Workers' Party of Singapore. 2006. *You Have a Choice. Manifesto 2006*. www.wp.org.sg/party/manifesto_2006.htm (Online Access 08/12/2006).

Workers' Party of Singapore. 2007. "Frequently Asked Questions," in: *The Workers' Party* website, www.wp.sg/wordpress/faq/ (Online Access 02/04/07).

Worthington, Ross. 2001. "Between Hermes and Themis: An Empirical Study of the Contemporary Judiciary in Singapore," in: *Journal of Law and Society*, 28:4, pp. 490–510.

Worthington, Ross. 2003. *Governance in Singapore*. London and New York: Routledge Curzon.

Xin Ren. 2003. "Towards a Secure Future," in: *The Hammer Online*, www.wp.sg/news/hammer_online/06_secured_future.htm (Online Access: 11/12/06).

Yang Yilung. 1985. "Time for one-man, one-vote," in: *Hong Kong Standard*, 13 October.

Yao, Souchou. 2007. *Singapore: The State and the Culture of Excess*. London and New York: Routledge.

Yap Neng Jye. 2006. " Reply to Liberal International on Statement about Chee Soon Juan, 15 December 2006," in: *News@Home*, 15 December, http://www2.mha.gov.sg/mha/detailed.jsp?artid=2188&type = 4&root = 0&parent = 0&cat = 0 (Online Access: 02/11/07).

Yen, Jeffrey. 2007. "Stop The Presses! EP 2," in: *Jeff's Blog*, 13 January, http://jeffyen.blogspot.com/2007/01/stop-presses-ep-2.html (Online Access: 01/20/07).

Yeo Lay Hwee. 2002. "Electoral Politics in Singapore," in: *Electoral Politics in Southeast & East Asia*. Singapore: Friedrich-Ebert-Stiftung, pp. 203–32, http://library.fes.de/pdf-files/iez/01361007.pdf (Online Access: 08/18/03).

Yeo, George. 2001. "Interview with BG (NS) George Yeo, Minister for Trade and Industry by Dr Albert Bressand and Catherine Distler of Promethee on 17 May 2001 in Paris," in: *Ministry of Trade and Industry* website, 23 November, http://app.mti.gov.sg/default.asp?id=148&articleID = 333&intViewCat = 1&intCategory = 3&txtKeyword = &txtStart = &txtEnd = &intOrderBy = 1&intYear = &intQuarter = 0 (Online Access: 02/26/07).

Yeung, Yue-man and D.W. Drakakis-Smith. 1982. "Public Housing in the City States of Hong Kong and Singapore," in: John L. Taylor and David G. Williams (eds), *Urban Planning Practice in Developing Countries*. Oxford: Pergamon Press.

Yip, Melanie. 2004. "The role of the Minister Mentor in Singapore's political future," in: *Radio Singapore International*, 11 August, www.channelnewsasia.com/analysis/2004/0811_ministermentor.htm (Online Access: 12/27/06).

Youngson, A.J. 1982. *Hong Kong: Economic Growth and Policy*. Hong Kong: Oxford University Press.

Zakaria, Fareed. 1994. "Culture Is Destiny: A Conversation with Lee Kuan Yew," in: *Foreign Affairs*, 73:2, pp. 109–26.

Zakaria, Fareed. 1997. "The Rise of Illiberal Democracy," in: *Foreign Affairs*, 76, pp. 22–43.

Zakir Hussain. 2006. "Praise for the 'elephant' spirit; PM praises grassroots push to open Buangkok station," in: *The Straits Times*, 5 May.

Zhang, Wei-Bin. 2006. *Hong Kong: The Pearl Made of British Mastery and Chinese Docile-Diligence*. New York: Nova Science Publishers.

Zürn, Michael. 2004. "Global Governance and Legitimacy," in: *Government and Opposition*, 39:2, pp. 260–87.

Index

eBooks – at www.eBookstore.tandf.co.uk

A library at your fingertips!

eBooks are electronic versions of printed books. You can store them on your PC/laptop or browse them online.

They have advantages for anyone needing rapid access to a wide variety of published, copyright information.

eBooks can help your research by enabling you to bookmark chapters, annotate text and use instant searches to find specific words or phrases. Several eBook files would fit on even a small laptop or PDA.

NEW: Save money by eSubscribing: cheap, online access to any eBook for as long as you need it.

Annual subscription packages

We now offer special low-cost bulk subscriptions to packages of eBooks in certain subject areas. These are available to libraries or to individuals.

For more information please contact webmaster.ebooks@tandf.co.uk

We're continually developing the eBook concept, so keep up to date by visiting the website.

www.eBookstore.tandf.co.uk

For Product Safety Concerns and Information please contact our EU
representative GPSR@taylorandfrancis.com
Taylor & Francis Verlag GmbH, Kaufingerstraße 24, 80331 München, Germany